Koi Kichi

P E T E R   W A D D I N G T O N

Koi Kichi

written by **Peter Waddington**

First published in 1995 by Peter Waddington Ltd. trading as Infiltration,
Unit 13, Millingford Industrial Estate, Golborne, Warrington, Cheshire WA3 3QE, United Kingdom.

Illustrations by Geoff Nuttall/Peter Waddington 1994, and Satoru Hoshino 1988.
Copyright Peter Waddington 1995.

Photographs supplied by Peter Waddington, Nigel Caddock – Nishikigoi International Ltd.,
Christoph Wolters and Mr. S. Baba.

ISBN 0 9526381 0 X Hardback
ISBN 0 9526381 1 8 De-Luxe

British Library Cataloguing-in-Publication Data.
A catalogue record is available for this book from the British Library.

Layout and colour separations by Messrs. Insight Reprographic & Scanning Services.
Unit 7, Farriers Way, Bootle, Merseyside L30 4XL.

Printed by Messrs. Kingprint, 36 William Moult Street, Taylor Industrial Estate, Liverpool L5 5AS

Finishing by Smith Settle, Ilkley Road, Otley, West Yorkshire LS21 3JP.

FOREWORD

When I was a child, I always longed for my very own goldfish pond but it never seemed to materialise, I think it was the lure of the water and the goldfish darting in and out of the lilies that fascinated me, coupled with the thought that one never quite knew what lurked in the depths of ponds!

In later years, when childish things had long been left behind, I became the owner of a house with quite a large back garden which was virtually all lawn. After a few months of tiresome mowing I began to dream of a beautiful pond, waterfall, pond plants, fountain and lots of fish swimming around. By building this feature I would, I reasoned to myself, save quite a lot of physical effort in mowing a boring lawn and, at the same time, realise a childhood dream.

Some well-meaning friend insisted on taking me to a large Water Garden Centre at Stapeley in Cheshire in order to purchase items for my pond project; it was there I saw my very first Koi. Looking back, the first things that struck me were the colours and the size - (some were all of 10 inches long!) A very young sales assistant informed me that they were 'Koi Carp' and had travelled all the way from Japan; prices incidentally started at £75.00! - and that was in 1971. The price immediately quelled my enthusiasm and I started to build my garden pond which took around three months of evenings and weekends to complete despite the brochure which insisted it could be finished in a single weekend. I gave every consideration to the aesthetic appeal of my pond and, needless to say, my goldfish all departed one by one. I was not at all happy, even though my friends tried to console me by telling me how beautiful the lilies, the fountain and the waterfall looked. I then started to buy books and magazines in order to try and find out where I was going wrong, alas, this was to

no avail as they taught me nothing. Soon afterwards I purchased several 4" Koi, only to watch them die after two or three weeks.

I was about to become resigned to growing water lilies which seemed to thrive in my pond when I saw an advertisement for a large Aquarist Exhibition soon to be held in Manchester where I worked as manager of a large record store. I still remember, quite clearly, going into the show early on the opening morning. I wandered disinterestedly around displays of tropical and marine fish, aquarium systems and related accessories before noticing, suspended from the roof at the rear of the huge hall, a large banner bearing the legend 'The British Koi-Keepers' Society'. I made my way through the hall to the stand situated beneath the sign to find a makeshift pond full of giant Koi, some of which were all of 15 inches long! The colours were incredible and I just stood there, mouth agape and mesmerised, watching these majestic creatures glide calmly before me. One tall man, who appeared to be manning the stand alone, approached me and asked me if I was interested in Koi, I replied that I was and enquired as to the prices of the Koi on display. At this point he seemed a little reticent to answer my question and told me that the Koi were on loan from an importer to be sold, at very special prices, only to members of the Society. It was then I joined the British Koi-Keepers' Society and became Member No. 61.

The tall man turned out to be Roland Seal, Chairman of the BKKS and, over the next few years, we became close friends sharing a common interest in Koi and Jazz/Rock music. And much of my time and energy was taken up with learning to handle complex subjects such as how to keep our Koi alive!

Roland and his wife Pauline together with Hilda and Eric Allen, (whom I met soon afterwards) by sheer enthusiasm and determination, opened many doors to the BKKS membership which helped us all progress in the hobby. One must bear in mind that, in those early days, keeping Koi meant shallow ponds, no bottom drains, no filtration – just plants, fountains, waterfalls and a lot of love and frustration. Roland and Eric helped set up a line of communication and information from Koi keepers in Japan and passed on to us, via newsletters or word-of-mouth, remedies and tips that helped to resolve some problems that were puzzling us all in the UK.

Soon afterwards the first of many BKKS visits to Japan was arranged; the feedback of information as a result of these visits helped us all immensely. On reflection, these early days of Koi keeping in the UK seemed like the 'dark ages' in a way, it always seemed to be an uphill struggle, learning from one mistake after another, only to find another creeping up behind! Roland, after visiting Japan to study keeping methods there, was way ahead of the rest of us. Even in those days he was experimenting with external concrete filters and continually complained that the UK Summer was not nearly warm enough to grow his Koi properly – even then he was thinking about some method of adding heat to his pond. My happier memories of the 'early days' were the social occasions of Koi keeping when members of the Society from all over England would gather, either at shows, seminars or meetings to 'talk Koi', 'argue Koi', discuss pumps, filtration, feeding, overwintering etc. etc., for hours on end. By the late 1970's the membership had increased to around 450 with no idea what was waiting around the corner in the 1980's when the hobby really took off to swell membership to over 5,000.

As I became more captivated with the fascination of Nishikigoi, and, at a time in my life when conditions allowed, I decided to become a Koi Dealer as a full-time occupation and surrender to Nishikigoi, for better or for worse. It was then that the real hard work and learning curve commenced and today, after over 70 visits to Japan since 1977 to buy and learn more about Nishikigoi, I am still little more than an enthusiastic amateur as there always seems to be so much more to learn and understand about the hobby of Nishikigoi in general.

It has taken around twelve years to complete this book as I was determined to carry out all research myself and not rely on any printed texts from previous publications that are available thus, hopefully, making it unique. Interviewing and questioning the Japanese Koi breeders has been a lengthy process. The only common language in many instances has been 'Koi Language', pencil drawings and notes etc. to be written up later the same day whilst the memory is still fresh. Researching the accurate details of the history of Nishikigoi has also produced some conflicting information from various sources where the language barrier again does not help. The whole project, however, has been immensely enjoyable and rewarding.

The book itself has been written for everyone interested in the hobby of keeping Koi, from those just starting out, right through to the experienced and dedicated enthusiast. I hope it will provide the reader with a complete insight to all the important aspects of the hobby in order to try and prevent some of the horrors and mistakes we all made in the early days. I have tried, in the main part, to keep simplicity to the fore without leaving any important stones unturned and to intentionally omit

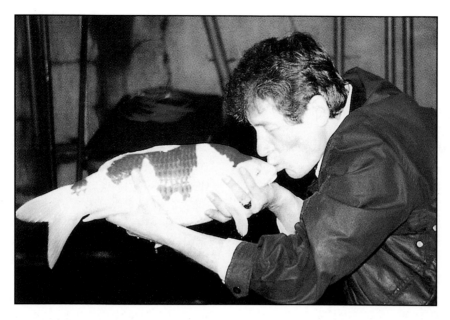

hopelessly outdated ideas and methods which only serve to confuse and produce the wrong results. However, many aspects of the hobby can be quite complex; hopefully the contents of the book should 'tell it like it is' in 1995. If it can save the reader some time, expense and/or grief in making needless mistakes then it will have served its purpose. Human nature though, being as it is, compels us to learn from our own mistakes rather than to learn from others.

One point must be stressed and that is that the hobby, like most hobbies, is both expensive and time consuming, albeit totally fascinating. The more one learns, the greater ones appetite for knowledge becomes and the hobby can then become an addiction. (I have to admit that I fall into this category.)

There is also something unique about many Koi enthusiasts – in my experience they usually appreciate other forms of beauty, be it music, art, gardening, animals etc., and they all have a common fascination with Nishikigoi. The popular Japanese term for this type of person is **'Koi-Kichi'** (Koi Crazy) hence the title of my book.

'It's a faint heart that never kissed a Kohaku!'

Looking back to when this book received its first rough printing in 1982, the only thing that hasn't changed in it since then is the title! - a healthy indication of how all aspects of Koi keeping have changed for the better over the past decade or so.

There are many entirely different subjects which go to make up the complete hobby of 'Koi Keeping'; in view of this I have prepared the overall book by dividing it into eight separate 'books', each covering a different aspect of the hobby and each, hopefully, following on from the last. This should allow the reader to make quick and easy reference to a specific subject. Each of the eight 'books' carry a single word title which should indicate the main subject in general and each of the eight 'books' close with a very special Nishikigoi, all of which are current Japanese Champions as of 1995 and some of the finest Koi ever produced to date.

Remember- 'It's a faint heart that never kissed a Kohaku!' (P.Waddington 1985)

They say that every person has one book inside themselves, this is mine, - Happy Koi Keeping!

Peter Waddington. ■

This book is especially dedicated to my late father and my very best teacher, Rhodes Waddington, also to Minnie Waddington - the best mum in the world. To my son, and best mate, Tim, my daughter Inez and her husband Julian who have both contributed in providing me with my gorgeous Granddaughter Ashleigh, my sister Carole, my brother-in-law Paul, my nephews - the strong, silent 'Wes' and the strong, loud 'Andy'. God bless all of you!

Sincere thanks also to the following:-
Roland and Pauline Seal, the late Hilda and Eric Allen, Bill and Margaret Fowler, Malcolm Waumsley, Val Frost, George and Beryl Woodward, Barrie Rowlinson, David Chadwick, the late Arthur Bailey, Rachel Bailey, Liz Donlan (nee Bailey), the 'super' Gerry Preston, Pete Reynolds, Pat Gaule, the late Malcolm Hardy, Peter Dobson, Mike and Inge Yates, Doug and Valli Bookless, Cyril Winterbottom, Paul Holgate, David Aubrey, John Cuvelier and many more for all the enthusiasm and hard work put into the hobby in the early days.

Howard Scott, Bill McGurk, Robert & David Goode, Carl Cheadle, Mary Harrison, Dennis Mitchell, Robbie Eccles and good ol' Tim for assistance in the formative years.

'Gentleman' Joe Wilmington, Syd Canavan, John Shelton & Family, the late John Lilley, Larry Groves, the unique Christoph Wolters, The Glaze Family, Dr. Nadra, Ray and Pat Talbot, Dr. Pasterski, John Mercer, Tony Pidgeley, John Fallows, Roy Charles Erlichmann, Trevor Reece, Steve Coleman, Alexander Lux, 'Big' Ian Stewardson, Trevor Pearson, Gerde Sauter, Jack and Maureen Howcroft, Peter Chalk, Mrs. Cynthia Miles, Greg Jackson, Joe and Norma Banks, Michel and Dominique Capot, Mr. & Mrs. Heinz Peter Mertens, Lou Cator, Ken Waterhouse, Bob and Maggie Coles, The Duke and Duchess of Worcestershire, Garry Bourne, Mary Riddoch, Jean Pichette, Helga Watson, Bill Ashley, John Hall, Reiner Behrens, Gordon Wilkinson, Barry Herbert, Dr. Dodo, Peter Tebby, John Robertson, Lee Roberts, Dr. Litschmann, Terry Holloway, Glyn Evans, Derry Evans, Isokazu Noma, Alan Chan, Brian Eckersley, Arthur Buckley, David Tuson, Richard Guildford, John Pattison, Jimmy Currie, Alan and Margaret Bradwell, John Craven, Jim Reilly, Graham Cheetham, Ryo Kamiya, Joe Wilde, Bernard Chadwick, Ernie Johnstone, Mr. Tsuchiya, Tony McCann, David Yates, Mike Donlan, Stan & Adam Douglas, Louis Hawksby, the late Derek Edwards, Tony West, Janet West, Steve Penney, Paul Valerio, Eric Cotton, Annick Caro, Ian Shotton, Ken and Lynne Boulton, Lance and Jan James, John Harrold, Paul Spencer, Peter Chester, Mick Lovet, Lawrence Hall, Dave Williams, another Dave Williams, John Davis, Mike Brighton, Alan and Margaret Rawlings, Chris Ball, Tommy and Ron Bradshaw, Ron Williams, John Rawlinson, Ed Clark, the late Derek Daws, John Pitham, Chris Ball, Nikki Chapple, Keith Phipps, John Phipps, the late Eric Devis, Fred Webb, Mr. & Mrs. Peet, David Noad, Keith Yoxon, Terry Porter, Dr. Sebastian, Scott Purdin, Bernice Brewster, John Cowell, Geoff Nuttall, Derek Fletcher, Keith Edwards, John Cook, Eric Paxton, Peter Granville, Alan Scandrett, Lance James, Gerry Whitehead, Di & Bob Lucas, John Robson, James Booth, Thongdee, Dave Rice, Dr. Gerde Schafer, Lord John Hunt of Worksop, Maureen Squires, Bill Haddock, Harry Green, Mr. and Mrs. Fielding, Dave Dyson, Chris Bilton, John Cartmel, John & Connie Chadwick, Norman Currie, Alan Rogers, 'Sandy', Roy Winterbourne, Maurice Dent, Rachel Gosling, Mark & Ritta Cooper, Steve Templeton, Ron Parlour, Barry and Linda Price, Stan Collinge, Derek Buckley, Bernard Channing, John Smith, Stan Teesdale, Baron Christoph von Conzendorf-Mattner, George Hurst, Joel and Ali Malach, Ron Sharp, Colin Barr, Keith O'Reilly, Mary Crompton, Paul Halewood, Geoff Claxton, Enda Lyons, Mike Howard, Ken, Pauline and Wayne

Smith, Bob Ashford, Mac Wilson, Ian Brown, John Woodall, Tom and Diana Burton, the late John Hurford, Julia Hall, Bill Oakley, Pete Waterman, Jim Bowcock, David Slater, the late, great F. Mercury, Andy Shepherd, Nick Van Loan, Rod Gilbert, Steve Hickling, Richard Jones, Graham Hutcherson, Naoki, Sue Finney, Norman Adamson, Adrian Barnes, Phil Adamson, Geoff Lambert, Merv Atkinson, Grant Clifton, Mr. & Mrs. Jolley, Itamar Shacham, Eugene Lim, all the 'gang' at the Queen Anne pub in Golborne and the 'Towler' pub in Bury, and many, many, many more for a mixture of many reasons, mostly Koi related, covering friendship, laughs, good times, trust, advice, discussions (sometimes heated), custom and a lifetime of fond memories.

Mr. Satoru Hoshino, Ojiya City for his vast knowledge of the history of Koi in Japan. Mr. Sakai from the Matsunosuke Company in Isawa for all his patience and time in teaching his secrets to a dumb 'gai-jin' (foreigner) like me. Mr.Kawakami, ('Torazo') Uragara, Ojiya; Mr.Tanaka, Yomogihira; Mr.Mano,(Dainichi) Iwamagi; Mr. Hiroi, ('Choguro') Araya; Mr. Hasegawa, Ojiya; The late Mr. Kozaburo Miya, Ojiya; Mr. Watanabe, (Jinbei) Budokubo; Mr. Sakai the elder, (Yamamatsu) Mushigame; Megumi Yoshida, Tokyo; Mr. Fujio Omo, Nagaoka City; Mr. Gamo, Isawa; Mr. Narita, Komaki; Mr. Masutani, Mihara; Mr. Sakai, Hiroshima, and many, many others for listening to, and answering with great patience, all my stupid questions!

Nigel Caddock for encouragement and enthusiasm for me to finally get down and complete this book. (Nigel was one of the few people I showed my original texts and ideas to, back in 1983) And for valuable assistance with many technical and artistic problems that arose during final production of the book of which I had no experience whatsoever. Especially the freedom of using his vast catalogue of photographs from his 'Nishikigoi International' magazine archives which amply covered the many gaps in my own photographs.

Dennis and Hilary Wordsworth, Phil Millson, Cliff Fleming and Rod Mathews, 'The 'A' Team' at Infiltration.

and finally!....................
Townes Van Zandt, Miles Davis, John Hiatt, John Prine, Pink Floyd, Chris Smither, Iris DeMent, Mickey Jupp, Weather Report, Deacon Blue, Leo Kottke, Bob Dylan, Jesse Winchester, Emmylou Harris, Nanci Griffith, Dire Straits, Pat Metheny, Mary Chapin Carpenter, Ry Cooder and others for providing inspiration and background sounds whilst I was transferring all my hand written texts and notes to a word processor.

Book One   'BEGINNINGS'

Book Two 'UNDERSTANDING'

Book Three   'ENVIRONMENT'

Book Four   'NISHIKIGOI'

Book Five 'CARING'

Book Six 'CYCLES'

Book Seven 'PEOPLE'

Book Eight 'MYSTIQUE'

BEGINNINGS

BOOK 1

'BEGINNINGS'
For my own part,
there is still a
tremendous fascination
as to how and why
Nishikigoi were
produced in the first
place. To be brutally
honest, they were
produced more by
mistake rather than by
intent and, for many
years after 'coloured
Carp' had been bred,
apart from the breeders
themselves, very few
others had ever seen or
even heard about them.
This section of the book
explains the history of
origin and development
of Nishikigoi in Japan
as well as covering the
introduction of
Nishikigoi to Japan
and the rest of
the World.

ORIGIN AND DEVELOPMENT OF NISHIKIGOI IN JAPAN

KOI-NO-BORI (CarpStreamers)

Carp, Latin name Cyprinus Carpio, have been around for quite some time and fossils have been discovered in South China which are said to be fairly accurately dated at 20 million years old. There are records which indicate that Carp were reared for food purposes in China five centuries BC although nowadays it is generally agreed that Carp originated in the area surrounding the Caspian Sea, hence the Latin name, and have been introduced, over the centuries, to most parts of the world for food purposes.

It is said, that during the 14th. Century, Carp were introduced into Central Europe via the Crusaders and were further distributed in later years by Monks to most other European areas, including Britain, for food rearing purposes.

Carp were introduced to North America during the 19th. Century from Germany and Japan. It is not certain as to when Carp were first introduced to Japan, but the first documented record of Carp in Japan was during the 8th. Century, presumably coming from China. German Carp (Doitsu) however, did not appear in Japan until August 1904 when 8 only arrived alive from the original 40 shipped.

Today Carp are still farmed in many parts of the world as an important food source. In Japan Carp signifies strength, so-much-so that 'Boys Day' is celebrated annually and many parents, with sons in their families, hang Carp streamers (Koi-no-bori) from their homes to celebrate the event.

the very ancient wild, black Carp known in Japan as 'Magoi'

Carp allowed to grow in large bodies of water are capable of attaining enormous sizes. The longest size recorded in Japan was for a specimen netted in Lake Biwa in the mid 1980's and transported for display in a public aquarium in Kyushu; sadly it could not adjust to captivity and soon died. It is said to have been almost 2 metres long (6.5 feet).

The Japanese word for Carp is 'KOI' and the 'NISHIKIGOI' (brocaded Carp) that are now kept and revered by many collectors throughout the world as the most beautiful of ornamental pet fish, are all direct descendants of the very ancient wild, black Carp known in Japan as 'Magoi'

As mentioned earlier, it is not exactly recorded when Magoi were introduced to Japan for food farming purposes. The main purpose was to produce animal protein where supplies of meat and fish were scarce at certain times of the year. One such area was Niigata Prefecture, a 'county' of tall mountain ranges, rivers, streams, forests and a climate varying from very warm in Summer months to very cold in Winter months when snowfalls could, and still do, exceed 10 metres.

In the middle part of the 19th. Century the main population of Niigata Prefecture comprised of farming people who produced rice, green vegetables and root vegetables on land carved out of the mountainsides. These people were mainly from peasant stock, renting and farming the land which belonged to the wealthy landowners. Indeed, it was not until the turn of the century that these people were allowed to own surnames by law. This privilege was only previously enjoyed by the Samurai classes. Even so, when surnames were allowed, the farming classes were only allowed to choose from a very small list of surnames permissible. This clearly explained to me why many modern day surnames in this area are the same, names such as Miya, Hiroi, Mano and Sakai are very common indeed and this is very confusing to the visitor wishing to purchase Nishikigoi.

The latter-day rice farmers of Niigata, endeavouring to make use of all available land, terraced the mountainsides into rice paddies and irrigated them by means of man-made mud reservoirs, sited above the paddies, which were part-drained periodically to feed the rice paddies below. These ponds filled again naturally with rain and snow water and were found to be ideal for growing Carp fry in the Summer months. Early books state that the fry were actually grown in the rice paddies themselves; this is an inaccuracy. Instead they were grown in the reservoirs which supplied water to the rice paddies. During the 1870's, many rice farmers began to diversify their labours by growing Carp in order to supplement their

standard Winter diet which usually consisted only of rice and root vegetables. It is recorded that the first area in Niigata to attempt to grow Carp for food was the village of Nijumurago during the Edo period in the first half of the 19th. Century.

It must be explained here that, even until quite recently, the Winters in the mountainous areas of Niigata kept the farmers and their families virtual prisoners in their own wooden houses. There was no possibility of travelling to the coast to purchase sea fish to add protein to their diet during Winter as the depth of snow made this impossible. Even today, roofs of cars and houses have to be cleared of snow, sometimes on a daily basis, to prevent them collapsing. Nowadays the area has narrow but good roads, automatic sprinkler systems to keep the roads free from snow, four wheel drive vehicles and mountainsides adjacent to the roads shored up with concrete or steel barriers to keep them free from serious avalanche problems to the traveller.

Snow Scene, Ojiya

Going back to the early days, the Carp fry were produced in early June and grown until mid-October before harvesting at around 10cms. long (4"). They were then dried and salted before being stored to be eaten during the Winter months. Valuable parent stocks were not allowed to be left in outdoor ponds for the Winter. Instead they were housed in small ponds built next to the house or, in many instances, inside the house by simply excavating a pond into the earth floor of the main room. By doing this it prevented losses from severe low water temperatures and natural predators that abound in the area. These 'house ponds' contained very few Carp, only the ones to be used for parents the following Spring. In those days there were no luxuries such as electric water pumps or air pumps and all members of the family had to ensure that aeration was added to the water by regularly disturbing the surface of the pond by hand.

After some years of breeding Carp in Niigata, the production quantities increased and stocks of salted Carp were in abundance. This brought food fish merchants from the large cities of Japan up to Niigata to purchase these for re-sale in their own areas.

No one seems to be sure exactly when the 'rice farmers-cum-Carp-breeders' started to find pigment irregularities in their food stocks but many locals in the area say it was between 1840 to 1844. Soon afterwards, producing 'coloured Carp' became a working class hobby and a Winter diversion to these people. To make a comparison, this was rather the same working class hobby as was pigeon fancying in its early years in Europe; today however, fortunes are paid for some pigeons.

I am assured that some farmers, who saw colour pigmentation occurring on some part of small Carp, kept these as their own pets. Some produced small areas of white whilst others produced random red scales; these were bred with similar Carp belonging to neighbouring farmers and the pastime began to gather momentum.

Even during the early 1900's it was only the Carp farmers themselves who kept their coloured Carp as a private pastime. In later years after a few 'outsiders' had seen and spoken about these rare fish, a few local businessmen, merchants, doctors and landowners started to keep these coloured Carp as a hobby. I mention the word 'local' as, in those days, it was almost impossible to transport the Carp alive for anything much more than five to ten miles as there were no methods of safe packing and transportation. In fact, the method we use today of transporting Koi by plastic bags containing pure oxygen and water was only first used in Japan as recently as 1960 shortly after the invention of the first plastic bag.

Before this method was adopted, moving Koi from area to area was a very risky business indeed, the late Mr. Kozaburo Miya recalled to me:-

"I was only eleven years old when my father instructed myself and my two brothers to accompany him, by cargo train, from Ojiya to Kyushu Island, in order to take some of our parent Nishikigoi to a new breeding area. We constructed a canvas pond and carried the Nishikigoi in wooden baskets, on our shoulders, to the railway station. We placed the canvas pond in the train and ran to the river to get water to fill the pond, it leaked badly, and, at every stop, we had to find more water. My father, my two brothers and myself travelled with the Nishikigoi and each took three hour periods of moving the water surface to provide aeration, even so, several were lost as a result. The journey to Kyushu took four days, my arms were very weak."

The Tokyo Taisho Exhibition held in 1914 first brought coloured Carp to the attention of the Japanese public. The exhibition was held to encourage the different Prefectures to advertise and display items which were unique to each Prefecture. The Carp farmers of Niigata transported their *'Hirogoi'* ('Coloured Carp', as they were then known) to Tokyo by rail in specially constructed wooden containers in order to display their unique hobby for the first time. The Japanese public were very impressed as no one before had seen such beautiful Carp. It is said that, after the Exhibition, some of the stock was placed in the moat surrounding the Emperors' Palace in Tokyo.

illustrations from the Tokyo Taisho Exhibition, 1914

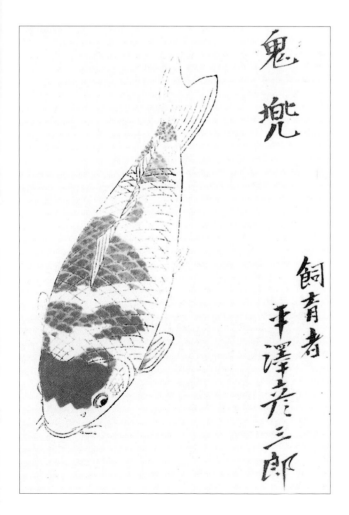

During the Exhibition itself, an artist was commissioned to make a full record of the 'Hirogoi' on display by painstakingly drawing and painting each one by pattern as the only means of identification. This 'one-off' record mysteriously disappeared shortly afterwards and was considered lost forever, fortunately the record turned up in Tokyo during 1987 on sale in a second-hand book store! Its present owner Mr. N. Takanashi has allowed me to reproduce some of the original exhibits in this book.

'Hirogoi' were bred for sale, albeit in a very small way, during 1916 for the local businessmen in the areas around Ojiya, Niigata as mentioned earlier. It is said that the Carp breeders in the village of Takezawa produced the first Hirogoi for sale but communications and publicity in these times were basic to say the least and very few were purchased at all.

Promotion was needed if these coloured Carp were to reach a wider market and, strangely enough, this was carried out by the Carp dealers, mentioned earlier, who visited Niigata to buy stocks of salted Carp for the table. Some purchased small coloured Carp and managed to transport them back alive to their businesses to sell to those wishing to keep them as pets. As a result of this minority interest, a few dealers started to build their businesses to cope with the gradual increase in demand as more and more Japanese became aware of Hirogoi. Much of the credit for 'spreading the word' of early Nishikigoi must go to the following people:-

The Niigata area was developed by the late Mr. Miya, (Miyakoya Co.), Mr. Hirasawa and Mr. Ichizo Kawakami.

The Tokyo area was developed originally by Mr. Akiyama and Mr. Saikichi Yoshida.

The Osaka area was developed by Mr. Tsujimoto and Mr. Takatsuki.

The Hiroshima area was developed by Mr. Konishi, Mr. Watanabe and Mr. Tamaki.

Obviously there are many other people in other areas responsible for similar work, but I feel that recognition should be given to the aforementioned who worked so hard to spread the joy of Nishikigoi (a term not used until after the second World War) to the rest of Japan and, indirectly to the rest of the world. Without the efforts of these and other 'believers' the farmers/breeders would almost certainly still be producing their Hirogoi as a private hobby shared only with their immediate contemporaries.

It is interesting to note that, in the time period between the names *Hirogoi* or *Irogoi* (coloured Carp) to the present day title Nishikigoi (brocaded Carp), they were known by other names along the way, notably *'Hanagoi'* (flowery Carp) and *'Moyoogoi'* (fanciful patterned Carp).

Because the 'hobby' in the early days was only a minor pastime in a very inaccessible area, very few actual records have been retained as to who first produced which variety and when. It was not until the late 1920's that pattern books were kept by some breeders by using coloured inks on a Carp outline to be viewed from above, as Nishikigoi were bred to be viewed. Variations in colour and pattern were logged annually as the specimen matured; this was the only way to maintain records until, in later years, colour photography became available. Mr. Kawakami in Uragara still proudly retains his father's pattern book of Taisho Sanke and Kohaku recorded in the 1930's, however, it is sad to say that most of these records have been lost or destroyed long ago.

DEVELOPMENT OF VARIETIES.

It is difficult to state, with total accuracy, how the varieties we know today were actually produced. As mentioned most records have been lost, the owners having no idea that their pastime would become so popular in years to come. During my research for this subject I have had several conflicting answers to given questions. Early Nishikigoi chronicler Dr. Matsui states that Asagi were first produced in the Takezawa area of Niigata in the early 19th. Century and breeders all seem to agree that Asagi were the first 'variety' ever produced. He further states that Kohaku were also produced in the same area at approximately the same time, but many breeders in the area dispute that Kohaku were around so early. However most agree that the Kohaku line, as we know it, was stabilised around 1930 by Tomoin in Niigata. Dr. Matsui and many breeders agree that Taisho Sanke was originated around 1915 and the breed stabilised in later years by Mr. Kawakami ('Torazo').

More records state that non-metallic Matsuba varieties were first produced in the early 1900's; Ki-Utsuri around 1921; Shiro Utsuri in 1925 and, during 1927 Mr. Hoshino produced Showa varieties from Ki-Utsuri and Kohaku. This variety was only stabilised as recently as 1960 by Kobayashi in Niigata.

Mr. Akiyama, who imported the Carp from Germany mentioned earlier, produced Shusui by cross breeding Asagi with German Carp during 1913. Dr. Matsui says that Mr. Akiyama confided to him that 'Shusui' appear naturally in a random spawning of German Carp i.e. some produce red bellies. It is also interesting to note that the original meaning of Shusui was *'Mr. Akiyamas' own blue Carp'*- it now translates as *'Autumn Water'* as a result of many simplifications in Japanese writing over the years.

As far as metallic varieties are concerned, I will try to explain the origin and development but would ask the reader to excuse the amount of inverted commas used as the original 'varieties' produced were a far cry from even the lowest grade examples destroyed today during culling.

In Niigata, at around the time of the birth of Hirogoi, there were two strains of Magoi present, one known as **'Tetsu Magoi'** - a brown-ish black Carp, and the other known as **'Asagi Magoi'** - a blue-ish black Carp. Tetsu Magoi produced some 'Matsuba- type' varieties (non-metallic) during a natural spawning and, when some Asagi Magoi lost black colour due to age, the 'Asagi' features appeared. The very few 'Matsuba' and 'Asagi' produced were kept as pets, the others salted and sold. The interbreeding of the 'Matsuba' from Tetsu Magoi and the 'Asagi' produced from Asagi Magoi resulted in very limited numbers of fry which were red- orange giving 'Higoi' and yellow giving 'Kigoi.' By breeding Asagi varieties with Higoi and Kigoi from Tetsu Magoi fry, this eventually produced some 'Aka-Matsuba' and 'Ki-Matsuba' varieties.

At around the same time, in a natural Magoi spawning, some 'Kinbo' and 'Ginbo' were produced showing a slight lustre on the dorsal fin. These were later bred with 'Fuji'- a very early variety of 'Shiro Muji' which had a slight lustre on its head (resembling Mt. Fuji). As a result, a small percentage of the spawning produced some metallic versions of Kinbo and Ginbo, resulting in 'Kin-Kabuto' and 'Gin-Kabuto'. These two strains were bred with 'Chagoi' from Tetsu Magoi to produce very limited numbers of the first 'Matsuba-type Ogon' which was simply known as 'Ogon'. 'Ogon' were then crossed with Kigoi mentioned earlier, to produce 'Yamabuki', these were then spawned with Kohaku and some 'Yamabuki-Hariwake' appeared.

As far as the true Matsuba Ogon is concerned, breeding during the early 1960's with two types of Ogon produced some 'Nezu-Ogon'. These were bred back to 'Ogon' parents and some of the fry produced Kin Matsuba and Gin Matsuba.

As recently as 1965 the first 'Purachina' appeared from an unknown breeder in the Utogi area of Niigata after he bred his own Yamabuki male with a female 'Fuji' loaned from the Miyakoya Company. During 1970, some offspring were sold to Mr. Itaru Suda in Kowada. The Yamazaki Company then purchased breeder stocks from Suda and cross-bred them with Shiro Muji 'Dia' (an all white, non-metallic Koi with random 'Dia' or 'Gin-Rin' scales) - soon afterwards 'Gin-Rin Purachina' appeared. Most metallic varieties were all developed in and around the Ojiya area of Niigata by Aoki, Yamamatsu (Matsunosuke), Hirasawa and Suda.

During the early 1960's, many Koi appeared with wild silver reflective scales on the side of the body only. In later years Mr. Uedera, in Hiroshima Prefecture, developed Gin-Rin varieties from Niigata 'Dia' stocks, even today Niigata breeders use the term 'Dia' in preference to 'Gin-Rin'.

As a point of interest I am informed, from several sources, that the first Hi-Utsuri fry appeared in a Takezawa mud pond due to a flock spawning which

Mr. Uedera, conservationist and breeder responsible for developing Gin-Rin varieties

occurred after one female Aka-Bekko had been washed out of one mud pond as a result of heavy rain and was swept into an adjoining mud pond when spawning took place.

Nishikigoi as we know them today did not appear overnight, the breeders of the 19th. Century and their descendants today have patiently strived to produce their dreams, each year getting one step nearer to their goal, only to find the goal posts move one step farther away each year! If one looks at pictures of Koi in the early Japanese Koi books, the Koi that were acclaimed as the best in the world at the time would hardly qualify for fishing pond grade today!

The first book produced for the Japanese market on Nishikigoi was as recently as 1966 by Dr. Kuroki. Before this book became available there were no printed references for enthusiasts and countless confusions arose in most aspects of the hobby in Japan. In the following year a lavish book was produced by Mr. Miya of the Miyakoya Company entitled 'The 100 Best Nishikigoi'; today this book is extremely valuable for collectors of Koi memorabilia. However, when one browses through the book, it is easily apparent that the then best Nishikigoi ever produced would not even receive 'Third in Variety' awards today in the smallest Koi show held in the UK! So much have standards improved in the past thirty years or so.

Today, however, Niigata Prefecture is still the world centre for high grade Nishikigoi production and, during late October, when the Ojiya Show is held, all the hotels in the area are booked solid with Koi enthusiasts and dealers from all parts of Japan, and in

Rice Paddies next to Nishikigoi Mud Ponds, Mushigame, Niigata.

recent years, from many other parts of the globe. This is the time of the year when all mud ponds have been harvested after the Summer growing period and the best Koi are exhibited in a two day event for all to see. There are several other important Koi producing areas in Japan today, notably Hiroshima, Isawa, Shizuoka, Saitama, Kyushu and Toyama as well as many smaller areas, yet the breeders of Niigata still remain at the top of the tree for **high class** Koi production. I have often asked these breeders why they still choose the Niigata area to produce their stocks in a climate of uncomfortable Winters and a multitude of answers will come forth. Some say the

Niigata water is the best in Japan; others say the Niigata mud is the best for growing strong Koi; others say the competition from 900 breeders in a 50 square mile area produces a strong competitive instinct to produce better stocks each year. Whatever the reasons are, and it may well be a combination of answers, the facts remain that the most famous names in Koi breeding choose to remain in Niigata. Names that are sacred to the serious enthusiast, Dainichi, Matsunosuke, Isumiya, Miyatora, Igarashi, Jinbei, Torazo, Maruju, Yamaguchi, Hoshikin, Hosoki, Tanaka, Suda, Hiroi Seiji and many other high grade breeders who seem to produce better stocks every year.

'The Mud', Niigata clay being replenished before the Summer growing season for fry

Importance of 'The Mud', Niigata clay being replenished before the Summer growing season for fry. After a few seasons the mineral values within the clay have been exhausted by the fry grown in previous seasons. Picture taken Spring '95 at 'secret' Tategoi ponds owned by Dainichi in Ojiya.

It is also a real fact that Niigata rice is renowned throughout Japan as the best rice in the world, reasons for this are given that the mud and water quality is responsible. In every instance the bloodlines and parent stocks favoured by Koi breeders throughout Japan are all from Niigata origins:-

Kohaku lines from Manzo, Tomoin, Sensuke, Yagozen and Dainichi.

Taisho Sanke lines from Matsunosuke, Sadazo, Torazo, Kichinai, and Jinbei.

Showa parents from Kobayashi, Maruju and Seijuro.

As far as Shiro Utsuri are concerned, few would doubt that Sakai and Omosako in Hiroshima produce the finest examples of this variety today, however the original parent stocks used to produce them were all from Niigata.

There are more details of bloodlines in a later section of this book where varieties are discussed in greater depth.

The 'boom year' for Koi in Japan was 1965 when the hobby really made an impact on the Japanese public. At that time around 3,000 breeders in all areas could literally sell all their production very easily to the eager home market. I am told that, during the early to mid 1960's, the Japanese public would buy a Koi for reasons such as:- the colour was the same as their favourite flower; the Koi only had one pectoral fin; the Koi had a big head etc. etc. - in short they bought them because they were cute!

Today the breeders are reduced to around 1,200, the main reason being that volume sales of regular grade Koi no longer have the volume buyers to purchase this kind of stock. The swing, since 1965, has been towards the small percentage of high grade stocks produced and today, as the hobby becomes more international and knowledge increases accordingly, the enthusiasts become more and more discerning in their purchases.

Above **Entering Nishikigoi to the All Japan Show.**

Left **Koi in show ponds as far as the eye can see.**

The All-Japan
Nishikigoi Dealers
Association
Anual Show

The remaining breeders understand the demand all too well and the competitive urge to produce the best is high. Obviously many more Koi have to be destroyed today during culling purely because they have no commercial value which means the fewer, albeit far better Koi produced, are more expensive. It is, therefore, the enthusiasts who dictated the increased price of Koi from the breeders by urging them to make more severe culls. Contrary to popular opinion, the price of high grade Koi increases every year due to the higher standard of quality produced, whilst the price of general grade stocks seems to decrease accordingly, which substantiates the supply and demand situation at the present time.

As far as the amateur side of the hobby goes in Japan today, it is extremely strong indeed with Zen Nippon Airinkai, the largest Koi Society in the world, serving its home members as well as members from many other parts of the globe. It produces a monthly magazine 'Nichirin' which also has an English text version and supports and encourages Local Chapter Shows in many parts of Japan. There is also a large independently-produced monthly magazine entitled 'Rinko' which is excellent and also available in English text. Each year the ZNA National Show is held in late November at different venues throughout Japan.

The All-Japan Nishikigoi Dealers Association hosts its annual Show in Tokyo during January, entries at this event can exceed 5,000 of the most incredible Koi in Japan and is well worth a visit.

Of course, there are some collectors in Japan at the very top end of the hobby with enormous collections of very famous Koi, one is Mr. Anabuki who produces a large calendar each year to display some of his Champion Koi. Another is the almost legendary Mr. Kato, who, it is said, has around 90 mud ponds in many areas of Japan to grow his Koi during the Summer months!

Closing this section of the book, I feel it right and proper to dispel a few myths that surround Nishikigoi that have added to the mystique which has escalated over the years, unfortunately they are now getting a little out of hand.

World famous Nishikigoi collectors, Mr. Kamiya (centre) and Mr, Kato (right)

■ The average lifespan of Nishikigoi is around 25 to 30 years, kept in good conditions. An early book mentioned a Higoi known as 'Hanako' which died in the late 1970's, and was reputed to have been around 200 years old! This was assumed by counting 'growth rings' on a scale put under a microscope, in the same way as growth rings on a tree are counted. This method of determining the age of a Carp has long since been discounted as a total inaccuracy as rings appear on scales when water temperatures reach around 50 degrees Fahrenheit, during Spring and Autumn. Water temperatures can fluctuate up and down at these times of the year and this temperature can be reached many times which produces more rings. Hanako may well have been a very old lady indeed, but I doubt if she would have reached her 50th. birthday before passing away; still it is a fascinating story!

■ The largest Nishikigoi ever produced is a subject that comes up from time to time. In truth, very few Koi, in relationship to the millions produced, have reached the one metre mark. At the time of writing no Kohaku, Sanke or Showa variety has exceeded 93cm., and there is a serious challenge and a significant financial reward to the first breeder who can grow one of these varieties to 1 metre. Of the few that have exceeded 1 metre, many are male Koi, usually very slim and often deformed in some parts of the body; varieties are usually Asagi, Chagoi, Kin Kabuto, and Hikari-Muji etc. etc. In over 70 visits to Japan I personally have only ever seen a genuine one metre Koi on less than ten occasions. According to many Japanese breeders, the largest Nishikigoi produced to 1988 was a Kigoi which measured 105cms.

■ Another question often asked by newspaper reporters and sensation seekers is 'How much?'- this is far more difficult to answer as few buyers of very expensive Nishikigoi wish it to be generally known how much was paid or, in some cases, where the funds came from. Also very few very expensive Nishikigoi are purchased without two or three unwanted ones being taken back in 'part-exchange'. In view of this, the 'witnessed' purchase prices paid for some very expensive Nishikigoi will certainly not reflect many higher prices that have been paid in private transactions. In open transactions there are prices that have been paid up to around 50,000,000 yen, which, at today's exchange rate at the time of writing, means £318,000.00!- very expensive indeed, but certainly not millions of pounds as many seem to believe.

I have asked many dealers, breeders, enthusiasts and historians in Japan, the truth of longevity, length and highest price of Nishikigoi and most answers substantiate these statements.

"In over 70 visits to Japan I personally have only ever seen a genuine one metre Koi on less than ten occasions"

97cm Yamabuki
All-Japan Show, January 1995

INTRODUCTION AND DEVELOPMENT OF NISHIKIGOI IN THE UK.

The first commercial importation of Nishikigoi to the UK was made by the late Mr. Gooding of G. H. Richard & Company in the London area during 1966, the shipment was made by Kamihata Fish Industries Ltd. from their Chiba depot.

In the following year, the late Mr. Colin Roe of Shirley Aquatics near Birmingham imported Koi to his premises and built quite a name for 'Koi Carp' – as they were then known to the very small band of enthusiasts interested at that time. Incidentally, Mr. Roe, together with Mr. Evans, also now deceased, wrote and produced the first ever publication in the English language on the subject of Nishikigoi, simply entitled 'Koi'.

Soon afterwards the UK importers started to increase in number – Robinson Fisheries in London, L. Cura & Co. in Hemel Hempstead, Stapeley Water Gardens in Cheshire, Aquatic Nurseries in London and from there the list increases rapidly.

I feel it should be recorded that these companies were the true pioneers of the hobby in the UK and thanks must go to these people for bringing Nishikigoi to the attention of the British fish keeper, and thus by doing so, provided a new variety to the traditional British garden pond which was previously a home for goldfish, shubunkins and orfe etc.

Equally important was the formation, in 1970, of The British Koi-Keepers' Society who pioneered the hobby from an enthusiasts viewpoint. This Society has grown over the years and nowadays has Local Sections in most areas of the UK. This growth in the membership is directly due to the hundreds of hard working members who have given time and labour, totally free of charge, in order to serve the membership at large. Today the BKKS has its own Judging and Standards Committee, Emergency Helplines for members, a National Show Committee who are responsible for staging the annual BKKS National Show, plus many Committees who run the Local Section Memberships to arrange monthly meetings, pond visits, inter-section visits and their own annual Koi shows.

The UK has also several other independent Koi Societies, notably The Yorkshire Koi Society; The Midland Koi Association; The East Midlands Koi Club; Heart of England Koi Society; North Lincs Koi Society; Wessex Koi Society; South of England ZNA Chapter and the recently formed Northern Koi Club.

During the turn of the decade 1979/81, the interest in the hobby of Koi keeping in the UK began to accelerate at an unforeseen pace. Around this time the majority of outlets where one could buy Koi consisted of garden centre outlets, water garden centre outlets,

Two of the founder members of the BKKS, Hilda and Eric Allen

'Nishikigoi 85"
UK Dealer Show

(Above) The Award Ceremony

(Right) National Television interest.

small back garden businesses and aquarium shops, usually selling other varieties of pet fish and accessories. I also started my Nishikigoi business trading from my home in a very small way, but specialising only in Nishikigoi and related accessories. I advertised under the name of Infiltration and started to visit Japan in order to purchase a better grade of Koi than those that were then available in the UK. I soon realised that I would have to move 'premises' before my neighbours made official complaints to the local council about endless cars and the odd coachload of visitors turning up at my house! I found a large industrial unit to rent and started to design and build the first 'professional Koi-only outlet' outside of Japan which opened for business in May of 1982. The initial reaction from enthusiasts was 'mixed' to say the least, everyone commented on how wonderful a specialist Koi-only outlet was for their needs, whilst others expressed doubts as to the viability. During the early to mid 1980's we began to build Koi ponds and design filtration systems for customers. At that time I was making seemingly countless visits to Japan to find more stocks and to carry on learning thus, our business, together with the hobby, began to grow.

Since our early days many more specialist Koi companies have formed in the UK bringing better Japanese Nishikigoi to enthusiasts all over the country. Companies, at the time of writing, such as Harrow Koi, Koi Water Barn, Shirley Aquatics, The Real McKoi, Japanese Water Gardens, Clearwater Koi, D.J's Koi, World of Koi, Quality Koi, Cascade Water Gardens, Selective Koi Sales, Q.S.S., How Kang Koi, Free Roberts Koi, Britkoi, Cotswold Koi, Cleveland Koi and many more.

1985 saw the first ever UK Dealers Show, 'Nishikigoi 85' held at Nottingham and organised jointly between Infiltration and Japanese Water Gardens. This event brought the Japanese-style Show to the UK, where Nishikigoi from different enthusiasts, for the first time ever, were entered in common water alongside each other in variety and size. Hitherto previous UK show rules would not allow Koi from different sources to be exhibited together for fear of transmission of disease. Fifty Japanese display ponds were imported for the event, the Judging was carried out on the evening prior to the show by a combination of UK enthusiasts, dealers and BKKS Judges together with enthusiasts and dealers from Japan. The event was a resounding success and a milestone in the UK hobby. After this, there followed many UK Dealer Shows, for the past few years these have been held in Telford, Shropshire.

There is no doubt whatsoever that those, in the UK, involved in Nishikigoi in the early days, in a minor hobby shared between a few friends sparsely distributed around the country, could ever have even dreamed it would reach the numbers it has today. As the numbers continue to increase so does the

All-England
Nishikigoi Dealers Show,
'B.A.N.D. '89'

demand for knowledge and up-to-date information, demand for high grade Koi is higher than ever with several private collectors owning specimens of exceptional quality. The hobby itself has improved in leaps and bounds in just about every aspect, especially in the methods surrounding pond design, construction, filtration and heating techniques etc.

Reading matter for the UK Koi enthusiast today can be found in several publications, notably 'Rinko' and 'Nichirin' (mentioned earlier) both printed in English on a monthly basis and available by subscription from Japan. UK publications include the high quality 'Nishikigoi International' magazine, capably edited and produced on a quarterly basis by Nigel Caddock, and the monthly magazine of the British Koi Keepers Society sent to all members. Nishikigoi are covered more and more in monthly aquatic publications such as Practical Fishkeeping and The Aquarist and Pondkeeper, in December 1994, a new magazine called 'Koi Carp' was launched on a monthly basis.

BKKS National Show-'KOI '94'

DEVELOPMENT OF NISHIKIGOI AROUND THE WORLD

It never ceases to fascinate me that a mountain farmer's simple private pastime of trying to produce beautiful colours to the humble black Carp, previously suitable only for food purposes, has spread to just about every corner of the globe. Today it appears that enthusiasts the whole world over are fascinated with the beauty of Nishikigoi.

In recent years, during my visits to Japan, I have come across enthusiasts and dealers from countries such as the USA, Canada, Thailand, Taiwan, Korea, Singapore, Indonesia, Brazil, South Africa, Cyprus, Germany, France, Holland, Belgium, Israel and the list continues to grow. Australia now has many Koi enthusiasts today despite their early days of a 'secret society' when the importation into Australia was banned for fear of these escaping into the eco-system and reproducing in their ideal climate.

Recently I have given lectures on the East Coast of America and Germany where I found very serious enthusiasts hungry for knowledge on all aspects of the hobby.

As far as Nishikigoi production is concerned in other areas of the world, there are several countries producing on a commercial basis. Today, Israeli-bred stocks are shipped to many parts of the world as are Chinese stocks, Taiwanese stocks, Korean stocks, Thai stocks and some American stocks. In my own opinion, these stocks can only help the overall hobby. In comparison with those produced in Japan the stocks produced by other countries are considerably inferior in quality, shape and colour, but find huge markets where price is the key factor which unfortunately has been governed, especially in recent years, by the continuing strength of the Japanese Yen against the continuing decline in strength of most other major currencies. This factor gives other Koi producing countries a very strong price advantage over the helpless Japanese breeders. However, many ardent enthusiasts,

Koi Show held in the USA.

who now collect Japanese-bred Nishikigoi, started out in the hobby with Koi bred elsewhere and many more will gain valuable experience with these cheaper Koi in the coming years. I often hear the comments on how the quality is improving in stocks from this country and that country, but the truth of the matter is that, in my experience, stocks in Japan seem to be improving in equal or greater rates as the years go by.

There is no doubt about it, Nishikigoi have brought keepers from all parts of the globe together to share this common interest. Today it is not uncommon for enthusiasts to travel to far-off lands to attend a Koi event and spend a few extra days 'talking Koi' to old and new friends alike, Nishikigoi have become truly international in this respect.

At the time of writing this section of the book, John Fallows (pictured right) is the owner of the current UK 'Supreme Champion', a Kohaku which took this award at BKKS 'Koi'94' held in August 1994 at Northampton.

International friendship brought about through Nishikigoi, Reiner Behrens (left) from Dusseldorf, Germany visiting John Fallows at his pond in Liverpool, UK to generally 'talk Koi'.

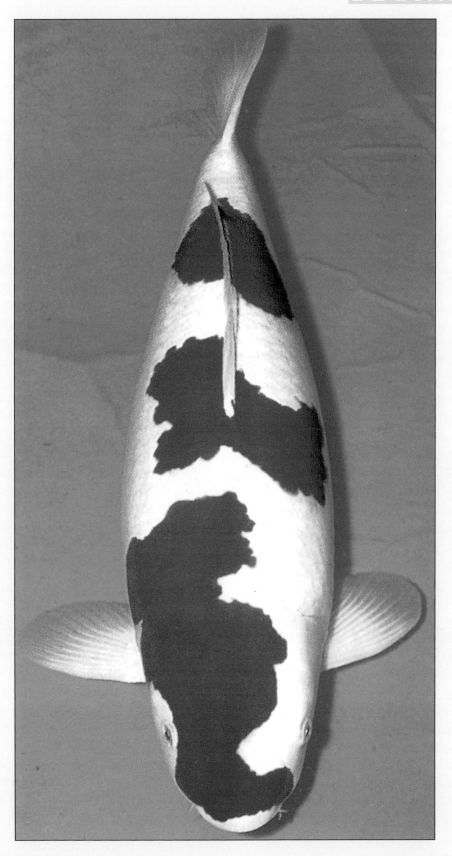

The face pattern on this Sandan Kohaku is so unique it almost appears to be unreal.
The edge of the head pattern to the left sweeps gently around the left eye whilst
the head area surrounding the right eye is pure white. The nose pattern is
extremely bold yet the white lips make a very pleasing contrast.
At the time of the photogragh this female was 65cm. (26")

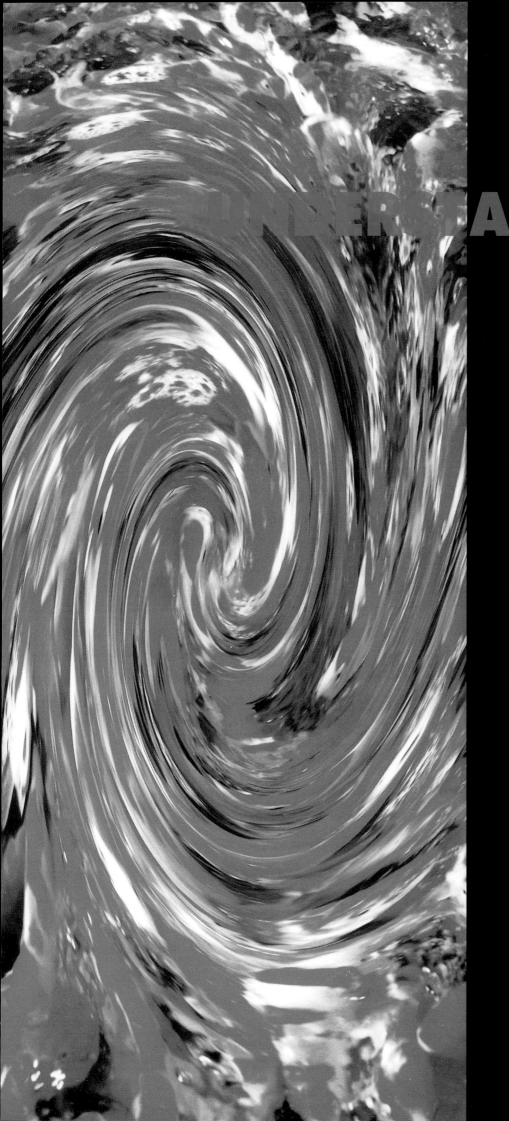

UNDERSTANDING

BOOK 2

'*UNDERSTANDING*'
Before going into detail on any aspect of Nishikigoi it is vital that I try to explain what the overall hobby can encompass and, at the same time, explain the basic water conditions which are necessary for Nishikigoi to thrive. By doing this, the information given in detail elsewhere in the book should have some form of introduction in this section.

WHAT KEEPING KOI CAN INVOLVE.

The overall hobby of keeping Koi encompasses many aspects other than the Koi themselves, and to many, these aspects are equally fascinating. The Koi keeper must also grasp an adequate knowledge of the following if he/she is to get the maximum pleasure from the hobby and all it entails.

* *Pond water conditions necessary for Koi to thrive.*
(This is covered later in this section of the book.)

* *Correct methods of pond design and construction.*
(See section 'Environment')

* *Correct methods of filtration.*
(See section 'Environment')

* *Understanding of water quality and how to maintain this.*
(See this section and also 'Environment')

* *Correct feeding techniques.*
(See section 'Caring')

* *Accurate methods of diagnosis and control of parasitic and/or bacterial problems.*
(See section 'Caring')

* *Breeding Nishikigoi.*
(See section 'Cycles')

* *Understanding and correct pronunciation of some popular Japanese Koi names and words.*
(See section 'Mystique')

Too many times have I heard newcomers to the hobby tell me "Oh! I don't want to get involved like the 'lunatics'- I just want a few pretty fish to look at." (My exact sentiments when I started!) More often than not these newcomers are usually the ones who become total addicts and perfectionists, and usually these are the ones who surprise us with the speed at which they become quite expert in the hobby. There is no given time period for 'apprenticeship' in Koi keeping and many who have only been in the hobby for a short period of time can be way in front of many who have been involved for many years. Like any hobby or pastime the enthusiasm and thirst for knowledge makes for quick, easy and enjoyable learning.

On top of this, Koi keeping is certainly not a hermits hobby, Koi keepers NEED other Koi keepers to chat to; to argue with; to help each other and to joke with,- if you need proof of this I suggest you visit a large Koi show and eavesdrop on some of the in-depth and very serious conversations that take place.

In short, keeping Koi is more of an addiction and a way of life rather than just a casual hobby. Most Koi breeders in Japan and most dealers outside of Japan are primarily in the business because they have become addicts; there are far safer things to tie up ones capital with than any form of livestock.

Another Japanese saying, roughly trans-lated, states 'To sell Nishikigoi successfully, first you must love them.' On many occasions I have witnessed Koi breeders harvesting their mud ponds to see their three to five year old tategoi for the first time in five months since they were placed outdoors to grow and improve. The wide grin that spreads all over their faces as they

Sanke

carefully lift them into transportation containers cannot be feigned - pure joy! This is what Nishikigoi is all about, there are disappointments from time to time, but the 'highs' more than compensate.

I, like most others had many set-backs, especially in my early days, Koi jumping out of a pond on the first night, pump failure resulting in many losses, ammonia/nitrite problems etc. etc.- always my fault and always preventable had I the knowledge and experience beforehand.

One experience in my early days more than compensated for my stupid mistakes and probably became instrumental in my decision to become a Koi dealer. This story started on my first visit to Japan in 1977 with a party of enthusiasts from the British Koi-Keepers' Society led by Roland Seal. In our Kyoto leg of the trip we visited a dealer called Umemura and many of us were rushing around, finding Koi and checking prices with a very harassed and overworked interpreter. I purchased six after deliberation but the final one was somewhat of a puzzle to me and I asked Roland as to the variety. Roland too was puzzled and we both agreed it was either a Sanke or a Showa or a 'bit of both'! This Koi was about 17" long and very cheap and, on return to the UK many friends asked me why I had purchased such an ugly specimen and I had to agree with them.

Some weeks later disaster struck, it was mid-Summer and my pond was crystal clear after a new filtration system had been installed. One evening, upon returning from work, I went to my pond to feed my Koi as usual; to my horror the white skin and fins of many Koi had become an angry red and panic set in. Telephone calls were made all over the country and someone diagnosed Columnaris disease. The remedy was to bring the affected Koi indoors to my garage system and inject all with a course of Gentamycin. (It was some three years later before I learned the truth of the matter which was the Koi were actually suffering with 'ultra-violet degeneration' or sunburn brought about by a combination of strong sunlight in a crystal clear, unshaded pond.) The courses of injections were administered as specified, the Koi recovered completely; I believed it was the antibiotic that was responsible when, in reality, it was the indoor situation that was all that was needed.

Only one Koi refused to heal and continued to deteriorate at an alarming rate, this was my 'Sanke-Showa' from Umemura. Friends advised me to put the Koi out of its misery by anaesthesia and their advice was good. By then the Koi had no pectoral, dorsal or tail fins, massive ulcerations covered the entire length of the body on either side of the spine and the swim bladder was clearly visible, plus 80% of all scales were missing. I really could not bring myself to kill the poor thing and, instead, decided to put it into a pond which had no stocks at all and contained some 2,000 gallons of stagnant, unfiltered, green water. For the next week or so I kept looking at the pond expecting to find a floating carcass but saw nothing other than gnat larvae and other water insects. I assumed that the fish was probably dead and decomposing at the bottom of the pond.

Showa

It was some 18 months later when I decided to modernise this pond by cleaning it out thoroughly and adding good filtration and a bottom drain to it. I started a siphon to empty the pond and waited for the level to drop before I was able to climb inside to make a

start. As the level dropped, the outline of a child's' red tricycle came to view, I took a net to it and lifted it out, as I did this an outline of a Koi darted past me and disappeared again from view. I rushed to find a bowl and waited until the water levels were low enough to catch the Koi, only then remembering that I placed my 'Sanke-Showa' in this pond some 18 months before and wondering how anything could survive without food for so long. After what seemed like ages I could eventually climb into the pond and finally had the Koi in a bowl, I carried the bowl to my main pond and released her.

I stood there for hours in total disbelief, the Koi was 22" long and female, every single scale had regenerated completely, all skin tissue had regenerated completely with no sign of any scars, every fin had re-grown, the shape and volume was perfect in every way but, more importantly, she was 100% true Showa with a superb pattern and colour pigmentation. Furthermore she was, by far, the best Koi in my collection!

Some two months later I took my Koi to Norfolk and entered her in the BKKS National Show. After benching her I went for breakfast and on my return found she had been awarded 'Best Showa in Size', later that day two Koi were being judged for Supreme Champion and the decision was so close that a coin was tossed eventually to decide; my Koi took second place and I was delighted. On going to the stage to collect my trophies from Roland Seal, he asked me where I had found such a Koi and how I had kept it so secret. I told him about the 'Sanke-Showa' from Umemura but he refused to believe me and it took me several weeks before he finally accepted my story.

In 1980 I sold my Showa to the Glaze family in the West Midlands where she went on to take several more awards. At BKKS Koi '94 held at Northampton, the Glaze family came to my stand and gave me their annual update on my Showa. She is now some 20 years old and her showing days are over, but she has grown and is the family pet and the true story has a true happy ending!

Before you all start rushing out to find an old red tricycle to throw in your pond, close down your filters and stop feeding your Koi for good, I would offer a few comments:-

■ Only one Koi was placed in 2,000 gallons of water.

■ The insect life within the pond may have been just enough for this one Koi.

■ Good fortune played a significant part to this story.

■ The standard of Koi in the UK at the time she won her awards was far, far lower than today's standards in the UK; no longer can such a Koi take this type of award.

However, on the positive side, looking back it was my first real experience with 'Tategoi' and conclusively proved to me that flesh and skin tissue can completely regenerate as can fins and scales given the right, albeit in this case, – uncontrollable, conditions.

Proof of how Tategoi develop.

Photograph 1 taken mid February 1995

Photograph 2 taken early June 1995

POND WATER CONDITIONS NECESSARY FOR NISHIKIGOI TO THRIVE.

"Why build all these fancy ponds and filtration systems when Koi are only coloured versions of our wild carp? – our wild carp do very nicely thank you in our muddy lakes, ponds and rivers!" This is a question that is often posed and, at least, deserves a serious answer.

As mentioned earlier, Nishikigoi were bred from the original black carp known in Japan as Magoi; these carp have a shape which is almost identical to our Nishikigoi. The so-called 'carp' we find in our UK eco-system of waterways also were originally introduced from these stocks. Unfortunately the majority of those originally introduced could not adapt to our severe Winters and many were lost, others survived. Some were cross-bred with German strains of Carp to **evolve** into what they have become today, a short, deep-bodied, stocky fish far removed from the cigar shape of the original. True, they still carry the Latin name 'Cyprinus Carpio' but have changed dramatically in shape and hardiness in order to survive in the harsh Winter and cool Summer conditions of Europe.

As our native 'carp' are far hardier than Magoi, Magoi, in turn are far hardier than Nishikigoi in a natural environment. To some extent our Nishikigoi are partially man-made, their genealogy has been interfered with in order to produce a variety of colours and varieties. As a result our Nishikigoi are to Magoi as say, thorough-bred horses are to wild horses, that is to say more pleasing to most eyes, yet not so resilient or strong if left to fend for themselves.

One of the first things I heard when I started in the hobby was **"Don't try to keep Koi, learn how to keep water, then the Koi will 'keep' themselves"**. This maxim is sound advice indeed although it was only years later that I really understood that the real secret of successful Koi keeping really is knowing how to keep good water.

I must point out here that there are many books available which cover every possible aspect of water quality. These have been written by eminent scientists who specialise in pollution, water make-up, de-salination methods, mineral content, all forms of algae and their effects etc. etc. Many of these books cover minute details of the water requirements for all forms of fish life and scientifically explain aspects such as pH; Ammonia; Nitrite; Nitrate; Dissolved Oxygen; Hardness; Metals and other pollutants which all can affect our Koi. Rather than bore the reader with page upon page of technical data taken directly from these textbooks, it is far easier to give ideal readings of the above, for our own specific application, and to supply simple, direct information as to how to control and maintain these within a Koi pond system.

I had no idea of any water requirements for my fish when I built my first pond, this, together with advice from water garden outlets to build myself 'a natural pond' led to my first pond design and construction disaster! Today the advice has changed little in many similar outlets since 1972 where 'a natural pond' means a 2 feet deep hole in the ground waterproofed by pre-formed GRP pond, plastic or rubber sheeting, adding planting baskets stuffed with special plant soil and containing lilies and other plants - *don't forget the oxygenating ones!*

Then a pump is needed to power a fountain and/or waterfall, in recent years other 'natural' items have appeared such as domestic cold water storage tanks full to the brim with assorted gubbins through which pond water is pumped until the silt becomes too much and the 'filter' overflows. After this has all been incorporated we add fish and then food. After this we add more food and then, yes — you guessed, more food! Hands up! I admit I did it in 1972! and people in all parts of the world are still doing it today, namely building very expensive sewers and calling them fish ponds. The penny finally dropped for me after constructing my first disaster when I realised that only God makes natural ponds and never in a weekend! – these usually evolve over decades.

Ironically though, natural ponds and lakes do hold the key to some of the basic water conditions which our Koi need if they are to thrive instead of to merely survive. If we look closely at natural conditions where fish life thrives and try to simulate some of these with modern technology as is done in up-to-date techniques of tropical and marine aquaria then we are on the road to keeping water properly.

Before we investigate the advantages of natural ponds it should be pointed out that there are very few of these remaining in the UK where modern man has not left his mark. Industrial and chemical pollution, removal of some fish species, addition of other species, weed cutting, control of natural predators and so on, all serve to alter finely balanced food chains. Still, we do have some excellent pond, lake and river systems left where we can try to incorporate the important features in our Koi ponds.

1. Depth.
The majority of our ponds, lakes and rivers where Carp are found have depths of more than seven feet (two metres). In Summer months Carp can be seen basking in shallow, warmer areas whilst in Winter they are usually to be found in the deeper areas. A common myth is that deeper water is warmer water, in truth in depths between 1

An efficient Koi pond system is quite simply a garden aquarium where the owner can control and regulate, by artificial means, every aspect of the requirements of the stock within the pond at all times of the year. It is also the most important 'tool' a Koi Keeper can have as the water conditions it produces and maintains will determine how well the Koi will thrive and develop.

foot to 10 feet there is little or no difference in Winter water temperatures at any of these depths in the same system. The reason that fish life generally chooses deeper water in Winter is that deeper water is not subject to the temperature fluctuations that would occur in shallow water during Winter say, when a sunny day is followed by a freezing night. All forms of fish life are particularly sensitive to water temperature fluctuations, it has been stated that a drop in one degree Fahrenheit to a Carp is equivalent to a drop of four degrees Fahrenheit to a human. If our Nishikigoi are subjected to a UK Winter in a shallow unheated pond, the temperature fluctuations will constantly weaken them on a day to day basis as they have no method of dealing with this situation which never occurs in deeper water. If this is allowed to continue throughout the Winter, losses will most certainly occur in Spring as a direct result of this constant weakening process.

Another good reason that our Koi are more suited to deep water is that of shape which is very important when showing Koi, good water depth grows our Koi with good shape whilst warm shallow water tends to produce a 'rugby ball' shape which is not so desirable. Another good factor for having a deep pond is that of protection against predators like the heron, it is rare that a heron will be able to successfully 'fish' in a deep pond with steep vertical walls, it is far easier for this bird to walk into a shallow pond and feed.

For many years now, most of the serious Koi keepers and dealers in the UK have added some form of heating systems into their Koi ponds. By using heat wisely the overall health and growth rates produced has been in comparison with growth rates in Japan, losses have been significantly reduced and more success and enjoyment has been experienced in the overall hobby.

Heating systems will be covered later as will recommended running temperatures in the section 'Environment' but it must be pointed out here and now that Nishikigoi are not true coldwater fish as many state. Furthermore no species of fish life 'hibernate' in Winter and cold water periods as many also believe. Some years ago in Niigata, Japan, an experiment was carried out where a series of filtered concrete ponds were linked together by a common channel and each pond was heated at different temperatures in 5° Fahrenheit differentials starting at 45° to 80° Fahrenheit. Nishikigoi were placed in each pond and left to their own devices. Within four days of the test starting, all stocks shoaled in the pond running at 70° Fahrenheit and stayed between this pond and the 75° Fahrenheit pond for one year, the duration of the experiment. As a point of interest all stocks chose to feed at all times.

It is also true that the vast majority of Japanese Koi that have been imported to the UK since 1980 have never had to experience water temperatures below 55° Fahrenheit, nor have their parents, they are always housed indoors for Winter nowadays.

2. Water changes & waste removal.

All our 'natural' ponds and lakes are fed by streams, springs and land drainage, each has both an inlet source for new water and an outlet exit for older water. When heavy rains occur the inlet stream swells which flushes out debris that has settled since the last heavy rainfall, this debris is taken via the outlet stream and eventually into our main river systems where this flushing effect is much more apparent. The efficiency of a natural flushing-out of these waterways can be witnessed by the necessity of constant dredging operations in our estuaries.

3. Water volume to stocking rates.

Even a very large man-made Koi pond system cannot compare in volume to a very small natural pond, stocking rates in nature

are minute in comparison to our stocking requirements for our Koi ponds. In view of this we have to provide efficient and constant filtration in order to be able to realise our high stocking requirements.

4. Natural food chains.

In natural waters there are natural food chains which supply all forms of water life within the system. This cannot be simulated in the same way in our man-made systems and has to be compensated by the feeding of correct foods on a daily basis.

5. Stable water readings.

The majority of our natural systems have very stable pH; ammonia; nitrite, nitrate and dissolved oxygen readings which have evolved over the years. This has been produced by a fine balance between plant, fish and insect life and any changes that occur to these readings will be extremely gradual indeed. Temperature changes from season to season are also on a very gradual basis in large bodies of water. As a result most wild fish seldom have to cope with constant severe fluctuations in any of the above and they are not armed to cope with these should they occur. In the same way our Nishikigoi have no means of rapidly adapting to constant fluctuations of the above.

6. Plant Life.

In nature this is vital to the natural food chains, it cannot be simulated with any accuracy within a man-made system. In view of this there is no reason to use plants within a Koi pond itself, other than that of pure aesthetic value. In my experience, large Koi and plants do not live in harmony together. As far as the system operation is concerned to provide excellent water conditions (see section 'Environment') plants and planting baskets only help to restrict water flow patterns and allow build-up of debris to accumulate thus reducing system efficiency significantly.

7. Green Water.

Most natural bodies of water have periods of green water conditions which provides valuable foods to some chains within the system. Most Koi keepers prefer to be able to see their stocks at all times yet green water conditions will come to many Koi ponds from time to time. Good green water conditions are very difficult to simulate for any period of time in a man-made pond as we come back again to the natural food chain, but there is no doubt that a period of good green water greatly enhances colour pigmentation in Koi. It should be pointed out here that there is both good and bad green water as there is good and bad clear water which will be explained later in the section 'Environment'.

8. Mud/Clay.

Our eco-systems are formed naturally from this type of matter to retain the water and there is no doubt that many vitamins and minerals in the soil are beneficial to the fish themselves. In Japan the mud ponds, which are totally man-made and have no inlet and outlet streams like our natural systems, are only used for growing during the Summer months when water temperatures are high. These are greatly valued for the quality of the clay in terms of the benefits of the minerals and vitamins it gives off. In a man-made pond we can simulate these conditions partially by the use of 'Re-fresh' on a regular basis.
(see section 'Environment')

9. Herons; Minks; Frogs; Kingfishers; Parasites; Anglers and Boats.

We don't need these in our Koi ponds so we'll just forget them altogether!

10. Natural Daylight.

All wild fish life receive a significant benefit from the vitamins produced in natural daylight. The daylight also produces fine moss-like algae to the pond walls which gives vital minerals to the Koi when eaten. If Nishikigoi are kept in systems which receive insufficient natural light, not only does colour and skin lustre suffer greatly as a result but these vital minerals and vitamins are also removed which reduces the overall health and natural resistances within the Koi. Good natural light conditions should always be taken into account when keeping Nishikigoi. For proof of this, one only has to observe how rapidly colours and lustre intensifies after a Koi is placed in good natural light conditions after being kept for a period of time in an environment which has little or no natural light.

In conclusion our Koi pond should try to simulate some of the above conditions such as depth, constant new water (not mains water unless for top-up purposes), adequate constant removal of heavy solids and debris, good dissolved oxygen content at least 8 parts per million, pH constant between 7.2 to 7.8, nitrite and ammonia readings of zero and stable plus nitrate readings as low as can be maintained.

Together with the above conditions the Koi keeper requires clear water with good natural light in order to enjoy the Koi, a filtration system that will allow high stocking rates and give good growth rates at the same time, an overall system that allows total control of all aspects required with a minimum of daily maintenance.

We cannot even think of 'natural' methods as a means of producing most of these conditions, instead we have to use human technology in order to simulate the requirements and, in some cases, try to improve on nature by these means, especially in the subject of stocking rates.

The Nishikigoi breeders of Japan nowadays, keep all their stocks from the October mud pond harvest in specially constructed indoor buildings. These contain oil-fired heated, concrete ponds for the stocks until selection is made the following May when the best tategoi will be returned once more to the mud ponds to grow and the remainder sold. These indoor ponds are filtered constantly and the stocking rates to water volumes are extremely high in comparison to the

Modern day Japanese breeders ponds for housing stocks during Winter.

stocking rates required by a private collector, again none of this operation is 'natural' by any stretch of the imagination. However, by using these methods, the modern day breeder can keep all his stock in excellent condition for the harsh Winter period and does not have to risk damages and heavy losses that occurred in previous years when no indoor facilities were available. In those early days, stocks had to be kept in outdoor concrete ponds as shown in the early Koi books where they were covered with bamboo and partially protected from the Winter snows and frosts, yet many valuable Koi were always lost.

These particular ponds (below) were built in 1990 in Kowada, Ojiya. They are double glazed in polycarbonate sheet to allow as

much natural light as possible and the gap between the two layers is approximately 2". A large reservoir full of 1/4" diameter polystyrene balls is connected to the cavity between the two layers of polycarbonate and the entire building can be totally insulated within three minutes by a vacuum pump which sucks the balls from the reservoir and pumps them into the cavities. In the event of a sunny Winter day, the process can be reversed and the roof area can be exposed in order to obtain free heat from the sun as well as increased natural lighting conditions.

The heating system to the water within the ponds is fuelled by oil. For any reader still holding opinions that Nishikigoi *NEED* cold water conditions during Winter I would suggest you look at the conditions of those kept in countries that have no real Winter as such. Warm climates like Thailand, Brazil, South Africa etc., are ideal for keeping Nishikigoi and growing them to maximum potential.

Standard indoor 'Winter Spending' ponds, 'Torazo', Uragara

The unique Maruten head pattern on this Koi looks like a jigsaw piece which will fit into the first 'hi' pattern on the shoulder. This female Kohaku was 75cm. (29.5")
when the photogragh was taken and the quality of the white ground
could be mistaken for a Koi half the age and size.

ENVIRONMEN

BOOK

'ENVIRONMENT'
It is vital that we all understand how to provide a perfect home in which to keep our Nishikigoi. This section is written to cover, in detail, all the aspects of this subject, including pond design, construction, filtration, equipment, heating, running operation, as well as how to mature and maintain a system.

TO BUILD A 'PROPER' KOI POND SYSTEM

'The cheapest way to build a Koi pond is to build it once, but build it properly'

I find it difficult to understand why there is no detailed information available that gives the enthusiast any real insight as to one of the most important aspects of the Koi keeping hobby; namely, how to plan, design, excavate, build, filter and landscape a 'state-of-the-art' Koi pond system as of now. Hopefully this section of the book will do all this and a little more because the quality of the actual system is the greatest 'tool' a Koi keeper can possibly have. A 'proper' system is one that enables the keeper to realise and maintain required water qualities mentioned earlier with the minimum of daily maintenance.

In 1995 there are many valuable innovations that significantly improve on many aspects of the way we used to design and build ponds a decade ago and today we can take advantage of these and incorporate them in our designs. There is nothing complicated about how a proper system should operate – it is, in fact, very simple in principle. But many choose, for reasons unknown to me, to try and make it complex, 'busy' and a nightmare to maintain, usually these systems are the ones with many problems. I am the last person to state that building a Koi pond is relatively inexpensive. I should point out, here and now, that it is very expensive to build any serious Koi pond, be it good or bad. In truth, it is a civil engineering project from start to finish and far more complex to actually install than say, a house extension. However one thing will always remain true and that is - *'The cheapest way to build a Koi pond is to build it once, but build it properly'* - a maxim I have used since I started in this business.

Before going on to the actual planning of the system it would be worthwhile to list what we and our Koi require of the system in order to incorporate everything into our design.

■ An overall system that is built to last.

■ A filter system which produces and maintains all the water qualities required namely:-

    a.   pH between 7.2 to 7.8 and stable.
    b.   Nitrite zero and stable.
    c.   Ammonia zero and stable.
    d.   Dissolved Oxygen content over 8 ppm at all times.
    e.   Nitrate as low as possible and stable.

■ Total control of water temperatures at all times of the year.

■ A pond and filter system that removes all mechanical debris to waste, on a daily basis, both efficiently and quickly, retaining none within the system at any time.

■ A filtration system with a biological stage that seldom requires any maintenance but if periodic removal of debris or dust is required, it can be carried out quickly, efficiently, safely and with no loss of biomass.

■ A system that requires a minimum of mains water for top-up purposes.

■ No toxic metals in any materials used and the ability to remove any heavy metals in mains water prior to reaching the pond.

■ A system design that gives the owner easy access to all equipment used for any servicing needed.

■ A system that can cope with high stocking rates of Koi to water volume.

■ A system that is aesthetically pleasing to the eye of the owner.

■ A system that can be enjoyed all year round.

■ A pond that contains only water and Koi – no pumps and pipework etc.

■ A system that has ample natural daylight conditions.

If all these are incorporated correctly, we should be well on the way to producing a very efficient garden aquarium and the best 'tool' we can have to keep water properly.

> **I must point out here why you will not find the following items mentioned anywhere else in this book and why. We are, after all, talking about a *'proper'* Koi pond system.**

✻ Butyl, plastic or any other form of pond liner - these are ideal for what they were designed for originally, to waterproof a shallow indentation in the ground. Koi pond walls need to be vertical, the Koi pond requires a minimum depth of 5 feet and has to incorporate 10" diameter bottom drains and other pipework connections. At these depths a liner has to withstand significant pressure, these connections weaken the liner and, if stretching occurs, these joints are the first to go. Stretching will occur after a period of time depending on ground conditions. When a liner is used in a deep pond, ground water tracks between the liner and soil constantly. This, sooner or later, produces soil erosion and the liner has to compensate by stretching because of water pressure inside the pond, after a while something has to give! Another important reason for not using these materials is that the contour of the pond base is the single most important aspect of the pond itself. It has to be formed to produce smooth, gentle slopes to the pond drains in order to constantly remove debris into the mechanical stage of filtration for periodic removal to waste. No matter how carefully a liner is installed, creases are always present thereby significantly reducing efficiency.

* Central Heating type water pumps or any other pump which has a cast iron impeller housing. In normal use these produce metals to the system, this is exacerbated when chemicals such as Malachite Green or Potassium Permanganate are added from time to time.

* Direct forms of heating are dangerous for the same reason as the above, do not pump pond water directly through copper or similar heat exchangers. Instead use indirect methods described later and be totally safe.

* Plastic domestic coldwater header tanks stuffed full of assorted 'gubbins' and ultra-violet clarifiers, fed by a pump in the pond and returning water to the pond by gravity and marketed and sold by the thousand as 'Koi pond filters'. These usually require regular cleaning if they are not to overflow constantly and water cannot possibly flow as is required. There is no method of removing solids except by constant manual attention which, in turn, destroys any small amount of biomass that may be present. These may be all very well for the small goldfish pond but are much more useful in what they were originally designed for, namely storing mains water in a loft!

The Initial Planning Stage.

The main cost centres for the overall project are as follows:-

- Waste removal costs.

- Building materials, readymix concrete for bases.

- Drains, pipework, valves and fittings.

- Filtration system.

- Heating system.

- Water and air pumps.

- Waterproofing materials.

- Electricity, water and gas supplies to filter house.

- Timber decking for filter house.

- Plant hire costs.

- Landscaping materials.

- Labour costs.

These all vary in direct ratio to the overall volume of the system to be chosen, a system of 10 tons (2,200 gallons) is significantly cheaper to install than one of 100 tons (22,000 gallons) in every example of the above cost centres. Every installation is different, some gardens cannot get an excavator on site, others can and are also able to dispose of waste soil elsewhere on their land thus not having to pay for this cost. Some can carry out the majority of the labour on their own which saves a significant proportion of the overall costs and so on.

THE BEST LOCATION FOR THE SYSTEM.

This depends on the position of the house in relationship to available space, ground conditions and the location of any underground mains supplies or sewage lines. I would suggest a position that can be viewed and enjoyed from the house at all times of the year.

THE 'STYLE' OF THE POND.

This can depend both on the aesthetic requirements of the keeper as well as the house and garden it has to blend in with. There are many points to consider when making this decision, the most important is to take children and pets into consideration.

Koi ponds are deep, pets and children are attracted to water, do bear this in mind when choosing this aspect of your pond.

The following styles should give some indication as to the choices that are available.

This is a converted swimming pool – not within most budgets but shows how Koi Kichi some Koi enthusiasts are!

In-ground Formal Pond

(Above) A flat stone coping is positioned to the perimeter of this pond to give easy access all round.

(Above right) This extremely modern Japanese system built in a suburban area is not at all typical of a Japanese Koi pond but the construction is of the highest quality.

(Below right) A formal coping from bricks has been chosen as a finish to this pond.

(Below far right) Brickwork edging again to both pond and filtration areas. Filtration system here is concealed under the timber decking which has a recessed hatch for daily entry purposes and the entire cover can be removed in less than 10 minutes if necessary.

In-ground Rock Pond

These superb examples show the importance of ensuring that the size of rockwork chosen is in keeping with the size of the pond in order to produce the desired overall effect. When rockwork is used that is too small for the surface area of the pond it never realises the true appearance of a 'rock pond'.

In-ground and Above-ground Informal Pond

An informal shape has been given by stone and brickwork to give a pleasing effect.

In-ground and Above-ground Formal Pond

A very neat finish is achieved by using brickwork and timber coping to finish the pond and disguise the filtration system.

The aspect of 'style' is a personal choice but the actual finish is very important for aesthetic purposes and one has to live with this and, hopefully, enjoy it for many years to come. In view of this I would strongly recommend that final landscaping requirements are taken into account during the initial planning stages.

Landscaping is an art form and one in which my company has no expertise, we can excavate, build, waterproof, install all equipment etc. but when landscaping is required we know our limitations and call in the experts who work in this field professionally.

CHOICE OF POND SHAPE.

Again no two are identical; available space, garden design and location dictates this. Avoid angular shapes such as triangles and complex rambling twists and turns as good circulation is necessary, by the current produced with the water returning to the pond from the filtration stages, in order to efficiently remove waste matter on the pond base constantly.

DEPTH OF POND.

I would recommend a minimum depth of 5 feet but 6 to 8 feet is far better for the Koi and for getting as much water volume within a given area as is possible.

Landscaping Japanese-style, these photographs were taken only weeks after the garden was completed yet give the appearance that the rocks inside the pond have been there since the beginning of time. Scenes of The Nishikigoi Centre, Ojiya City, Niigata

GROUND CONDITIONS AND LOCATION OF POND IN RELATION TO THE HOUSE OR OTHER OUTBUILDINGS.

These should be very carefully considered during the initial planning stages. An in-ground pond which is to hold a 7 feet depth of water when finished requires an initial excavation of 8 feet. Sometimes ground water table poses a problem, sometimes footings for house or outbuildings have to be considered if the pond is to be sited close to the house. If these problems are envisaged then the following is strongly advised before continuing with the project.

■ There are specialist on-site, de-watering companies who can usually assist in keeping excavations dry until the project is finished and running.

■ A Chartered Surveyor specialising in building and excavation should be employed for both his opinion as to the suitability of the pond being built anywhere near to existing buildings, as well as his insurance indemnity, should any of his recommendations be inaccurate and any problems occur during excavation.

(In my own experience of this, my company was once asked to excavate and build a 9 feet deep pond less than four feet away from the owners house, when I urged the owner to bring in a surveyor for a report he told me that he would arrange for someone else to excavate the pond and we could site all the equipment etc. Some weeks later the owner of the pond telephoned me at midnight, very distressed, to tell me that part of his house wall had cracked and was in danger of falling into the pond excavation. He was some 200 miles away but I managed to get a specialist company close to him to attend to the problem. Within one hour, four large vehicles and eight operators began to start driving steel piles all around the pond perimeter to a depth of 12 feet. The house wall was propped up and made safe by six the following morning after thirty or so neighbours had telephoned the Police complaining about the noise. I don't know what the final account came to, but I suspect it was far more than the £150.00 that the Surveyor would have charged for his fee!)

This advice is not intended to discourage any reader from making a Koi pond and I hope it does not deter anyone from doing so. However it is far better that I point out any pitfalls well in advance and then I cannot be accused of omitting important areas or situations which could arise as a result.

Finally, before a spade, pickaxe or JCB is employed, it is vital that every aspect of the total system is fully understood, specifically:-

■ Final water levels in both pond and filtration areas should be pegged out.

■ The area for the pond should be pegged out, allowing for wall thicknesses.

■ The area for the filtration housing should be pegged out, allowing for wall thicknesses and checked that it is large enough to accommodate all necessary equipment and allow good access for maintenance. Prior to actually commencing the pond, it is vital that all aspects of 'proper' filtration systems are explained in full – this subject will be covered next in order that the correct system for the actual pond water volume is selected.

■ All pipework and service channels should be pegged out.

■ All excavation depths should be noted by taking into account final water level, depths of water required and thicknesses of concrete bases.

■ A sewer outlet has to be found to take waste and overflow water.

After this is completed, a work plan should be made to ensure that the excavations are made in a proper pattern in relationship to the position of waste skips, dumper trucks etc.

Once all the above have been completed we can now start the actual installation. I have prepared two examples of full installation from start to finish whereby I can detail every aspect and the overall work plan.

The first is a fictional system which will hold around 50 tons of water (11,000 gallons) and is designed purely as a top class Koi pond for keeping good Koi from an enthusiasts viewpoint.

The second one is my own system which is well under way at the time of writing and is intended to be used to house and grow various stocks of good grade Koi very quickly. It will hold around 120 tons of water (26,000 gallons) and will operate in a very similar way to the first pond but will have extra facilities to realise its extra requirements.

These are both large ponds by any stretch of the imagination but the planning and installation methods and requirements are identical for smaller systems whereby everything can be reduced accordingly.

In a book of this type where it is vital to cover all aspects of a specialist subject thoroughly, it cannot be done without actually naming and describing specific items referred to and the sections 'Environment' and 'Caring' do, inevitably, mention several brand names of goods and their usages. I must point out that all items mentioned are, in my own personal opinion, the best to use for a particular application. Furthermore I can categorically state that I have been paid no monies or services for including them in this book. There are alternatives to many of these items, some I have tried, others I have not and new items will be introduced in the future. However the ones mentioned are ones which I use on a daily basis, some for many years, and find them to be the only ones I can honestly recommend to the reader. In my own opinion, it is pointless, time-consuming and a waste of space to confuse the reader, for whom this book is written, with a host of alternatives to the one that produces the best results for me.

BASIC PRINCIPLES OF ALL FILTRATION SYSTEMS DESCRIBED

The operation principle for all filtration units described is identical, be it for large or small volumes of water. Obviously, the larger the pond volume - the larger the filter system required and, as volumes reduce, the size of filter system necessary reduces accordingly. In every instance the first stage of the filtration system is 'gravity-fed' from pond drains and the main water pump running the system is sited to pick up water from the final stage of filtration and return it to the pond itself. When the water pump is switched on, this slightly reduces water levels in the filtration stage and slightly increases them in the pond. Gravity then ensures that the levels in both pond and filter are maintained by drawing water from the pond drain/s into the filter to compensate the differential of level. As the pump action continues, the combined action of both pump and gravity ensures water levels are maintained and thus water flow is supplied constantly to the filtration system.

When all pumps are turned off, water levels in both pond and filtration are identical. As mentioned before, water is supplied to the first (mechanical) stage of the filter system directly from the bottom drain/s sited in the pond base during construction. The siting, description and installation of drains is covered in greater detail later but the actual drain sump is positioned at the lowest point of the pond. The actual base of the pond is formed to give a gentle, but effective, fall to the entire diameter of the sump perimeter. In this way any items heavier than water, such as fish waste, leaves, dust and general debris are taken into these sumps continually, aided partially by the Koi themselves but mainly by currents from points strategically located in the pond walls and powered by the return water from the filter stage. A well-designed pond should never have to be cleaned as the cleaning operation is taking place constantly.

The drain/s are connected to the prime mechanical filtration unit via individual UPVC or ABS plastic tubes.

(Note:- Never link bottom drains together with a common pipe, this only results in the one nearest to the filtration stage working properly whilst the others are useless and totally wasted.)

The connecting tubes are installed into the base of the pond during installation which is detailed later and have to be of a bore that will supply ample requirements of water to the filter by 'gravity'. This is very different in principle to the bore of tube required when water is pumped through it. In view of this, the connecting tubes from drains to filtration stage in the following two detailed examples are all 4" bore.

Furthermore, the specification of all pipework and fittings used in every stage of all systems detailed is to BSP 'Pressure' specification which is solvent weld. These are more expensive than those found readily available in plumbers' merchants and only specialist suppliers stock these items. However, it should be pointed out that the type of pipework and fittings sold at plumbers' merchants and DIY outlets, be they 'push' fit or 'glue fit' are intended for use in domestic house drainage applications where water is seldom, if ever, retained in these pipes. The domestic drainage pipework and fittings take water from a toilet, a washing machine, dishwasher or a bath into the main sewers, after which the pipes are empty. The system I recommend is made specifically for retention of water at all times and is the only specification I will use in a Koi pond installation.

Still on the subject of actual bore of tubes, in many instances I have come across those building their own filter systems who attempt to connect tanks together in order to get water flow transferred from tank to tank by first supplying water to the first stage correctly in 4" bore tube. They then connect tank to tank by 3 individual 1.5" tubes, thinking that this will allow the required 4" bore flow-rate to take place throughout each tank. Please note, and don't take my word for this, you can calculate this for yourself, it takes 7.114 x 1.5" tubes to equal the bore of a single 4" tube. Severe flow restrictions/ water starvation occurs as a result of adopting this method, due to insufficient water flow as a result of too few small bore tubes and the friction loss that is produced.

Correct type of plastic fittings for Koi Pond construction.

Requirements of a 'Proper' Koi Pond Filtration System

Basically this must serve a dual purpose, firstly it must remove all mechanical waste matter from the pond, take it into the filtration stages and 'settle' it out for efficient daily discharge to sewer. 'Efficient daily discharge' is an important maintenance requirement and is one where a minimum of good water is wasted whilst all debris is removed in a very short time. A good system should never allow this debris to collect and build-up in any of the units. In truth, the filter should always be as mechanically clean as the pond once discharge has been carried out.

If build-up of this matter does take place within a filter chamber, it is usually in an area where both water flow and dissolved oxygen content is extremely low. This creates a home for unwanted anaerobic bacteria to colonise and re-produce, eventually this can cause bacterial and/or viral problems within a pond system.

This stage of primary filtration is termed as **'MECHANICAL FILTRATION'** and is, quite simply, a method of removing all solids quickly and efficiently. To further clarify this, 'mechanical' stages, within a system, are those which have to be discharged or cleaned periodically. There are several types of mechanical stages used today namely:-

- **Filter Brushes**, these are used in many systems as a prime mechanical stage whereby water fed by bottom drain/s is passed through them, much of the debris and solids are trapped in the brushes thus preventing it from passing into the next stages of filtration.

- **Settling Chambers**, these are usually large chambers fed by the bottom drain/s where heavy solids are encouraged to 'settle out' before being taken into the next stages of filtration.

- **Sand Pressure Filters**, the same as the ones used in swimming pool filtration. In a Koi pond application, water is pumped through them and the silica sand within the chamber, traps the solids within the vessel.

The problem with all of the above is that of the discharge of debris to sewer, this usually can only be carried out accompanied with a huge wastage of good water as well as being very laborious.

To date, the most efficient mechanical stage of filtration is one I designed in 1984 and first offered for sale in late 1985 after testing it on my main system. Initially this was viewed with scepticism and, in some areas, total ridicule. Today, however, this is not the case and every manufacturer of Koi pond filtration in the UK now produces a derivative of my original 'Vortex Unit'. It is, by far, the most used and most efficient mechanical stage offered today and its operation is that of total simplicity. This unit is covered in greater detail later. It is a circular unit, diameters and overall depths vary in relationship to the volume of the pond in question. All units have vertical walls for the top 25% of their depth at which they come inwards, internally, for a 1" to 2" recess, depending on size, and walls continue downwards vertically for a further 25% of their depth. At this point the unit becomes conical and the base is taken to a central narrow drain point directly underneath the base of the cone. The structure is then fitted on a base which supports the entire unit, it allows the conical shape to become free-standing on to a concrete base as well as allowing space for exit pipework and fittings. These units are moulded in glass fibre and the circular design greatly aids the strength.

Operation of the mechanical Vortex Unit:-
The pipework line/s from the pond bottom drain/s are fed *tangentially* into the side wall of the Vortex unit, entering at a centre which is approximately one third below the top of the unit itself. The pipework is bonded into position by glass fibre to make a watertight joint. *Note:- If more than one drain tube is bonded, make sure they all enter the unit at the same level in order to each produce a similar flow-rate.* A centrally positioned large bore exit tube (bore of this tube again varies with size of unit and flow-rate required) is bonded into the unit to take water to the next stage of filtration, the top of this tube is usually 5" to 8" below the water level of the system. By bonding inlet tube/s tangentially and transferring water to the next stage from a central position within the chamber, then, once the system is started, the water flow into the Vortex unit begins to spin gently and constantly. As a result, the majority of solids entering the unit from the pond drains are taken downwards, by 'centripetal' action, to the base of the cone and collect in the drain point. The water exiting via the central tube has to rise in order to make its exit, by then much heavy waste matter has already been removed to the base of the cone. The drain outlet directly below the base of the cone is taken to the discharge sump and stopped by a ball valve. Daily maintenance is a quick turn of the valve when all the sludge collected in the base of the cone is instantly removed. After two to five seconds, clear water comes to view and the valve can be shut off immediately. This operation removes all the sludge accumulated daily with no wastage of good water and a minimum of time and effort.

Note:- If entry tubes are bonded in straight lines instead of on a tangent, the operation of the unit is wasted as no 'spin' is produced.

Vortex System

During 1990, after the 'Vortex principle' had been well tested, I decided to apply this unit to my larger filter systems by linking four identical vortex units together tangentially; the first unit being the prime vortex unit and the next three to do the biological stages as described next. By doing this, all units produce a 'spin' in water flow and any mechanical, finer debris is deposited at the base of each cone; this produces a 'mechanically clean' filtration system. These are fully covered later in this section of the book.

The second purpose of a 'proper' Koi pond filtration system is that of **'BIOLOGICAL FILTRATION'** — Koi, in urination and gill action, produce toxic substances that become totally dissolved in the pond water and cannot be 'strained' out by any mechanical means. These toxins consist of ammonias and nitrites which, like mechanical solids, are also heavier than water. If these are allowed to build up continually, they will quickly destroy the mucus membrane on the delicate gill filaments of the Koi. Eventually the gill surfaces will then vegetate, decay and deaths will occur.

The most effective way of removing these toxins is to pass them constantly over 'surfaces' of a suitable 'biological media' whereby all surfaces are supplied with a constant flow of water per square inch per minute.

It is important here to understand that a good biological stage is not intended to be a 'strainer' as is a mechanical stage. Instead if we can provide the maximum amount of 'surfaces' within a given chamber and guide the water constantly through these surfaces without any restrictions to actual flow rates we can then stimulate good aerobic bacteria to colonise on these surfaces. The bacteria thrive on the toxic nitrites and ammonias given off by the Koi and reproduce rapidly once a constant source of 'food' is available. Once all the surfaces become biologically 'mature' the ammonias and nitrites constantly entering the first stage of the biological filter are completely removed by the bacteria as food and, as a result, the water returning to the pond contains none of these toxins. The bacteria, in turn, give off their waste product by way of dissolved, non-toxic nitrates.

To put all this in a nutshell, the bacteria in the biological stages of the filter are totally dependent on the Koi within the pond for their constant food supply whilst the Koi within the pond are totally dependent on the bacteria within the biological stages of the filter for the removal of toxic nitrites and ammonias.

After a biological stage is totally mature, if the Koi stocks are removed, the biomass can be lost in a very short period of time. Conversely, if the biomass is destroyed for whatever reason, the Koi will soon begin to suffer with a build-up of their own toxic substances. This whole process is more commonly referred to as '**The Nitrification Process**'. Later in this section, detailed information will be given as to how to mature a new biological filter and how to maintain the biomass on a permanent basis.

As far as the best choice for a 'biological surface' is concerned, any non-toxic material will support bacterial activity, from crushed stones, gravels, even chunks of crushed glass will do! Many other materials are advertised and sold as a media that will provide an excellent surface to stimulate a good biomass. Unfortunately all these forms of 'surfaces' are generally placed within the filter chamber in depths of around 8" to 12" and the top surface is usually around 6" below water level. They are usually supported on perforated trays so the water can pass upwards through them. Irrespective of how good the initial mechanical stage of the filter is, fine dust etc. will build

up under these trays and, after a period of time, flow restrictions will occur and the media requires cleaning. This is laborious and generally results in much of the biomass being lost. Furthermore, these 'solid' bodies of media generally only support a good aerobic biomass on the top surface of the media to a depth of around three sixteenths of an inch. Therefore the maximum surface area of the biomass within a given chamber, using this type of media, is the square feet obtained by multiplying the length and width of the chamber in question.

As stated earlier, the best choice for a non-toxic material which provides a surface for biological activity is one that can satisfy the following requirements:-

1. It must give the greatest useful surface area for potential biomass within a given chamber.

2. It must produce no flow-rate restrictions at any time.

3. It must not deteriorate in water.

4. If rare periodic cleaning is necessary, it has to be done quickly and efficiently, without removal of media and without any significant loss of biomass.

The only material I have used on my own systems and specified on the systems of my customers since 1985 for this purpose, is a material made in Japan specifically as a surface for biological filtration in water applications. It is supplied in flat sheet form 2metres x 1metre x 3cms. thick, mid-blue in colour and very firm and abrasive to the touch. It is a polyester based material, which is dense yet very porous. If used simply as a flat sheet in a 'baffle' application it is of little use other than for mechanical purposes. Its real effectiveness is realised when used in a cartridge form, first taught to me in 1984 by Mr. Sakai of the Matsunosuke Company in

Isawa, Japan. The cartridges are tailored to fit a given filter chamber, for smaller pond systems up to 15 tons (3,300 gallons) we use 'horizontal flow' cartridges, whilst for larger systems we use 'upward-flow' cartridges.

Cutting Filter Matting accurately by means of a circular saw, using a knife-edged blade to give a perfect fit to a specific filter chamber.

In the case of the horizontal-flow filter systems the cartridge sits on the base of the unit. In the case of the larger, circular, upward-flow systems the cartridge is tailored to sit on the recess of the vortex unit mentioned earlier, this fits very tightly and requires no support tray at all.

When I first introduced this material to the UK in cartridge form, many complained that it was only a series of 'holes' and, as such, could not possibly filter a Koi pond. It took many years to promote and prove; today these cartridges are accepted by most as the best media by far, for this type of application.

■ If one closely inspects a cartridge and sees the surface areas formed by the square channels it is easily apparent to see why a tailored cartridge can produce a surface area of more than five times that of the previously described 'solid' media applications.

■ Because of the open channels, it is impossible for any flow restrictions to ever occur.

■ It is made to last indefinitely in water.

■ If cleaning is ever required, this can be done in situ by a pressure washer, without disturbance or removal of the cartridge, very quickly indeed. (On my own main system which holds many Koi at peak times of the year, cleaning has taken place twice in five years with no loss of biomass.)

WARNING:- The material I refer to is the 'genuine article'- beware of other materials manufactured by the same Japanese manufacturer and offered for sale as 'Japanese Filter Mat' – this is not made for water filtration, but rather for drainage purposes under roads before the final surfaces are applied. It is sold in 2metre x 1metre sheets but is both thinner and infinitely softer, green/blue in colour and does not last so long submerged in water but is far cheaper than the material made specifically for water. The genuine article is firm enough to form into an upward-flow cartridge without using anything to 'stick' it together. By tailoring the cartridge slightly larger than the shape of the chamber, the entire cartridge remains in place simply by pressure of the outer walls of the chamber. This forces it to compress slightly and the minimum of support is required under the cartridge. If you are confused, a good test is – if you can roll it up and carry it under your arm, it is not the genuine article!

■ In any biological stage of filtration, good biological activity seriously takes up considerable dissolved oxygen content, it is vital that heavy aeration is supplied to all cartridges so that maximum biomass can be formed on all surfaces. This is generally produced by air pump and air stones.

Finally on this subject, whilst the nitrates, given off by the bacteria as their waste product, are not a significant problem at normal levels, nitrates can affect growth rates especially in smaller Koi if allowed to build up, it is also true that nitrate levels in mains water can be high. I have never found nitrates to be a problem except in being the instrumental cause of green water conditions which can easily be resolved by using ultra-violet clarifiers on the return line from the filtration system to the pond. But this, in itself, does not actually remove the nitrates within the system. There is no doubt that plants can be successfully used to absorb nitrate build-up situations in an outdoor Koi pond. Waterfall header pools and watercourse returns to the pond are ideal situations in which to plant watercress which is excellent for this purpose. Once established, the root mass of a bed of watercress grows rapidly taking its nourishment from the nitrates within the water constantly passing through it. If this form of filtration is necessary for removal of nitrates, it is important to regularly cut back the plants before allowing them to flower as the nitrate intake reduces quite significantly after flowering takes place. Many allow the watercress cuttings to enter the pond to provide excellent food supplements for the Koi.

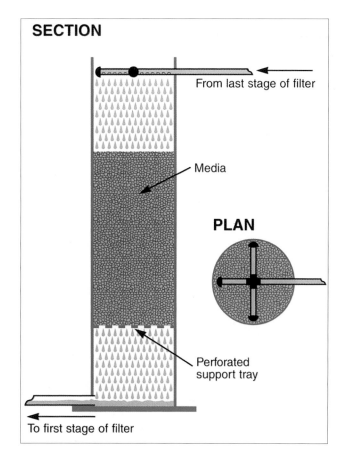

SECTION

From last stage of filter

Media

PLAN

Perforated
support tray

To first stage of filter

Nitrate Filtration

Nitrates can be a problem to those trying to grow large numbers of Koi fry in an indoor situation where maximum growth rates are important and plants difficult to grow. A simple, successful method of removal in this situation is basically to incorporate a separate filter housing from the main system and pump a small volume of water into it from the last chamber of the main filtration system and allow it to return to the first stage of filtration on a continuous 'trickle' basis. In this type of filtration a tall tubular container is more suitable for the job.

The principle of this is to take water from the last stage of biological filtration via a small submersible pump or a small, valved by-pass from the main pump and trickle this through a 'spray bar' assembly at the top of the chamber to give good distribution of water flow to the media before returning it to the start of the filter. Ideal forms of media for this operation is the sintered glass or

similar types of material such as 'Siporax' and 'Biohome' widely available. The water here passes downwards through the media which is supported on a suitable tray, the media is never submerged as water exits to the first stage of the filter via the exit tube. Size of unit depends on amount of water within the system and the stocking rates. For example, a 23 ton (5,000 gallons) system, at a medium stocking rate should be nitrate free, after maturing, with a system specification as follows:-

Chamber made from 12" diameter UPVC tube, 48" tall with UPVC plate welded to the base. A perforated UPVC media support tray should be welded in position approximately 12" above the base. The exit tube to the first stage of the filter should be made in 1.5" bore and the spray bar assembly formed in 1" bore tube. Depth of media should be 24" and the flow rate approximately 40 gallons per hour.

In this type of application it is essential that the exit tube is slightly higher than the water level of the system.

Once again, the problem of nitrates seldom affects the vast majority of Koi ponds and very few would have to consider incorporating this type of unit, I have included this for the benefit of a minority of readers.

FILTER SYSTEMS, FLOW PATTERNS AND DISCHARGE OPERATION.

The subject of proper Koi pond filtration still continues to puzzle even many experienced enthusiasts in the hobby. However, to the more confused newcomer, the wide range of systems available and their various forms of operation together with well-intended advice from a 'friend-in-the-know' and sometimes the initial firm belief that filtering a Koi pond properly is 'kids stuff' all tend to lead to more confusion and, usually, into making the wrong choice. Unfortunately this wrong choice is only apparent after a given time period when all the inefficiencies come to the surface and this usually proves to be expensive and time-consuming to rectify.

If one looks carefully at what we require from a proper filtration system before even thinking about building or buying one and if one understands every aspect of what is required beforehand then the real choices and methods available should be significantly reduced. In turn, so should the confusion.

In truth, a Koi pond filtration system is running constantly, 24 hours per day, 7 days a week and 365 days per year. Over a one year period the entire water from the pond will pass through the filtration system between 2,000 to 3,000 times. In the case of a 10,000 gallon (45 tons) system, the filtration stage will handle between 20 to 30 million gallons per year of water, debris/dust,

It is absolutely vital to ensure that the proper filter allows for ample, unhindered water flow, both in size of feed and transfer pipework used as well as ensuring the correct 'pattern' of flow to the biological surfaces.

mulm, uneaten food and leaves etc. plus a very significant amount of Nitrites and Ammonias!- (to give the reader an impression of 30 million gallons of water, this would be an area measuring around 1,000 feet by 1,000 feet by 5 feet deep.) In the case of a 2,500 gallon (11.3 tons) system, the filtration stage has to cope with between 7 to 10 million gallons of the same water and assorted debris over the same period. The amount of debris produced, even in a low stocking situation, is very significant, especially in an outdoor environment.

In view of the above, whereas the debris etc. has to be taken out of the pond continually it is vital that it is not allowed to be retained within the filtration stages and thus continually be allowed to build up day after day after week after month and so on.

Unfortunately, most flat-bottomed or gently-sloped-bottomed filter units produced around a decade ago using the 'upward-flow' principle produce these undesirable conditions of build up of mechanical waste matter. If these are used with 'solid'-type biological media held by support trays in mid-water much more of the debris is trapped and allowed to build up constantly. To try and reasonably maintain these types of systems properly involves constant physical effort in the cleaning operation resulting in a significant fluctuation of water qualities together with unhappy Koi.

It is absolutely vital to ensure that the proper filter allows for ample, unhindered water flow, both in size of feed and transfer pipework used as well as ensuring the correct 'pattern' of flow to the biological surfaces. A proper filtration system 'channels' water how we need it to be 'channelled' for maximum efficiency. This will remove heavy solids to waste points constantly as well as ensuring all biological surfaces receive a constant supply of pond water at all times and at a constant flow rate. The greater the efficiency of a flow pattern also significantly reduces the actual surfaces required within a given filter chamber.

In earlier days, several large, square, concrete chambers were often linked together, each with several 4" bore tubes or small transfer ports. As a result, the water flow 'tracked' in direct line with the entry and exit of the water flow and consequently large surfaces of media received little or no water flow which resulted in many stagnant areas in much of the filtration units.

In 1995, however, it is possible to build or purchase proper filtration systems that will handle the flow rates required, that provide the correct flow patterns and will ensure that all mechanical debris etc. can be efficiently discharged to waste with a minimum of daily maintenance. The actual design of the systems described here are extremely simple in both principle as well as in running and discharge operations, there is nothing complicated about them in any way. Similar systems have been in daily usage in many gardens throughout Europe and the USA for many years as they have in my own ponds and, providing daily or weekly discharge is carried out as specified, there is very little extra maintenance required.

As mentioned earlier, I personally use only two flow patterns in order to channel pond water efficiently through a filtration system. For ponds with a total volume of less than 17 tons (3,750 gallons) the 'horizontal' flow pattern is ideal and economical, for larger systems I use the 'upward-circular' flow pattern.

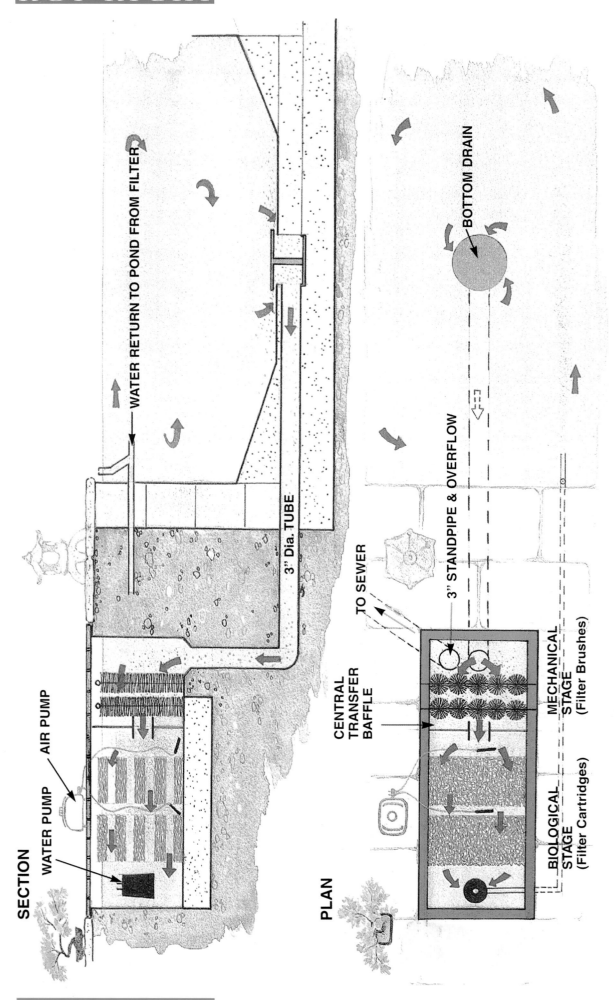

SECTION

WATER RETURN TO POND FROM FILTER

3" Dia. TUBE

AIR PUMP

WATER PUMP

PLAN

TO SEWER

CENTRAL
TRANSFER
BAFFLE

3" STANDPIPE & OVERFLOW

MECHANICAL
STAGE
(Filter Brushes)

BIOLOGICAL
STAGE
(Filter Cartridges)

BOTTOM DRAIN

Filtration system for volumes up to 5.5 tons (1,200 gallons)

1. HORIZONTAL-FLOW FILTRATION.

a. For systems up to 5.5 tons (1,200 gallons)

The external dimensions of the chamber itself is 58" long, 24" wide and 19" deep. If a ready-made unit is purchased a concrete base should be made to support it, make this 46" long, 24" wide and 4" deep. The top of the concrete base must be 18" below pond water level.

The system operates as follows:-

Pond water is taken from bottom drain via a 3" bore tube and enters the filter at the base of the mechanical stage. Water then passes through the 10 filter brushes in the mechanical stage, where most of the heavy solids are retained, and into the biological stage via the central transfer in the baffle plate which divides the mechanical and biological stages. On entering the biological stage, heavy aeration disturbs the flow and water passes horizontally through the first tailored filter cartridge which is 9" long, heavy aeration then disturbs the flow again before it passes through the second 9" long tailored filter cartridge. After exiting the second filter cartridge the water is picked up by the submersible pump and returned to the pond. Actual flow rate required in this instance is between 450 to 550 gallons per hour.

The discharge operation is as follows:-

Switch off submersible pump.

Place 4" pipe stop in central transfer baffle to isolate biological stage from mechanical stage.

The 3" standpipe located in the base of the mechanical stage during normal running is perforated at water level and acts as system overflow. This standpipe, when removed, takes water from the mechanical section directly to sewer or 'soak-away' via a 3" tube.

Remove 3" standpipe from normal position and place immediately into the socket where pond drain enters the filter. This prevents water escaping from the pond into the sewer and allows the mechanical stage to be discharged completely.

Rinse brushes in situ with hosepipe; dirty water is taken to sewer.

Lift 3" standpipe and allow drain line from bottom drain to filter to be purged if necessary.

Replace 3" standpipe to original running position and mechanical stage will re-fill from the pond drain.

Remove pipe stop from transfer baffle.

Switch on submersible pump.

Replace water discharged to waste.

Depending on stocking rates and feeding rates, this operation is usually done weekly and takes less than 5 minutes to complete — the biological stage is not disturbed in this operation.

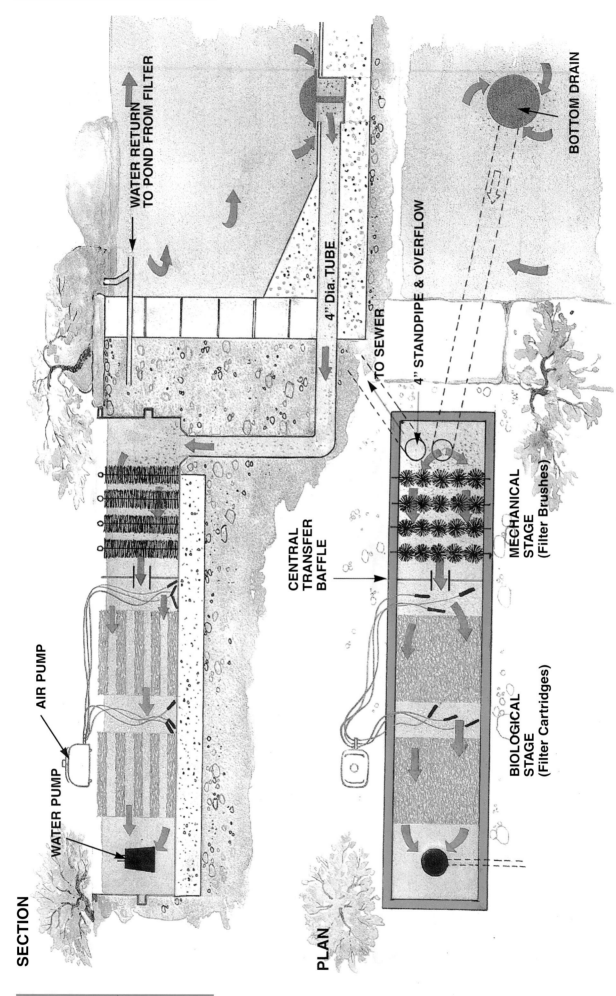

SECTION

AIR PUMP

WATER PUMP

WATER RETURN
TO POND FROM FILTER

4" Dia. TUBE

TO SEWER

PLAN

CENTRAL
TRANSFER
BAFFLE

4" STANDPIPE & OVERFLOW

BOTTOM DRAIN

MECHANICAL
STAGE
(Filter Brushes)

BIOLOGICAL
STAGE
(Filter Cartridges)

Filtration system for volumes up to 12 tons (2,600 gallons)

b. For systems up to 12 tons (2,600 gallons)

The external dimensions of this chamber are 112″ long, 24″ wide and 19″ deep. If a ready-made unit is purchased concrete base requirements are 96″ long, 24″ wide and 6″ deep. Again the top of the concrete base must be 18″ below pond water level.

This system is fed by a 4″ bore tube from the pond drain and waste to sewer also run in 4″ bore tube. The mechanical stage holds 20 filter brushes and the biological stage holds two 18″ long tailored filter cartridges. Actual flow rate required is between 950 to 1,150 gallons per hour. Again heavy aeration is vital prior to each filter cartridge.

The running operation and discharge operation is identical to that of the previous system.

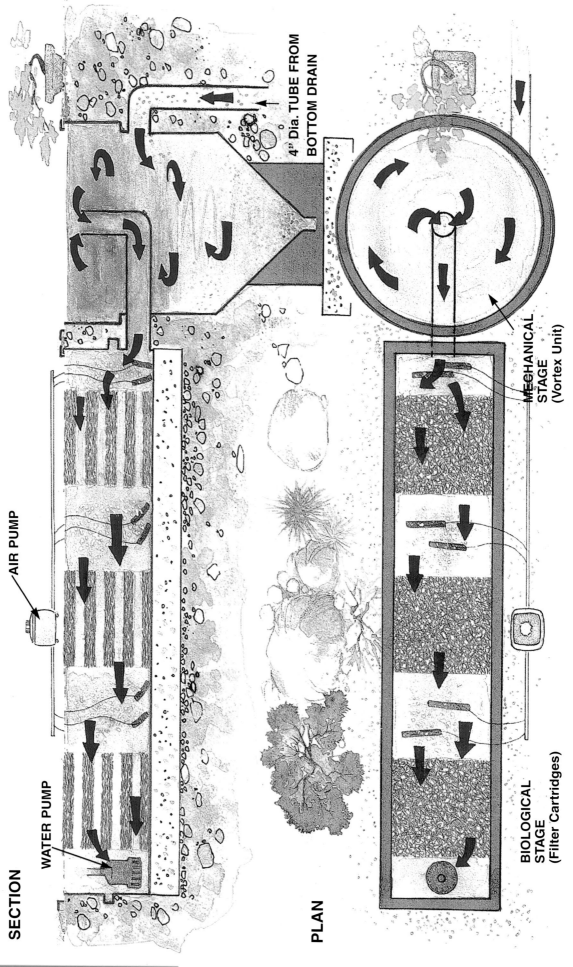

SECTION

AIR PUMP

WATER PUMP

4" Dia. TUBE FROM BOTTOM DRAIN

PLAN

MECHANICAL STAGE (Vortex Unit)

BIOLOGICAL STAGE (Filter Cartridges)

Filtration system for volumes up to 17 tons (3,750 gallons)

c. For systems up to 17 tons (3,750 gallons)

By installing a vortex unit correctly between the pond drain and horizontal flow stage, much more volume can be filtered properly. In this instance no filter brushes are necessary as the vortex unit takes care of the mechanical filtration. The horizontal flow chamber identical in external dimensions to system b., does not require a transfer baffle and three 18" long cartridges can be used in the biological stage again with heavy aeration prior to each cartridge.

The vortex unit illustrated has an internal diameter of 40" and an overall depth of 49.75", concrete base dimensions for this are 46" square and 6" deep. The top of the concrete base for the vortex unit should be 49" below pond water level. Debris/sludge is discharged to waste from the vortex unit daily via the 2" bore drain in the cone of the base terminated with a 2" ball valve.

The 4" tube connecting pond bottom drain should enter the vortex as shown on a tangent and a 4" slide valve fitted to this line prior to entry to the vortex in order that the drain line can be purged periodically.

To purge the drain line in this example, the main pump should be switched off and a 4" pipe stop should be placed in the 4" bore tube centrally exiting the vortex to the biological stage. The 4" slide valve should be closed and the 2" drain from the vortex drain opened to waste. When the vortex is empty the 2" valve should be left open and the 4" slide valve opened, any build-up of debris within the bottom drain line can be purged to waste quickly. Once this is completed the 2" vortex drain can be closed, the 4" pipe stop removed, the pump re-started and the system topped-up to running level.

A 2" bore overflow should be taken from the surface of the horizontal-flow chamber to waste by connecting this to the same waste line from the vortex unit after the valve. The actual flow rate required for this system is between 1,200 to 1,400 gallons per hour.

Please note, the horizontal-flow systems specified here all work very efficiently indeed because of the widths and specified depths of the chamber which is only approximately 18" by 18". Biological activity is constantly maintained by a combination of heavy aeration, which disturbs the water flow, together with the specified required flow rates.

On several occasions attempts have been made to link these units together 'in-line' to increase biological filtration capacity, this does not work as the flow rate has to be increased significantly. If more than one unit is to be employed correctly they should be sited in parallel and a separate pump placed at the last stage of each unit to give identical flow rate to each unit.

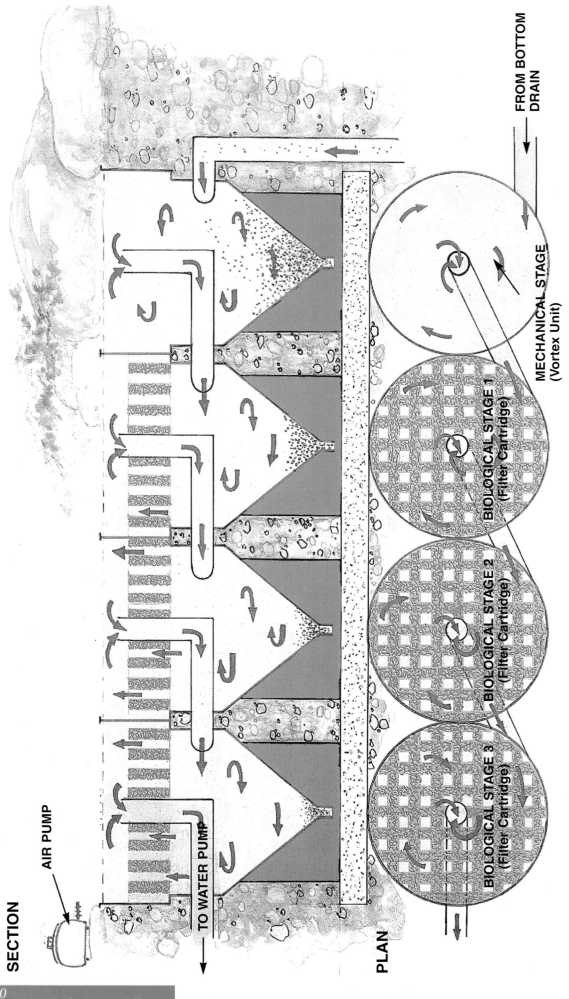

SECTION

AIR PUMP

TO WATER PUMP

PLAN

FROM BOTTOM
DRAIN

MECHANICAL STAGE
(Vortex Unit)

BIOLOGICAL STAGE 1
(Filter Cartridge)

BIOLOGICAL STAGE 2
(Filter Cartridge)

BIOLOGICAL STAGE 3
(Filter Cartridge)

Filtration system for volumes up to 30 tons (6,600 gallons)

2. UPWARD CIRCULAR FLOW FILTRATION.

a. For systems up to 30 tons (6,600 gallons)

This system comprises of a prime vortex unit fed tangentially via 5″ bore tube, to three biological units. The vortex unit receives water from the pond drains by separate 4″ tubes, a 4″ slide valve is placed in each tube prior to entering the vortex unit tangentially. Internal diameter of each unit is 40″ and overall depth is 49.75″. Concrete base requirements for this system is 162″ long by 46″ wide and 6″ deep, the top of the concrete base is 49″ below pond water level.

Actual flow rate required for this system is between 1,800 to 2,000 gallons per hour.

The water supply to each biological stage enters the chamber below the filter cartridge and is allowed to circulate freely. Any solids are taken to the base of each chamber for periodic discharge whilst the water flow exits the central outlet of each unit by having to travel upwards in a circular motion to ensure constant water supply to all surfaces of the cartridges which are 8″ deep. Heavy aeration is supplied to all cartridges by way of airstones placed inside the cartridges at required intervals.

Daily discharge of this system is very quick indeed, each unit has a 2″ bore drain which is taken to a 2″ ball valve prior to waste exit. A quick turn of each valve purges the sludge from each unit in seconds and the system is mechanically clean once more. The main system overflow should be placed in the first or second biological chamber in 2″ bore tube.

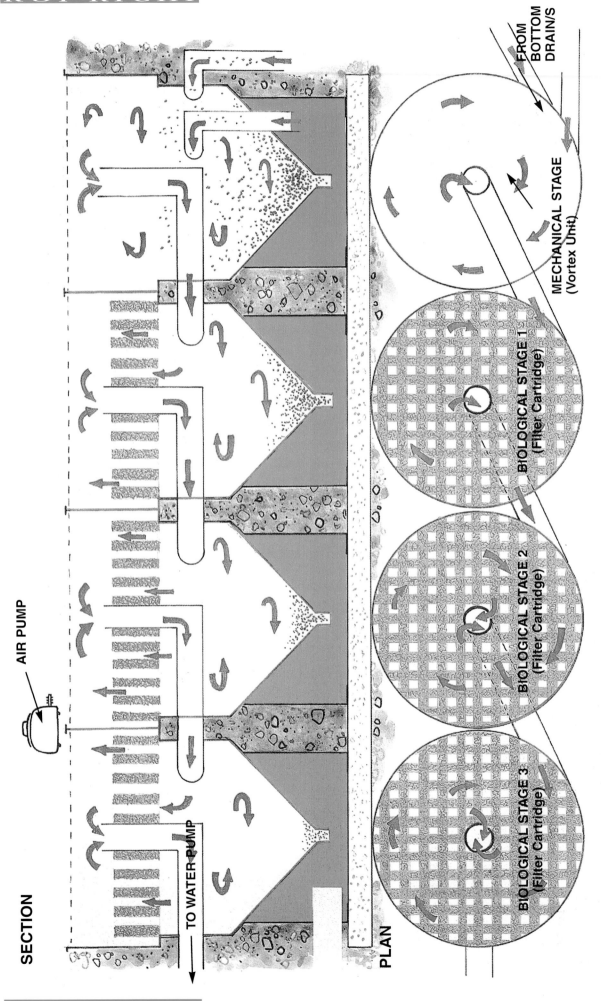

SECTION

AIR PUMP

TO WATER PUMP

PLAN

FROM BOTTOM DRAIN/S

MECHANICAL STAGE
(Vortex Unit)

BIOLOGICAL STAGE 1
(Filter Cartridge)

BIOLOGICAL STAGE 2
(Filter Cartridge)

BIOLOGICAL STAGE 3
(Filter Cartridge)

Filtration system for volumes up to 55 tons (12,100 gallons)

b. For systems up to 55 tons (12,100 gallons)

This system is identical to the previous one in operation and discharge respects but far larger in size. Each unit has an internal diameter of 54" and an overall depth of 74.5". Concrete base requirements are 222" long, 60" wide and 6" deep, top of the concrete base to be 73" below pond water level. The tube connecting each unit together is in 6" bore to allow for required water flow, the drain to each unit is in 3" bore and the filter cartridges are 10" deep.

Actual flow rate required is between 2,500 to 3,000 gallons per hour.

These systems can be sited in several configurations if space restrictions are limited and, if larger volumes of water need to be filtered, they can be used in independent banks. (see chapter 'Tomorrow's World' later in this section)

Alternative layout, upward circular flow filtration units.

A 'PROPER' KOI POND SYSTEM FROM START TO FINISH.

The following example is a fictitious system, the overall volume will be approximately 50 tons (11,000 gallons) water. The finished system is planned to include:-

Dimensions (approx.) -
maximum length . . . . .21 feet,
average width . . . . .12 feet,
maximum depth of water . .6.25 feet.

1. MAIN POND.

Required style is that of an in-ground 'rock pond', viewing requirements are that it can be enjoyed at all times of the year from the house living room window which is 7 feet away. An extension will be made to the existing patio directly to the front edge of the actual pond, this will be finished as a straight edge to the entire front of the pond and finished in York stone. The reasons for this are threefold; namely the edge will give an effective stark contrast to the otherwise large, informal rockwork landscaping, it will give an unhindered view from the house and an area of easy access for feeding and inspection purposes. Final landscaping required is to have a Japanese flavour using gravels, stone ornaments, large rockwork and plants to complement this style.

The pond base will have three standard 10" diameter bottom drains, each to a separate 4" bore pipeline to filter housing, each line will have a 4" slide valve prior to entry to first stage of filtration.

Two surface power skimmers (see photograph below) will be installed to remove any leaves and surface debris, these are standard swimming pool-type units fitted with a grille to avoid any damage to the Koi.

Final waterproofing will be made by the use of G4 resin to give a black finish to pond and waterfall areas. There are several other types of products available for waterproofing concrete structures but we have used this for many years with perfect results. The three coat application permeates the porous rendered concrete and produces a varnish-like finish when dry.

2. WATERFALL/WATERCOURSE.

This has been requested to give a main focal point from the house, the watercourse return will be part of the actual pond and the Koi will be able to swim up to the water entry from the actual waterfall itself. When the landscaping is mature, this feature will obscure the filtration housing directly behind it. The flow of the waterfall can be controlled completely by valves and can be varied as and when required from zero to full capacity. This will not affect any flow-rates through the main filter system as any water flow reduced by regulating the waterfall will be returned directly to the pond by open pipe built into the pond wall.

3. FILTRATION HOUSING.

This has been sited to the side of the plot. Approximate internal dimensions, after 6" block wall has been built to the perimeter, will be 21 feet long, 7.5 feet wide and the top of the concrete base will be 6.25 feet below final water level of the system. This housing will accommodate the following equipment and facilities:-

a. Filtration system

This is identical to the largest-capacity system described previously and consists of the prime mechanical Vortex chamber, fed tangentially by the three pond bottom drains each incorporating a 4" slide valve prior to entry to the Vortex. These slide valves allow easy purge of any debris that may be allowed to build up in the drain lines over a period of time. The water exits the centre of the Vortex unit and is transferred tangentially by 6" bore tube to three Biological units, also linked tangentially to each other by 6" bore tube. The drain from the base of each unit will be in 3" bore pipe-work, terminated by a 3" ball valve on each line.

The main system overflow will be sited in the first biological unit in 2" bore pipework.

b. Disposal of waste from the system.

The base of the housing incorporates a sump area built into the base of the housing, the four 3" bore ball valves and the 2" bore overflow will all discharge into this sump. A float operated submersible sump pump will be fitted to this sump and, when any waste matter is emptied into this chamber, the level of waste water will operate the float switch on the pump and the waste matter will be pumped directly into the sewer via 1.5" bore tube. A non-return valve should be fitted directly above the pump to stop any water in the line from returning to the sump. The floor of the filter chamber is also formed to drain away any rain water entering the chamber to run to the sump.

c. Heating system.

This will be fuelled by natural gas, the boiler will be a 80,000 Btu/hr. normal domestic model linked to an independent 130,000 Btu/hr. stainless steel heat exchanger unit via a pressurised top-up system and driven by a standard central heating type motor.

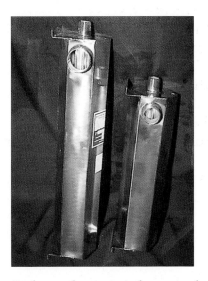

Independent stainless steel heat exchanger unit.

Note:- Balanced-flue regulation requirements have to be met in full and a professional 'Corgi-registered' gas heating installer should be consulted here.

The pond water to be heated is independent of the main filtration system and will be taken by a half horse power surface pump from the individual 2" lines from the two surface skimmers in the main pond. Each surface skimmer will be controlled by a 2" ball valve prior to entry to the suction inlet of the pump. This pump will then push water through the stainless steel heat exchanger and back to the pond via a 2" bore tube built into the wall and will enter the pond at 4 feet below water level. The temperature will be controlled by an independent thermostat, the sensor sited in the last biological unit. In this method of indirect heating, there will be no possibility of any toxic metals coming into contact with pond water. (There are more details on heating at the end of this section of the book.)

d. Mains water metals purification system.

After the mains water supply line has been fed to the filter house, this will be connected to the inlet of the purification unit and, after the water has passed through the unit, it will be taken to enter the second biological unit and regulated by a ballcock-type valve. Once the levels of the system drop during periodic discharge, this valve will automatically top- up the system.

The reason that the mains water feed is sited in the second bio-logical unit is purely because the system overflow is sited in the first biological unit. By adopting this method, any new water added can only go to overflow after it has passed through the total system.

Note:- during the 'maturing' process, (covered later) new water will have to be run through the system from time to time. The ballcock valve mentioned earlier will not allow this in normal running levels, however, by adjusting the system overflow by 1" below water level, this will allow constant new water to be added as necessary. The puri-fication system is backwashed automatically on a daily basis by an electric valve, the discharge water is routed to the discharge sump.

e. Aeration system.

The cartridges in the three biological units require heavy aeration constantly, this is effected by a 100 litre per minute air pump which will drive a total of ten 50mm. long-life air stones via heavy duty airline. These are fitted at the bottom of each cartridge by pushing them partially down the channels of the cartridge at desired intervals. Four will be placed in the first cartridge and three each in the next two cartridges. The air pump should be sited on a shelf, above the water level of the system if possible, to ensure that if electricity supply fails for any reason, the air in the airlines can not 'back-siphon' and thus drag water into the air pump and flood the unit.

f. Main water pump for filtration system.

Required constant flow rate for this system will be approximately 2,750 gallons per hour actual, which results in the total volume of the pond being passed through the filtration stages once every four hours or six times every day. Once the system is completely mature, the water returning to the pond from the filtration system is, in effect, 'new' water and the Koi, in theory, are living in 66,000 gallons per day.

Please note:- All pump performance figures do not allow for any restrictions placed upon the output flow. All pipework and fittings produce friction loss to some degree and allowances must be made for this. In this particular instance, where a waterfall is incorporated and a by-pass return made direct to the pond via a pipe run of some 25 feet, a surface pump capable of pumping 4,000 gallons per hour is required. In view of this, and taking into account item 'g' overleaf, a three quarter horse power motor should be used here.

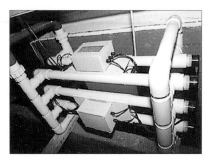

Ultra-violet steriliser system.

g. Ultra-violet steriliser system.

A six-bank 180 watt unit will be fitted in the return 2″ line of the pump mentioned in item 'f' over; this will prevent 'green water' situations caused by photosynthesis due to a combination of nitrates and sunlight, and will also help to reduce some parasitic and bacterial problems.

h. The housing itself.

The roof of the housing will be finished approximately 1 foot above pond water level and constructed in tanalised hardwood planks. These will be bolted (to allow for quick removal if required) to the walls of the structure after a steel support girder has been centrally placed along the length of the housing. Gaps will be made in the planks to allow for expansion. An access hatch is built into the decking to allow for entrance to the housing and wooden steps are sited underneath.

All mains services, namely water, gas and electricity are controlled from here.

Please note:- All electrical appliances, splash-proof plugs and control gear MUST be protected by a suitable Residual Current Device (RCD). This unit will ensure that, in the event of an electrical problem, the circuit breaker will 'trip' rendering the system safe by isolating the electricity supply. Correct installation is vital, not just to make the system 'trip' if a fault develops, but also that it does not 'trip' as a result of poor installation. The nature and importance of the vital inclusion of an RCD in the system is such that a professional Electrical Contractor should always be consulted.

There is also ample space in this housing to store, in wall cupboards, items such as water test equipment, medications, foods etc. etc., plus larger items such as nets and inspection bowls.

4. GENERAL INFORMATION.

To avoid a 'cluttered' visual appearance in the filtration housing, all feed lines and return lines should be carefully planned and the majority installed prior to the main filtration system being sited. In this example, for instance, the feed lines from both power skimmers, the return lines from both the heating system and the filtration units can all be fixed, with pipe clips screwed to the walls of the filter housing, behind where the filtration units are to stand **prior** to installing them. These will all be out of sight and require no maintenance at all. The drain lines from each filter unit should also be run as close as possible to each other in parallel and fixed to the floor, again by pipe clips and not sited over areas where they are a potential danger for the operative tripping over them.

All other equipment that is plumbed in the pressure pipe lines should be able to be removed quickly and easily should maintenance/repairs ever be required. In this instance, both water pumps, stainless steel heat exchanger and ultra-violet system should all have union ball valves fitted on both inlet and outlet points for this purpose.

The apparently 'simple' task of gluing a 'few bits of pipework and fittings together' is, in practice, not nearly as quick and easy as it seems. The solvent used instantly 'fuses' the fittings to the pipework and second chances are rare if mistakes are made. In larger size bores of pipework, tolerances are almost non-existent and errors can be expensive if measurements are not exact. Take your time when doing this work, clean all joints and tubes with the special cleaner solution prior to applying the solvent, push pipes and fittings together as a 'dry run' if necessary before the final fixing. In large installations such as this example there are hundreds upon hundreds of joints required; leaks caused by inexperience or rushing to finish the job can be very expensive and even more time-consuming to rectify.

As far as the air pumps are concerned I have no hesitation in recommending the 'Hi-Blow' range, manufactured by the Takatsuki Mfg. Co., Japan, these are available in numbered models which denote the output of air in litres per minute. They range from 20, 40, 80, 100 up to 200; to date I have not seen any to equal these for reliability, performance and silent running.

'Hi-Blow'
Air Pump.

The choice of water pumps is as wide as it is varied in types of pumps available, but do consider all costs including the running costs when choosing a pump for a particular application as well as reputation, build quality, warranty, performance and head figures quoted. There are usually three types of pump used in a Koi pond system and all should be continuously rated to run on a permanent basis.

Different types of water pumps for Koi pond applications.

1. Submersible Pumps. An example is shown on the right of the photograph. These are excellent for use in filtration systems where no sand filters, heavy pipework restrictions or excessive return pipe runs are present, they are also intended for use as 'sump pumps' which are installed in a sump and are float operated, the float automatically switches the pump on and off as necessary. Running costs vary with the size of motor used and there are many different makes and models on the market. The Oase 'Aquadex' range are particularly excellent.

2. Central Heating Pumps. An example is shown on the left of the photograph. These motors have to be installed externally, preferably below water level in a dry chamber, and cannot be submerged as the ones described above. Only use the stainless steel or phosphor bronze models for Koi pond use. These are generally expensive to buy but slightly cheaper to run in comparison with output performance. Again, do not use these when driving a sand filter or in a situation where pipework restrictions and long pipe runs can present problems. 'Grundfos' make an excellent range of these motors.

3. Centrifugal Pressure Pumps. An example is shown to the centre of the photograph. These are widely used in swimming pool applications where a sand filter has to be powered, they also have to be mounted externally preferably below water level in a dry chamber. If they are installed above water level, then a suitable non–return valve should be fitted prior to the suction inlet to avoid the re-priming operation should electricity supply be switched off. These pumps are very powerful in comparison with the first two examples but running costs are higher and should only be used when the job in hand is too great for the previous types of motor. Most makes of this type of pump are generally very reliable, I have found 'Starite', 'ITT Marlow' , 'Sequence' and 'Espa' all to be excellent.

WORK PLAN FOR EXCAVATION AND CONSTRUCTION.

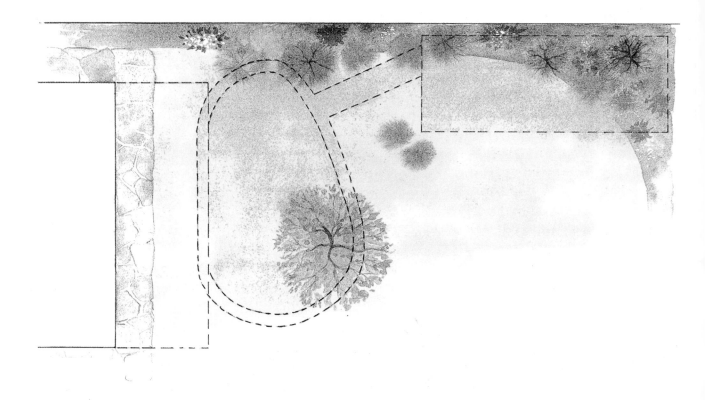

Fig. 1

This is the site plan, final water levels have been decided and pegged, the areas for pond, waterfall/watercourse and filtration housing have also been marked out. An excavator can easily be used on this site as access is wide enough and the plan is to first excavate the filtration housing, next the waterfall/watercourse area and finally the pond itself.

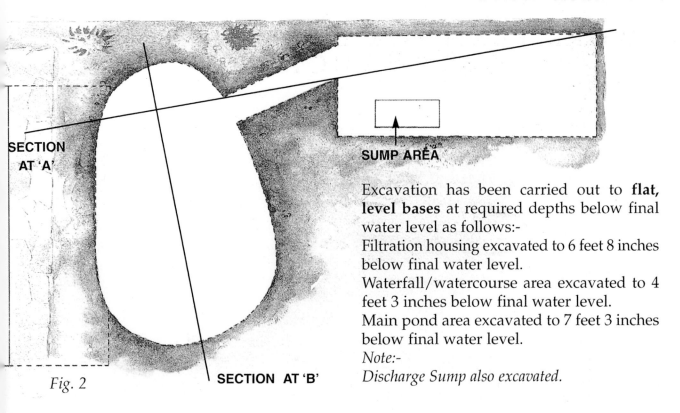

SECTION AT 'A'

SUMP AREA

Excavation has been carried out to **flat, level bases** at required depths below final water level as follows:-
Filtration housing excavated to 6 feet 8 inches below final water level.
Waterfall/watercourse area excavated to 4 feet 3 inches below final water level.
Main pond area excavated to 7 feet 3 inches below final water level.
Note:-
Discharge Sump also excavated.

Fig. 2

SECTION AT 'B'

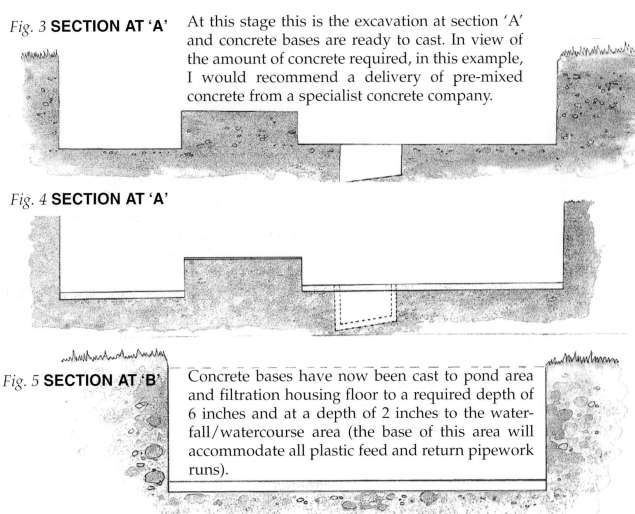

Fig. 3 **SECTION AT 'A'**   At this stage this is the excavation at section 'A' and concrete bases are ready to cast. In view of the amount of concrete required, in this example, I would recommend a delivery of pre-mixed concrete from a specialist concrete company.

Fig. 4 **SECTION AT 'A'**

Fig. 5 **SECTION AT 'B'**   Concrete bases have now been cast to pond area and filtration housing floor to a required depth of 6 inches and at a depth of 2 inches to the water-fall/watercourse area (the base of this area will accommodate all plastic feed and return pipework runs).

At this stage, things begin to start taking shape, the walls to the filtration housing are finished to required height, finishing 1 foot above water level as planned. These walls are built in 6 inch wide concrete block work. The area of the wall where the three 4" drain tubes enter the housing should be finished later when all pipework installations are complete.

The walls of the pond should be commenced for five courses only as follows:-

On straight runs use 18 inch by 9 inch by 4 inch solid concrete blocks and lay them on the 9 inch dimension to form a 9 inch thick wall.

On curves use solid concrete common bricks and lay as illustrated. The bottom drains are now ready to be sited as follows:-

■ Mark a central line along the length of the pond base.

■ Divide the line into three equal sections and then mark the centre of each section. This is where the centre of each drain sump is to be located.

■ Carefully mark out pipeline runs from drains to the point where they will start to rise vertically under the watercourse exit to the pond. Then glue a 90 degree elbow to each line as required, next carefully glue drain sumps to other end of the tubes. At this stage, the tube from the sump of each drain should be totally horizontal but will be one inch above pond base due to the depth of the drain sump. It is best here to pack under each drain line at 2 feet intervals, with small 'chocks' of 1 inch timber to make the tubes totally horizontal. After this, each drain sump and line should be filled with water to level of the sump top which gives excellent stability and also ensures everything is watertight.

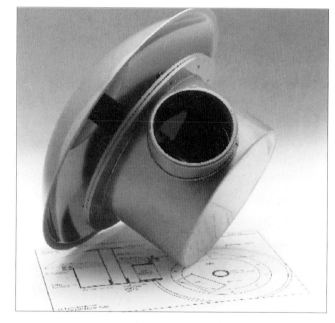

Standard 10" diameter Koi pond bottom drain with 'dome' shaped cover, originally designed by the author in 1979 and first marketed commercially in 1981. These are now widely used as vital equipment for serious Koi ponds. The purpose of the cover, which is some 18" in diameter and is fixed to the sump to give a gap of half an inch between top of sump to the cover, is that good water directly above the sump is not wasted, as would happen without a cover. But rather dirt and debris from the pond base is taken instead and 'sucked' in all around the 18" diameter of the dome.

Fig. 6 **(Prior to second base being cast)**

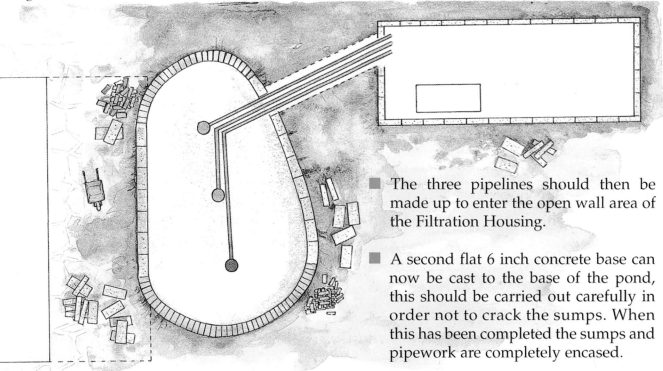

■ The three pipelines should then be made up to enter the open wall area of the Filtration Housing.

■ A second flat 6 inch concrete base can now be cast to the base of the pond, this should be carried out carefully in order not to crack the sumps. When this has been completed the sumps and pipework are completely encased.

We are now at the stage where all pipework runs must be made up and laid along the base of the waterfall/ watercourse area. In this example they are as follows:-

Two 2" lines from each power skimmer (the actual power skimmers cannot be sited until the walls are continued).

One 2" line from the heating system, this will exit in the pond wall to give a 'clockwise' current to the pond water at 4 feet below water level.

One 2" line, a valved by-pass from the main filtration system pump, which can be used partially all the time and increased depending on waterfall requirements. This also should exit in the pond wall to also give a 'clockwise' current, this can be around 2 feet below water level.

Fig. 7 **SECTION AT 'A'**
(Second base cast to pond)

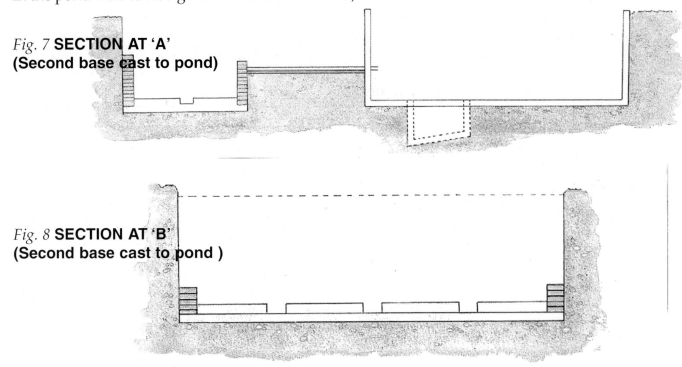

Fig. 8 **SECTION AT 'B'**
(Second base cast to pond)

Fig. 9 **SECTION AT 'A'**

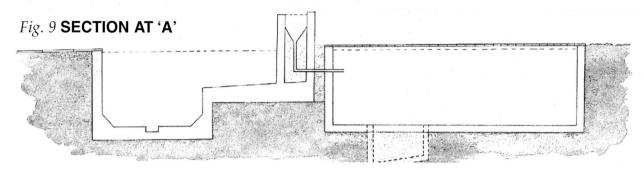

All pipework in the base of waterfall/ watercourse area has been encased into a concrete base and a gentle slope has been formed to the base which will take any debris into the pond and then to the bottom drain. The waterfall header tank has now been formed in concrete block in preparation for final landscaping. Slopes have been formed to the base of the pond walls and the pond base very gradually sloped to the perimeters of the drain sumps.

All filtration equipment and other items can be made up and installed in the filtration housing after feed and return pipework has been installed behind the filter units as mentioned earlier.

Fig. 10 **SECTION AT 'B'**

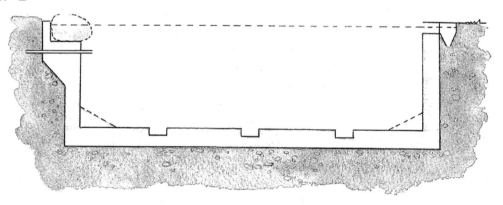

This shows how to correctly install large rockwork to this type of pond in order to give the effect of a natural 'rock pool'. It is important that rocks are selected that are large enough to give a correct effect to the size of the pond itself, and two thirds of the rock is actually under water. The majority of the weight is supported by the main pond wall as a proportion of the rockwork is overhanging the vertical wall, even so the wall has to be reinforced as shown. Behind the rockwork, a wall is incorporated that ends 1" above water level, this cannot be detected once gravel landscaping is taken to the rockwork.

On the opposite side of the pond a power skimmer is sited.

Prior to any rockwork being sited, the whole structure should be completely finished and a 0.5″ render applied to all internal surfaces, this should be mixed with a suitable fibre additive to add strength, after which a final 0.25″ fine 'trowel finish' coat of render is applied. This is a task for an expert! After the render is completely dry, the entire surfaces of the pond should be checked by hand to see if everything is smooth to the touch.

When the pond has been checked for smoothness and everything is in order then waterproofing can be carried out as follows:-

1. Ensure entire surfaces of structure are **completely** dry.

2. Apply a single coat of G4 clear resin to the entire surfaces, by brush and/or roller.

3. When first coat becomes 'tacky' apply a second coat in G4 black resin.

4. Repeat No. 3 after second coat becomes 'tacky'.

Note:- Neither concrete nor G4 resin will form a watertight seal to plastic drains or pipework in view of this, after the G4 has been applied and has dried fully, seal these fine cracks with a film of non-toxic mastic or silicone sealant, this will do the job permanently.

After three days fill the pond to level with mains water, ensure that the three 4″ slide valves to the Vortex unit are closed. Check that the pond is watertight by leaving it full for a day or so.

Next, drop the pond level for approximately 2 feet by opening the 3 inch ball valve drain to the vortex unit and partially open one slide valve, water will exit into the discharge sump and then be pumped to waste. Once the level has dropped, close both valves.

Ensure that the rockwork ledge is dried off, the rockwork can now be carefully bedded in mortar. The reason for leaving water in the pond at this stage is to reduce the risk of damage to the pond structure should an accident occur and a rock fall into the pond. Once all rockwork has been positioned, the spaces between the rocks should be pointed as should the area behind the rocks and between the retaining wall. All mortar should be given a three coat application of G4 after all mortar work is completely dry. This is the method that should also be used when landscaping the waterfall/watercourse area.

The entire system should be emptied by pump and thoroughly steam cleaned in order to remove any un-cured mortar etc.

After this, the pond can be filled via the mains water purification system; this unit incorporates a flowmeter and the exact start reading should be noted prior to starting to fill.

When full to overflow level, the water should be stopped and the final reading taken. By taking the first reading from the last reading, the figure will usually come out in 'tons/cubic metres' of water; gallons can be obtained by multiplying the figure by 220.

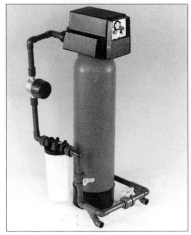

Mains water purification unit for removal of heavy metals.

At this point all the system should be checked for running operation very carefully:-

1. Ensure all control valves are in the 'open' position and all drainage valves in the 'closed' position.

2. Open fully the two control valves that supply water from the power skimmers, switch on skimmer pump and check the 'pull' on each which should be the same, adjust by control valve if necessary.

3. Switch on the main pump that powers the filtration system and check running operation, ensure waterfall and by-pass can be regulated as required, check that flow of current in the pond is visible

4. Switch on central heating pump for heater circuit and gas heater, check system fires up. Adjust thermostat by hand and check operation is working correctly.

5. Ensure U/V system is operational.

6. Check all drain valves are fully operational and that automatic water top-up system is operational as water level drops.

7. Check all pipework and fittings are leak free.

8. After two days, the system is ready for Koi stocks, see 'Maturing a Filter' later in this section of the book.

Impression of finished system.

'TOMORROW'S WORLD?'

My new pond, mentioned earlier, is identical in many ways to the one described previously as far as construction and style are concerned but it is being constructed as a 'growing' system as opposed to a good display system to house a good private collection. At my business premises all Koi are kept and offered for sale in various filtered display pond systems – these are all inside a building for security purposes as well as to reduce heating costs which would be significantly higher in an outdoor situation.

Furthermore my display ponds are not designed for growing purposes and this is the main reason why I decided to build this new system. My requirements from this system are as follows:-

■ The ability to grow stocks quickly with perfect shape and pigmentation.

For this I need a large volume of outdoor water, a heating system, good depth, good current, good dissolved oxygen content, perfect water quality and ample supplies of good quality food.

■ An overall system that requires little daily maintenance and a filter system that can handle high feeding rates and stay mechanically clean and biologically sound together with the minimum of periodic maintenance.

For this I need to be able to use more than a single filtration system as in the previous example, so that periodic total clean-out can

be made to one system very quickly whilst the other systems run as normal, thus not disturbing operation of the system in any way.

The pond itself is a more circular style of shape than the previous system, approximately 24 feet across and 8 feet deep, a rough estimate for the total volume of the system will be around 120 tons or 26,000 gallons. The pond base has four bottom drains each with diffuser tops as opposed to standard 'dome' shaped covers – these were first introduced to the UK by Prokoi Enterprises and I have found them to be excellent in use. During installation of the bottom drain sumps, heavy duty airline is run inside the pipeline and attached to the diffuser top of the drain before fixing the top to the sump.

The 9" diameter rubber diffuser is perforated with thousands of tiny holes and,

Diffuser bottom drain.

when powered by an air pump, it produces a 9" diameter column of gentle aeration from the base of the pond to the surface. This has no adverse effect on the efficiency of the drain itself as far as the removal of debris is concerned as the flat drain cover is underneath the diffusion. It does, however, increase dissolved oxygen content more so than do standard pond airstones.

The larger surface of the pond will require three surface power skimmers and these will be used to power the gas-fired, 100,000 Btu/hr. heating system – the operation will be identical to the last example.

During construction of the pond walls, five 2" tubes were installed at equal intervals, all entering at mid-water level and all terminating parallel with the wall in a clockwise direction. These will provide a constant current to the whole pond which is vital for exercising the Koi if growth, together with perfect shape is to be achieved – without this current the Koi would become too fat. The style of the pond is a 'rock pond' as described in the last example, but final waterproofing will be by fibreglass (GRP) lamination. There is no doubt that this is the best method of waterproofing a system albeit the most expensive.

Note:- Like landscaping and good plastering/ rendering, glass fibre laminating is a task that should be carried out by an expert rather than an amateur; it is both sticky and messy and the fumes produced are both heady and dangerous. Furthermore, it is important to use non-toxic resins and flow coats for use in Koi ponds. My company uses a specialist contractor for any ponds which require this work as a good laminator has the expertise to produce a non-toxic perfectly smooth finish which is vital in this task.

A professional pond lamination, showing base coat, mat and laminated mat.

The filtration housing for this system is large, by any stretch of the imagination, but consideration has to be given to regular access for quick daily maintenance and easy and quick periodic maintenance. Construction of the housing is identical to the previous system but the depth is shallower as the units used will be 40" in diameter and 50" deep which means that the top of the concrete base of the filtration housing will be 49" below the final water level of the system.

As you can see from the plan (right), the system incorporates four separate banks of filtration, each one consists of a prime Vortex unit linked tangentially to two biological units. Each prime Vortex unit gets its supply of water from its own diffuser drain. Prior to the 4" drain tube entering the Vortex tangentially, the tube is fitted with a 4" slide valve. Prior to that a 'tee' piece (the outlet of which is reduced to 3" and stopped by a 3" valve) is fitted. Prior to this, an outlet for the airline which takes aeration to the diffuser drain from the air pump has to be fitted to allow the slide valve to be fully closed when necessary (See drawing opposite).

The reason I have included this 'tee' assembly after the airline exit and before the 4" slide valve is that, by heavy feeding, there is a likelihood of a larger than normal build-up of waste matter collecting in the drain lines. By switching off the pump at the end of one of these banks of filters, the 4" slide valve can be closed and the 3" valve opened. By watching the water discharged through the sight glass assembly, one can 'purge' the drain line quickly and with a minimum of water wastage.

The last biological unit, in each bank of filters, supplies water to its own pump. All four pumps are identical and, in view of this, each bank of filters should run at identical flow rates of 2,200 gallons per hour actual, which is 8,800 gallons per hour total. This results in the entire volume of water being

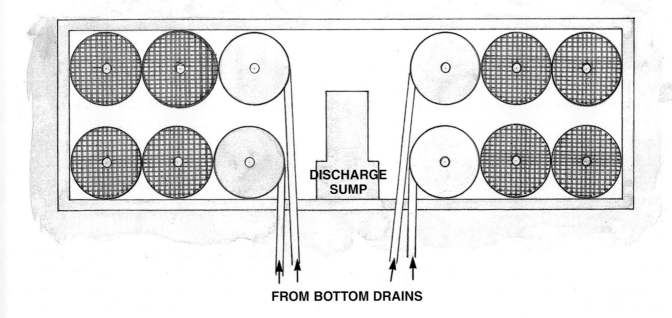

DISCHARGE SUMP

FROM BOTTOM DRAINS

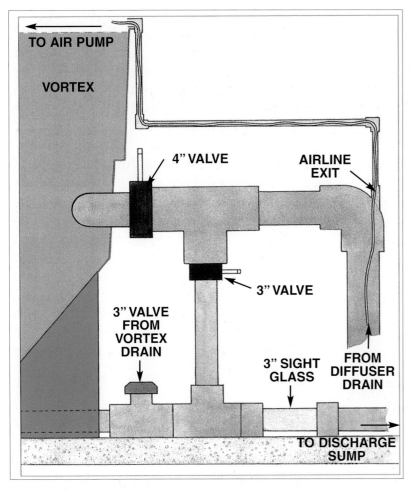

TO AIR PUMP

VORTEX

4" VALVE

AIRLINE EXIT

3" VALVE

3" VALVE FROM VORTEX DRAIN

3" SIGHT GLASS

FROM DIFFUSER DRAIN

TO DISCHARGE SUMP

Correct pipework installation for diffuser drain.

passed through the filter systems once every three hours or 8 times per day. When the system is fully mature and the filtration stages producing 'new' water back to the pond, the Koi will be living, theoretically, in 208,000 gallons of water per day.

The five 2" return lines in the pond, mentioned earlier, are supplied water from the four filter pumps and one heater pump fed by the power skimmers. This will give a clockwise current to the pond of 11,500 gallons per hour and is vital to give exercise to the Koi in order to develop the correct shape discussed earlier. There is a waterfall incorporated but this is fed on a separate feed from the base of the watercourse and will only be used for aesthetic purposes when required, or for situations when more dissolved oxygen content is required, it will have no adverse effect on the system operation at all.

A large discharge sump is built into the floor of the filtration housing and all waste removed to sewer via a float-operated pump. This discharge sump will take waste from the drain cones of each filter unit by separate 2″ ball valves (12 in total) plus the main system overflow and the four 3″ valves to purge drain lines.

The housing will also be used to accommodate all other equipment mentioned in the last example and will be decked by timber in the same way.

The main reason for using these four independent banks of units is for that of ease of periodic total clean-out which will be necessary with very heavy feeding and can be carried out by the following method:-

1. Select one bank of filters and shut-off its pump.

2. Close the 4″ slide valve connecting it to the pond.

3. Open the three 2″ drain valves from each unit and allow them to empty completely.

4. Leave valves open and pressure wash each filter cartridge thoroughly.

5. Shut three 2″ valves, open 4″ slide valve and the system refills.

6. Switch on main water pump to system.

This will take around 10 minutes to complete whilst the other three systems are running as normal and only a small amount of biomass will be lost during this cleaning process. The next system can be cleaned in the same way a week later and so on. Even if one system is cleaned each week on a rota, it means that every bank will be cleaned once a month and no debris will be allowed to build up in any bank of filters and the biomass will not suffer at all.

Once mature, the total system should take an average of no more than four minutes per day to maintain. That's the basic principle behind it all, the truth will only be known after all the theories have been put to the test!

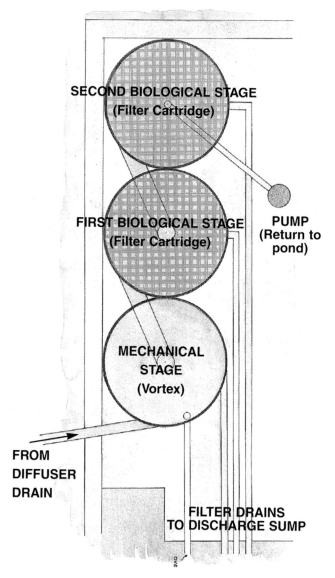

Close-up detail of single bank of filters.

FINAL LANDSCAPING, WHAT TO USE AND WHAT NOT TO USE.

The wrong choice of trees and shrubs that surround a pond can result in problems within the water should leaves, berries or sap etc. enter the pond. Many also choose some form of timber in filter covers or 'log-style' pond edging landscaping — the correct timber and the correct choice of preservative, if used, should be chosen carefully in order to avoid a potential disaster.

1. PLANTS/TREES/SHRUBS.

Many Koi pond systems are surrounded by conifers and heathers to give a pleasing effect which requires little maintenance. Many intersperse Acers amongst these to add to the effect but large deciduous trees are rarely purposely planted near a pond system as leaves can produce problems in Autumn which results in the pond having to be netted at this time of the year.

There are many plant and soil foods, lawn fertilisers and treatments, and insect pesticides on the market which can be applied by hand or by spray. It is important that none of these are allowed to enter the water of the pond system and great care must be taken when using any of these products.

I have been advised by a plant specialist some plants which should not be sited near Koi ponds for a variety of reasons, obviously the toxic effects of these depends on the amount of leaves, twigs, seeds, berries etc. within the volume of water in question. I must admit that I have seldom come across problems directly as a result of toxins produced by plants in general. The only one I can recall was when a small pond was full of large pine cones and this had a serious effect on the Koi — once the cones were

removed and water changed the Koi improved dramatically.

The following plants and trees are not recommended to site near a Koi pond:-

Laburnum (Leguminosae)
Seeds are very poisonous.

Taxus (Taxadiaceae) Yew,
nearly every part is poisonous.

Sambucus (Caprifoliaceae) Elder,
the bark, leaves and berries can be poisonous.

Salix (Salicaceae) Willow,
leaves can be poisonous.

Wisteria (Leguminosae)
Seeds and twigs can be poisonous.

Hedra (Araliaceae) Ivy,
berries and sap can cause problems.

Digitalis (Scrophulariaceae) Foxglove,
the whole plant can be poisonous.

Convallaria Majalis, Lily-of-the-Valley,
berries can be poisonous.

Ilex (Aquafoliaceae) Holly,
berries are poisonous.

Rhododendron (Ericaceae)
plus Azaleas (mainly Japanese species)
- bark can be toxic.

It should be pointed out here that there is no real problem if small amounts of any of the above find their way into a pond and are removed periodically.

2. TIMBER.

A 'log effect' edging to a pond wall can be very pleasing, this is usually achieved by siting logs on to the pond wall to give an un-even finish above water level and to disguise the pond wall as follows:-

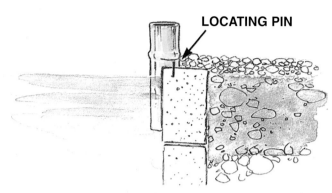

LOCATING PIN

Face View & Section correct way to site logs.

In a 'rock-style' pond, logs can also be used at random intervals in between boulders to give a pleasing variation to the overall effect.

Most types of logs can be used but pines should be avoided if possible – before fixing these into position I would recommend them to be tanalised for preservation purposes. Many timber suppliers can offer this service nowadays and tanalised logs are safe for pond landscaping methods. I would recommend Oak, Ash, Bamboo or Birch for this purpose.

If timber is required for filtration housing covers as in the examples previously described, I would suggest a strong hardwood for this purpose. Again this can be tanalised by the supplier and used as supplied to give the natural colour of the timber chosen. If staining is required then a standard wood stainer can be used before sealing this, prior to installation, with either G4, a clear poly-urethane varnish or a yacht varnish. Do not use wood stainers or dyes on any pond timberwork unless they are to be sealed as above prior to use. All forms of Creosote are lethal to fish life and great care must be taken if fences have to be treated near the pond system.

It is always prudent to check with a manufacturer or supplier as to the potential toxicity of any wood treatment or finish prior to purchase.

There are rocks, and there are Rocks!

MATURING AND MAINTAINING A SYSTEM.

Every new system has to be matured before all water readings are perfect and remain so, the finest filtration system available has to 'live' before the necessary results are produced. The 'Nitrification Process' mentioned earlier, now takes on a real meaning and, when a new system is started, daily attention has to be paid as to all the water readings and their fluctuations and the keeper has to know what to do if problems start to manifest themselves.

Assuming a new system has been filled with water and circulated for two days or so to test running operation etc., a full water test at this point will reveal no ammonias or nitrites and probably a neutral pH, this is to be expected as there are no Koi stocks in the system. A new system cannot be matured until Koi stocks are introduced as the biological surfaces cannot support a biomass until ammonias and nitrites are 'fed' at a constant rate and these are produced by the Koi themselves.

At this stage there are many who advocate that stocks should be introduced very gradually and increased very slowly to give the filtration a chance to cope, I personally think that this method takes much longer to mature as only a small percentage of the surfaces will support a healthy biomass due to low stocking rates and very gradual increases in these stocking rates. In my opinion, it is better to add a good stocking rate from day one and carefully monitor all readings in the way described below. In my experience this produces a stable system in the shortest possible time period. If water temperatures are over 58 degrees Fahrenheit it should take between four to six weeks to develop an operational biomass, at lower temperatures it will take longer.

The Japanese breeders adopt the above method every year out of sheer necessity. From early June to mid October, when all their stocks are growing in mud ponds, all their indoor ponds have been emptied and scrubbed clean, the media in their filters has been removed, washed and stored and the filter chambers thoroughly cleaned. Aproximately one week before they start to harvest their mud ponds during mid October all indoor ponds are filled with spring water or well water, the filter media is placed back into the chambers and all systems are started up once more.

All these ponds receive enormous volumes of stocks from mud ponds harvested regularly between mid October to early November. They are placed in these 'immature' systems and usually an appropriate anti-parasite medication is added immediately. On many occasions I have seen these newly harvested Koi; to the first-time visitor it is a distressing sight as all the Koi are usually lying motionless on the base of the ponds and many laying on their sides. This is basically because of the fluctuating water qualities as the filters start to mature. However, by constant expert monitoring of water conditions and correct addition of new water to dissolve the toxic waste products, within four to five days these systems are almost fully mature and the Koi are in perfect condition and looking for food. Feeding is carried out very sparingly over the next few weeks to allow all systems to mature fully after which the feeding rate can be increased to normal levels.

Make a chart to keep next to the pond and divide it into columns from left to right as follows:- Date; Water temperature; Dissolved Oxygen; pH; Nitrite; Ammonia and a wide column on the right headed 'Additions/ Action taken', take all these readings prior to Koi being introduced. There are many makes of water test kits available on the market, they all are easy to use with step-by-step instructions, an excellent range of accurate budget-priced test kits which give reasonable water quality indications are manufactured by the 'Tetra' company.

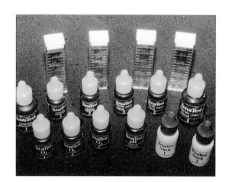

Water test kits.

For those requiring far more accurate readings for daily professional purposes, there are many test kits available albeit significantly more expensive. These range from reagent- type kits right through to digital versions.

When Koi have been introduced, after ensuring water temperatures have been equalised, add 'ABA-N1' to the surfaces of the biological media at the rate of 5mls. per ton (220 gallons) pond water.

'ABA' (Aqua-bacta Aid) is a liquid preparation of various forms of live bacteria which speeds up the maturing process of the media surfaces, it is available in 'R1' form (regular) for maintaining mature filters and 'N1' form (nitrifying) for the start-up process. Once this has been introduced, mark the last column on the chart opposite

'ABA' (Aqua-bacta Aid)

the respective date, 'ABA N1 added at 5mls/ton', at this point introduce a constant supply of mains water to the system which will exit the system at the rate of approximately 10% of the pond volume per day, via the overflow.

For the first five days, after introducing new stocks, one should be aware that this is the period when some Koi, trying to adapt to new water make-up, tend to jump, especially where water currents enter the pond, it is, therefore, wise to cover these areas in particular until the Koi have had time to adjust to the water conditions.

On the second day, take all water readings and log them on the chart, do this on a daily basis for at least four weeks. The Koi can be fed sparingly from day 2 and mechanical stages of the filters discharged as required. On every third day, re-dose with ABA-N1 as per day 1 for a total of 10 applications over a 30 day period.

Remember, ideal readings are:- Dissolved Oxygen in excess of 8PPM; pH between 7.2 to 7.8; Ammonia zero; Nitrite zero and a water temperature that fluctuates very little on a day-to-day basis.

Fluctuations will certainly begin to be seen in Ammonia and/or Nitrite, usually around day 7, this is because the biological surfaces are not yet anywhere active enough to remove all these dissolved toxins produced by the Koi and some are returned to the pond which causes a constant build-up and readings start to show on the water tests. At this stage immediate action needs to be taken to reduce these, if no action is taken at this stage, readings will continue to climb and the Koi will become very distressed as a result.

To reduce the levels of these readings, pond water levels should be reduced several times a day by discharging mechanical stages to waste. This should be replaced by mains water as quickly as possible and the new water added to the pond constantly should be increased to 25% to 30% per day and feeding stopped during this period.

In Japan, many enthusiasts use 'Zeolite' to absorb some quantities of ammonias and nitrites not removed in the biological stages. Zeolite is a form of porous rock that can absorb up to 8 times its own weight in nitrites and ammonias before it becomes ineffective and then requires to be re-charged. It must be pointed out here that there are more than 150 types of zeolite and many are not suitable for Koi pond purposes. The one mined in Japan for Koi pond usage can be periodically re-charged in a high salt solution by placing it in a bowl, covering it with water and adding salt at the rate of 1 kilo per 10 litres of water, after 24 hours this can be rinsed and used again. Some other forms of zeolite require to be re-charged in high temperature ovens which is very time consuming. In the UK many enthusiasts use zeolite to replace sand in sand pressure filters at the last stage of filtration prior to actual pond return stage.

If pH fluctuations occur either upwards or downwards, these too can be corrected by adding new water, but a better choice would be to introduce a pH 'buffer' to the water flow in the filtration stage. I have found that crushed oyster shell is particularly effective here. It is generally available in 20 kilo sacks which will easily handle ponds up to 25 tons of water and quickly bring the readings to around 7.5. This can be divided and placed in a fine–mesh nylon material such as greenhouse shading tied into bags which are suspended in the water flow through the filtration stages. It is totally safe to use and can be left in place permanently or removed when the system is totally mature.

By noting all these readings on a daily basis and controlling new water as necessary, it becomes easy to realise when and how much new water is required to control the overall situation. Once the biomass becomes much

greater, the need for constant new water becomes far less and this can be reduced accordingly and feeding can continue. Eventually, the fluctuations will stop and all readings will be perfect and stable, new water can be stopped and the only new water required will be to replace any discharged to waste in daily servicing. The system now is fully mature and the Koi and biomass are totally dependent on each other.

To maintain this situation, I would suggest water readings be taken once a month and ABA R1 is added to the biological stages of the filter once every month at the rate of 2 mls per ton.

Finally on the subject of water quality, most Koi keepers have to use mains water for their Koi ponds; this water has been processed by the water authorities before reaching our homes and is specifically processed for human drinking purposes. Most impurities have been removed and chlorines and fluorides are added during treatment, many of the impurities removed for human drinking purposes contain important vitamins and minerals found in the clay of our natural lakes which are excellent for our Koi stocks and greatly enhance mucus and skin conditions.

Re-Fresh'

This product is widely used nowadays to replace these minerals and vitamins back into our Koi pond systems and results can be witnessed after two to four weeks of usage in overall condition and greatly improved skin quality after it has been absorbed into these parts. 'Re-Fresh' can be used in all water temperatures and, after the initial dosage, only needs to be replaced in direct relationship to the amount of water discharged by daily servicing etc. Initial dosage is 250 grams per 4 tons water (880 gallons) – this should be measured out and placed into a large plastic bowl, pond water is then added and then mixed by hand thoroughly to ensure all lumps have been removed when it takes on a texture similar to emulsion paint. This is then added to the pond water and turns the whole system very 'muddy' for some three days or so before clarity returns. Top-up dosages should be carried out at monthly intervals when total water discharged should be estimated, e.g. if 1,760 gallons have been replaced then 500 grams 'Re-Fresh' should be added accordingly. Please note, it is not at all dangerous to overdose with this product and its make-up is that of Montmorillionite Clay together with vitamins and minerals.

The use of large boulders, granite lanterns, sculptured trees, moss, formal paving and raked gravel – Japanese landscaping at its finest.

HEATING A KOI POND.

By now, the reader will have gathered that I strongly believe that Koi in the UK need higher temperatures than our annual ambient temperatures. If a pond heating system is incorporated then I would recommend the following monthly running temperatures for the health and good growth rates of the Koi together with maximum economy of running costs for the keeper.

The biggest source of heat loss by far to our ponds is that lost by 'wind chill', many take steps to reduce this during Winter months by covering the pond in some way. If this is to be done I would suggest the cover used should allow as much natural light to the pond as possible, and to try and prevent the cover from resting on the pond surface, a 6" gap is more preferable if this can be made.

The following graph is for estimated monthly ambient pond water temperatures for a ficticious outdoor uninsulated system somewhere in Central England – all temp-eratures are given in Fahrenheit. It also shows recommended monthly running temperatures for the same pond with a heating system.

As the thermostat used in a good heating system can work to minute tolerances, the readings shown for the heated pond are formed by way of a smooth line. The ambient temperature readings, however, are shown by an uneven line which reflects quite significant fluctuations that do take place.

By maintaining a minimum temperature of 55°F, the Koi can take food all year round and the pond can be safely medicated all year round should this be necessary. At no time does the heater have to take water temperature over 15 degrees above ambient. Obviously the greater the volume of water to be heated, the greater the running costs and a suitable cover here can save dramatically on fuel.

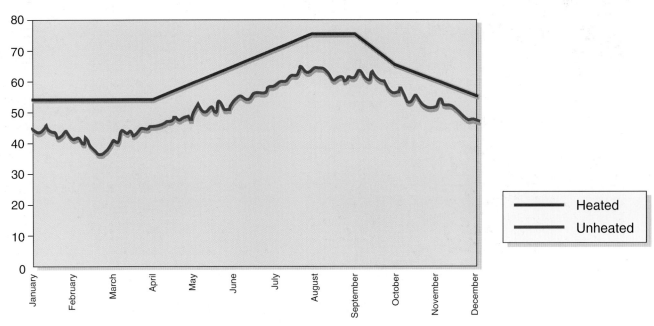

Average UK ambient water temperatures vs. a heated pond.

The most important time of the year to use a heating system is during the Summer months, as mentioned earlier Koi need water of 65°F before any significant growth is produced. By using the heater wisely at this time of the year, together with a good diet, the growth rates produced are excellent. Colours of the Koi in higher water temperatures do tend to fade a little but these return better than ever when temperatures fall to around 55°F.

The 'indirect' heating system described earlier in this section powered by Natural Gas is, by far, the safest to adopt in a Koi pond system together with the cheapest running costs as far as the UK is concerned. In larger systems the external stainless steel heat exchanger unit can be replaced by a 1" bore stainless steel loop line submerged in a reservoir where pond water is passed through to slightly increase efficiency. I have come across isolated instances where a free supply of wood is available and a wood burning boiler has been installed. Other options for those with no Natural Gas supply are propane, oil or electricity, which are far more expensive to run. A stainless steel in-line electric heater is cheap to purchase and both quick and simple to install, but if this is to be run properly, controlled by thermostat constantly, then running costs can only be met by the wealthy Koi keeper. Many use electric heating during off-peak times when electricity costs are cheaper, I would not recommend this form of usage as quite significant temperature fluctuations can occur on a daily basis.

A female Maruten Sanke, 65cm. (26") long and with all the 'sumi' hallmarks of Kichinai bloodline. I particularly like the bold single stripe of sumi on the left hand pectoral fin and the delicate quality of the texture of the red pattern.

'NISHIKIGOI'
This section of the
book explains
Varieties,
classifications,
pattern styles,
bloodlines and
appreciation aspects
of the Koi
themselves. It also
covers Nishikigoi
shows, the rules and
judging stages, plus
aspects of importing
and buying
Nishikigoi.

NISHIKIGOI VARIETIES, PATTERN STYLES AND CLASSIFICATIONS.

The reason for classification is that there are many varieties of Koi but, for show purposes, some minor varieties and sub-varieties have to be entered alongside each other in the same classification. If this was not so, and Koi entered by variety only, there would probably be in excess of fifty 'varieties' entered. As a result many 'first' awards would be given purely because many Koi had no competitors within the size group. I have included all major varieties still produced today and, for Kohaku, Sanke and Showa varieties, I have also included some popular examples of pattern styles for identification purposes.

Describing varieties and pattern styles by way of illustrating them with actual photographs is very difficult. Location of all photographs required is almost impossible, backgrounds vary, sizes vary and picture qualities vary. In view of this the 'Koi' illustrated here are ficticious examples, each hand painted on to a standard female Koi shape to give the reader an accurate impression of each example. All paintings shown in this section were hand painted by Mr. Satoru Hoshino of Ojiya City, Niigata, specifically for this book. These were commissioned from a list of varieties and pattern styles I prepared for him. The quality of his work and attention to fine detail reflects the hours spent in completing all 71 paintings plus his vast knowledge of the subject of Nishikigoi in general.

KOHAKU.

(a white Koi with red pattern.)

At an auction for food fish held in Niigata Prefecture during 1891, a female 'Menkaburi Tancho' patterned Kohaku and a male 'Gotensakura' Kohaku were purchased by Kunizo Hiroi. (great grandfather of Satoru Hoshino, the artist mentioned earlier and interviewed in a later section of this book) In those early days of Nishikigoi, most Kohaku had 'gotensakura' pattern which comprised of many small patches of red pattern and individual red scales as opposed to todays' heavy 'block' patterns. Mr. Hiroi bred these two Koi during 1891 and the offspring, in later years, were developed into 'Gosuke' bloodline. In the late 1890's some Gosuke fry were purchased by 'Jiemon' and their offspring sold to 'Genjiro'who, in turn, sold his offspring to 'Gorobei'. Around 1921, Gorobei Kohaku were purchased by 'Tomoin' who later sold his offspring to 'Yagozen'. Back once more to 1891, Gosuke sold other fry to 'Genpachi' who, in turn, sold offspring to 'Manzo'. Today Tomoin and Manzo lines are used as parent stocks by the most successful of Kohaku breeders, notably Dainichi, Sakai, Torazo, Hoshikin, Miyajima, Igarashi etc. whilst other, equally successful breeders prefer Kohaku from Sensuke and Yagozen lineage to produce high grade offspring. I have discussed with many breeders as to development of Kohaku from one year size to adult stages and the pattern change and stability of pattern depends purely on the bloodline of the parent stocks. Some lines produce patterns that vary little at all, whilst others change quite significantly. On many occasions I have witnessed small Kohaku with creamy skin and 'yellow' pattern sell individually at incredible prices to breeders at local village auctions. These Koi would be ridiculed by most in the UK as being 'junk grade' and would be hard to even give away. I nicknamed these as 'Kihaku' because of their yellow pattern. The

*Kuchibeni
(lipstick pattern)*

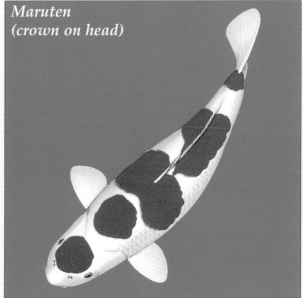

*Maruten
(crown on head)*

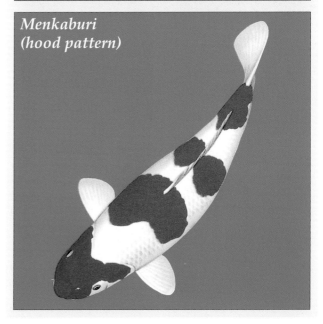

*Menkaburi
(hood pattern)*

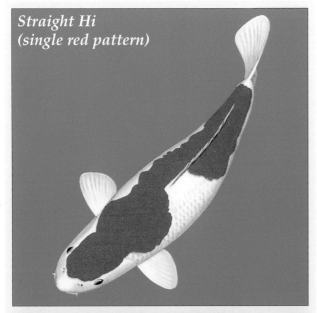

Straight Hi
(single red pattern)

Inazuma
(lightning strike pattern)

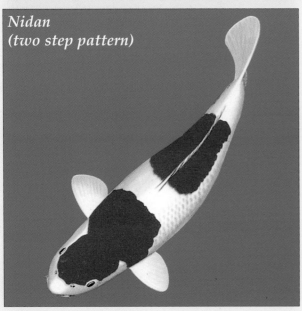

Nidan
(two step pattern)

professional breeders, however, will try to purchase as many of these examples as they can afford, fully aware that the future potential is that of the highest grade possible. I know of few breeders who do not breed Kohaku each year, Kohaku is still the most popular and potentially the most valuable variety of Nishikigoi. I have included some common patterns here, these are by no means a yardstick of any kind in choosing Kohaku, instead they are included simply as identification for the most common patterns. For instance if you are looking in a pond of 200 three year old Kohaku and wish to ask to see one closer, it is far easier to identify it to the breeder by describing the pattern rather than just asking to see one you are pointing at which can be confusing and time wasting. As I mentioned earlier many do not fall into common pattern descriptions at all, nonetheless they are all true Kohaku and entered in Kohaku class at shows with one exception, and that is the Tancho Pattern shown. This again, is true Kohaku, but, for show purposes, it is entered in a separate 'Tancho' class.

To try and give 'pointers' as what to look for when selecting Kohaku is extremely difficult and the price quoted is a very good yardstick to work on.

For many years I have tried to point out to many enthusiasts that there are many 'cheap Koi' and many 'good Koi'- unfortunately I have never come across 'good cheap Koi'.

In small sized Kohaku priced very cheaply at your local dealer, the future potential as far as pigmentation and skin quality will not be good at all, but if you are new to the hobby then these may be an ideal choice to experiment with. In later years, when you are more confident with your keeping abilities, it may be worthwhile to try a better grade Kohaku, perhaps with a much lighter red pigmentation, and observe developments in skin and pigmentation compared with the cheaper stocks given the same conditions and keeping methods.

In good quality Kohaku, Sanke and Showa varieties the delicate orange-red pigmentation can be gradually improved to a very vivid orange-red colour, still retaining an even texture overall, by feeding a good quality colour enhancing food. Many Japanese breeders rarely feed colour enhancing foods until after the Koi are two years old, hence the orange-red pigmentation in good grade smaller sizes.

When choosing larger sizes, try to look for clean, creamy skin, and a potential, when fully grown, to produce a good edge (kiwa) between the pattern and the white pigment. Also look for an even texture to the red pigmentation (not one that has scales varying in colour) and a pattern that is pleasing to your eye. Many like a break in red pattern before the tail although this is, by no means, essential.

Note:- Even the finest Kohaku, Sanke and Showa varieties produced will always show a more intense red pigmentation on the head area as opposed to the pigmentation on the rest of the body. This is simply because the pigmentation only has to show through the skin on the head region, whereas it has to grow through both skin and scales elsewhere; this is not so apparent in Doitsu examples.

Also in these varieties the 'edge' of the red pattern is always much sharper at the 'end' of the pattern (nearer to the tail) as individual scales are fully highlighted. This is not so obviously apparent at the beginning of the pattern.

Do try to avoid Kohaku with 'windows' of white pigmentation appearing in the pattern areas, as it is usually a sign of heavy or total loss of pigmentation in future years.

Sandan
(three step pattern)

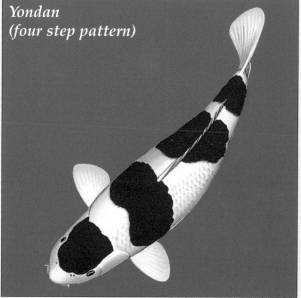

Yondan
(four step pattern)

Tancho
(single crown pattern on head)

TAISHO SANKE.
(TAISHO SANSHOKU)

(a white Koi with red and black pattern.)

Kuchibeni
(lipstick pattern)

A three coloured Koi first produced in the Taisho Era of Japan's history and long since abbreviated simply to 'Sanke'.

During 1921, 'Torazo' developed his famous Sanke bloodline which is responsible for producing other famous bloodlines in later years. The 'Jinbei' bloodline originated from a female Torazo Sanke, a male Tomoin Kohaku and a male Sanke purchased from Isumiya with no bloodline. The true Jinbei bloodline was stabilised around 1960 and was largely responsible for producing 'Matsunosuke' bloodline which was stabilised in 1965.

Several other true lines of Sanke were also produced, for instance, in 1950, 'Sanba' bloodline were stabilised and sold in 1953 to Genpachi (not the Kohaku Genpachi) and then to Naoshichi in 1965, all these lines are now extinct.

Maruten
(crown on head)

However Sanba fry were also sold to 'Sadazo' in 1955, offspring from these were sold in 1965 to 'Kichinai' who developed Kichinai bloodline in later years.

The famous bloodlines used today in Sanke production i.e.- Torazo, Matsunosuke, Jinbei, Sadazo and Kichinai, all originated from early Torazo and Sanba bloodstocks.

I personally find Sanke the most beautiful and interesting variety of all as pattern changes can be so surprising, with each passing year, as the Koi develops. I have included some common patterns here for identification purposes, all are true Sanke and entered in Sanke class for show purposes, with one exception and that is of Tancho pattern which is entered in a separate 'Tancho' classification.

Aka Sanke
(heavy red pattern)

Again, bloodline has to be taken into account when selecting small sizes in Sanke. Many high grade small sizes show little, if any, black ('sumi') pattern at all, indeed many show no black pattern until they are two years old. Some Torazo fry show black pattern at three months old which disappears at twelve months old to re-appear around three years later. Matsunosuke bloodline produces very faint blue-grey patterns in good examples even up to four or five years old, which increases and intensifies significantly as the Koi matures. On the other hand, some Sadazo and Kichinai lines remain almost identical in pattern from five inches to adult sizes and if one is growing Sanke from small sizes it is advisable to make a photographic record annually to witness the changes during growth. By studying many examples of Sanke bloodlines, it is not very difficult to be reasonably accurate in determining bloodlines of other Sanke as the styles of each individual bloodline is almost like a trademark. Generally speaking, try to avoid heavy black patterns in small sizes as these will increase dramatically in years to come to produce far too much black pattern overall. In larger sizes try to look for a creamy white skin, good edges between white and red pattern and a pleasing black pattern which, if removed, would leave a good Kohaku. Look for an overall pattern which pleases your eye and bear in mind, once again, that symmetry is not important at all. (see 'appreciation' section)

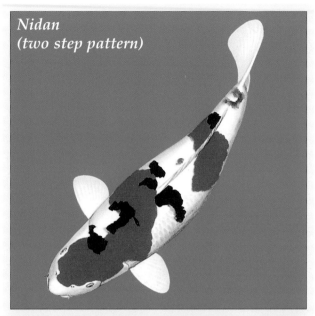

Nidan
(two step pattern)

Menkaburi
(hood pattern)

Subo sumi
(black pattern only falls on white skin)

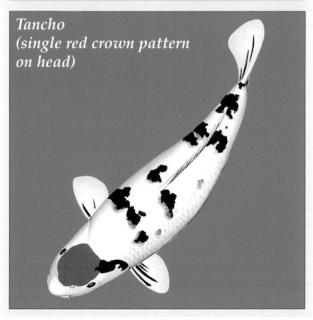

Tancho
(single red crown pattern on head)

SHOWA SANKE.
(SHOWA SANSHOKU)

(a black Koi with red and white pattern.)

A three coloured Koi first produced in Japan's Showa Era and now abbreviated simply to 'Showa'. As mentioned earlier it is recorded that Hoshino produced original strains of Showa in Niigata during 1927 from Kohaku and Ki Utsuri parents. However to date there is no actual bloodline although many breeders use offspring from Kobayashi stocks produced in Niigata around 1965 which are rumoured to have had some Hoshino blood in them. It is only in very recent years that Showa have taken on a red pigmentation which is akin to good Kohaku and Sanke. Before this the red and black pigmentation was very dull which led some breeders to experiment during breeding by using female Showa with male Sanke and Kohaku. As a result the stunning Showa seen today in Japan are worlds apart from those yellow-orange examples first produced by Kobayashi around 1965. I have included several styles of Showa for identification purposes only; all are entered in Showa classification at Shows again with the exception of the Tancho pattern which is entered in 'Tancho' classification.

Many newcomers to the hobby are confused between Showa and Sanke varieties and this is very understandable as both are red, white and black. Perhaps the following will take away the confusion:- The black pigmentation on Sanke is rarely found on the head, nose and mouth areas and very seldom, in any quantity, below the lateral line. If any black pigmentation is found on the pectoral or tail fins it is usually seen in thin stripes. The black pigmentation on Showa is often found on the head, nose and mouth areas and generally in quantity below the lateral line and belly areas. If black pigmentation is present on the pectoral fins it is usually in a block pattern stemming from the ball joint

Maruten
(crown pattern on head.)

Hi Showa
(heavy red pattern)

Kindai Showa
(heavy white pattern)

of the pectoral fin and known as 'Motoguro'. Generally speaking there is more black pigmentation on Showa than Sanke although many breeders today are producing some true Showa stocks that do resemble Sanke at a glance, but after close inspection, the correct identification can be made. There is no doubt that Showa varieties are, by far, the most interbred of all the varieties of Nishikigoi and many breeders find them difficult to produce with quality and in any quantity. It is said that only 30% of the fry hatched in a Showa spawning are, in fact, Showa and these can be seen after three days of hatching as black in colour, the other 70% are destroyed at this stage. Of the 30% that are placed in mud ponds to grow it is estimated that a further 40% of these will have to be destroyed in subsequent culls because of head and mouth deformities which are commonplace in Showa varieties. The development of Showa from small to large sizes can only be explained in relationship to the parent stocks of the breeder in question. On my early visits to Japan, I saw many small Showa which were muddy brown in appearance with no pattern definition and often wondered why these stocks were housed in indoor heated ponds for Winter as, I thought, they would have very little commercial value if any at all, and I certainly could not sell these in the UK. After a few more visits were made I discovered that these Koi were very expensive indeed, the breeder knowing how they would develop in the future. During 1979 I purchased two such muddy brown 'Showa' and gave them to a friend to grow for me in a large aquarium; he knew very little about Nishikigoi and I forgot about them for about 18 months. My friend, later contacted me to ask me to collect them as they were too big for the aquarium. On my arrival I could not believe that these were the same Koi I had purchased at five inches long, they were around 14" long with intense red, white and black colours and excellent definition, a very far cry from the Koi I originally purchased. During the mid 1980's I purchased another

Tancho Showa (single red crown pattern on head)

similar style of small Showa from Mr. Gamo in Isawa and brought it back to watch it grow. My staff asked me why I had paid £400.00 for this totally unsaleable Koi. A few months later a lady customer asked me why I kept this small Koi in the pond which contained my best stocks and I explained my reasons. Some weeks later the lady bought the Koi for exactly the same amount I had paid for it. It was kept in an outdoor, heated pond for 18 months and the lady made several telephone calls during that period to say how well the Koi was developing and, by the way, had christened her by the name of 'Killer'! Some months later, 'Killer' was entered in the BKKS National Show, she was then over 18" long, she took the award for 'best Showa in size', then the award for 'best Koi in size', and then the award for 'best Adult Koi in Show'. There is no doubt that Showa can be confusing in small sizes, some look terrible whilst others look stunning! Over the years I have found superb Showa from Yamaguchi in Koide, Hashino in Tsunan, Dainichi, Isumiya, Hasegawa, Sakai in Hiroshima and Matsunosuke and Gamo both in Isawa.

'UTSURIMONO' VARIETIES.

SHIRO UTSURI,
- a black Koi with white pattern.
HI UTSURI,
- a black Koi with red pattern.
KI UTSURI,
- a black Koi with yellow pattern.

It is best to cover these varieties next to the section on Showa, as these varieties all originated from Showa stocks although today parent stocks are bred from Shiro Utsuri and Hi Utsuri. Ki Utsuri are not bred today in any great numbers and I have yet to see a really good example of this old variety. In short a Shiro Utsuri is a Showa without red pattern and a Hi Utsuri is a Showa without white pattern, these are all entered into a show under the 'Utsurimono' class-ification.

There is no doubt that Sakai and Omosako from Hiroshima, at the time of writing, produce the best Shiro Utsuri in the world. In adult sizes the white skin and black ground can dazzle, whilst the ones with potential in small sizes have a yellow skin and a blue-grey sumi! — very confusing, especially for the novice.

Shiro Utsuri

Hi Utsuri

Ki Utsuri

'KAGE' VARIETIES.

KAGE SHOWA,
    – a Showa with black shadow pattern.
KAGE SHIRO UTSURI,
– a Shiro Utsuri with black shadow pattern.

Still on Showa varieties and best kept to this section are the 'Kage' varieties. Kage translates as 'shadow' and is, in my opinion and experience of these patterns, something of a misnomer as many Showa and Shiro Utsuri show Kage patterns during development and then lose the Kage effect after reaching maturity. However in larger Japanese Shows, Kage varieties are entered in the 'Kawarimono' classification which will be detailed later, I have opted to include these here as they are really pattern styles of Showa and Shiro Utsuri

I have also seen the odd Kage Hi Utsuri from time to time, but, in general these are almost one-off examples, and I know of no Japanese breeder today who specialises in these varieties, more often than not they are a by-product in Showa or Koromo Showa production.

Kage Showa

Kage Shiro Utsuri

'BEKKO' VARIETIES.

SHIRO BEKKO,
— a white Koi with black pattern.
AKA BEKKO,
— a red Koi with black pattern.
KI BEKKO,
— a yellow Koi with black pattern.

This classification today usually refers to Shiro Bekko which is, in truth, a Sanke without red pattern. However the classification still allows for Aka Bekko, a Sanke without white pattern except for the finnage, and Ki Bekko, rarely produced nowadays, which is a yellow Koi with black pattern. As many newcomers also get confused between both Aka Bekko and Hi Utsuri and Shiro Bekko and Shiro Utsuri, the way to differentiate is with the black pattern forms as described earlier under Showa and Sanke varieties. The word Bekko is translated as 'tortoise-shell' which was the effect given by early examples of this variety to the breeders. The examples shown here are all entered in a show under 'Bekko' classification.

When selecting Bekko varieties look for a clean, unblemished head, good skin and pleasing patterns, together with good shape. In adult Koi look for good edge between pattern and base colour.

Shiro Bekko

Aka Bekko

Ki Bekko

'KOROMO' VARIETIES.

AIGOROMO,
— a white Koi with red pattern and the edge of each red scale tinged with black.

SUMIGOROMO,
— a white Koi with a black-ish pattern, the edge of each black-ish scale tinged with red.

BUDOGOROMO,
— a white Koi with Sumigoromo appearance, the edge of the pattern resembles a bunch of grapes in effect.

This classification includes Aigoromo, Sumigoromo and Budogoromo which are all entered in 'Koromo' class for show purposes. Aigoromo were first produced in Niigata by Matsunosuke by crossing various lines of Kohaku together for several years before the Koromo effect was evident. Many believe that Aigoromo were produced by crossing Kohaku with Asagi but this cross breeding was used to produce Goshiki.

Koromo Koi are very popular in the UK and good class examples are difficult to find, in recent years Matsunosuke has produced many good Sumigoromo. In choosing these varieties look for pleasing pattern, almost like good Kohaku, with good white ground. The pattern seldom changes in these varieties from small size to large size as it does in Kohaku, Sanke and Showa varieties.

Aigoromo

Sumigoromo

Budogoromo

GOSHIKI.

GOSHIKI,
> – a white Koi with a 'Koromo' effect throughout the body.

GOSHIKI-SANKE
> – a Sanke with Koromo effect throughout.

I have included this variety after Koromo because they are very similar in appearance, however Goshiki are entered in 'Kawari-mono' class in Japanese shows whilst UK shows enter these in 'Koromo' class. There are many styles of Goshiki being produced especially in recent years, this variety resembles Aigoromo but the reticulated black edging to the scales is apparent throughout the body on both the white ground and the pattern pigment.

Koromo and Goshiki varieties can be very striking indeed, small high grade Aigoromo can resemble 'dirty' Kohaku which turns into true Koromo effect as the Koi matures. Today in Japan there are many different styles of Goshiki which are being developed by specialist breeders, one in particular is Goshiki - Sanke that is being produced by 'Choguro' in Araya, Niigata, this also is entered in 'Kawarimono' class for show purposes.

Goshiki

Goshiki-Sanke

ASAGI/SHUSUI.

ASAGI.

Asagi were the first real variety of Koi ever produced, they are blue or blue-grey in colour; some have a red belly which can sometimes come up to the lateral lines and cheeks of the Koi. The scales upon the back are edged in a darker grey giving a highlight to each individual scale. For show purposes these are entered in a separate 'Asagi/ Shusui' classification.

SHUSUI.

Shusui is a doitsu (scaleless) version of Asagi, usually with large mirror scales along the lateral lines and/or to the right and left of the dorsal line. In many cases this variety also has a red belly and cheeks and is entered to shows in 'Asagi/Shusui' class-ification.

Shusui and Asagi are varieties where symmetry of pattern is desirable, the large doitsu scales on the Shusui should form an identical pattern down each side of the Koi, look for striking blue pigmentation and a clear, unblemished head. There are several styles of the above such as Narumi Asagi and Hanna Shusui which show much more red pigmentation, some of these can be very striking in appearance.

Asagi

Shusui

'KAWARIMONO' VARIETIES.

This is a collective name for non-metallic Koi which, with the exception of Goshiki, do not fall into any of the varieties described previously. They are, however, true varieties but compete against each other in a show under 'Kawarimono' classification.

BENIGOI OR AKA MUJI.
Benigoi is an all red Koi; look for examples free from small black blemishes.

KIGOI.
Kigoi is an all yellow Koi; some are albino with red eyes, try to find ones free from orange blemishes.

SHIRO MUJI.
An all white Koi seldom seen nowadays. Several years ago I purchased a very beautiful albino example with pure, milky white skin.

Benigoi or Aka Muji

Kigoi

Shiro Muji

MAGOI.

This is the original black Carp from which all Nishikigoi were bred, many Japanese enthusiasts usually keep one large Magoi in their collection to remind them of this fact. As this is not classified as a true Nishikigoi, many shows do not allow Magoi to be entered. However I have seen several 'Jumbo' specimens which are breathtaking, displaying large bronze scales and incredible volume, all these examples have been bred by the breeder specifically for selling as pets and not for food. Some of these specimens are very expensive indeed.

Magoi

CHAGOI.

In recent years there has been a world-wide resurgence of interest in this very old variety; it is an all brown Koi and one of the fastest growing varieties available. They are also popular as pets becoming very tame indeed. Colour pigmentation varies from cream brown right through to chocolate brown depending on the breeding stocks used. I have seen many Chagoi almost reaching the one metre mark, with fantastic volume and shape, these are very impressive to behold.

Chagoi

SORAGOI.

A blue-grey Koi and another quick growing variety.

Soragoi

Ochibashigure

OCHIBASHIGURE.
Ochibashigure was originated by cross breeding Soragoi and Chagoi to produce almost Kohaku-style patterns, a good example of this variety is very beautiful indeed.

Hajiro

HAJIRO.
This is a black Koi with white tips to the nose, tail, dorsal and pectorals.

Hageshiro

HAGESHIRO.
Similar to Hajiro but with a white crown on the head.

KUMONRYU.

This is a black doitsu Koi with random white patterns, some examples are extremely vivid in the contrast between the black and white colours. Unfortunately the patterns are seldom stable and changes occur seasonally.

Kumonryu

KARASU.

A black Koi with a red belly.

Karasu

Midorigoi

Aka Matsuba

MIDORIGOI.
These are usually doitsu (scale-less) Koi and were one of the first attempts by Japanese breeders to produce a green variety, some do take on a yellow green colour especially in small sizes.

AKA MATSUBA.
This is another early variety which resembles a red Asagi and can be very beautiful, the scales on the back and flanks are edged in black to form a pinecone effect. The depth of red pigmentation varies from orange-red shown here to very intense red depending on parent stocks used. There are many other varieties which could be included in Kawarimono but these would only confuse the issue as many are no longer produced and others are almost one-off examples generally produced by accident, such as Suminagashi, Matsukawabake, Yotsushiro, Raigo, En-yu, Huck-shu, Koshi-no- hisoku etc. In Kohaku, Sanke and Showa varieties some 'kanoko' patterns are still thrown out in very small numbers during a few spawnings, (kanoko pattern is a 'dappled effect' to the red pigmentation, similar to gotensakura mentioned earlier) These rarities are also classified under Kawarimono for show purposes.

METALLIC VARIETIES.

These varieties are responsible for bringing Nishikigoi to the attention of many new-comers to the hobby, the impressive sight of a shiny golden Koi has started many into taking up Koi keeping as a hobby. I will cover these metallic varieties in three sections to fall in with show classifications, namely 'Hikarimuji' classification which covers all metallic single colour varieties, 'Hikari Utsuri' classification which covers all metallic Showa varieties and 'Hikarimoyo' classification which deals with any other metallic varieties of more than one colour.

When selecting these varieties the aspect of lustre is very important; dull specimens are infinitely cheaper than those with good metallic lustre. In small sizes check the nose and mouth areas first, if the lustre is good in these areas there is every chance that the Koi will retain and improve this shine as it grows. Another important aspect of all these varieties is that of an unblemished head.

'HIKARIMUJI' OR 'HIKARIMONO' VARIETIES.

YAMABUKI OGON.
A metallic gold, single coloured Koi, try to avoid those with orange blotches on the skin.

Yamabuki Ogon

PURACHINA OGON.
A metallic platinum, single coloured Koi.

Purachina Ogon

Hi Ogon

HI OGON.
A metallic red, single coloured Koi, rare and not often seen but a good example is a sight to behold. Depth of red colour varies from light red, shown here, to intense red in some examples.

Orenji Ogon

ORENJI OGON.
A metallic orange, single coloured Koi.

Kin Matsuba

KIN MATSUBA.
A metallic gold Koi with pine cone effect to the scales.

GIN MATSUBA.
A metallic silver Koi with pine cone effect to the scales.

Gin Matsuba

ORENJI MATSUBA.
A metallic orange Koi with pine cone effect to the scales.

Orenji Matsuba

AKA MATSUBA OGON.
A metallic red Koi with pine cone effect to the scales, unfortunately rare today.

It is worth pointing out here that there are still some examples available of the original 'Cream Ogon' and 'Cream Matsuba' which are somewhere between Yamabuki and Purachina in colour.

Aka Matsuba Ogon

'HIKARI UTSURI'

(METALLIC SHOWA VARIETIES).

KIN SHOWA.
This is quite simply, a metallic Showa.

KIN HI UTSURI.
A metallic Hi Utsuri.

GINSHIRO. *(below right)*
A metallic Shiro Utsuri.

KIN KI UTSURI. *(below)*
A metallic Ki Utsuri.

The previous varieties are all entered in a show under 'Hikari Utsuri' classification.

Kin Showa

Kin Hi Utsuri

Kin Ki Utsuri

Ginshiro

'HIKARIMOYO' VARIETIES.

(Metallic varieties of more than one colour other than Hikari Utsuri varieties)

YAMATONISHIKI.
A metallic Sanke.

HARIWAKE.
A metallic white Koi with metallic yellow/gold pattern.

SAKURA OGON.
A metallic white Koi with metallic red pattern.

Yamatonishiki

Hariwake

Sakura Ogon

Kikusui

Kujaku

KIKUSUI.
A doitsu version of Sakura Ogon.

KUJAKU.
Possibly the most popular metallic variety in Japan; a metallic five coloured Koi made up of white, black, yellow, red and brown pigments. There are many other rarer varieties that are included in 'Hikarimoyo' classification such as Ginsui (metallic Shusui), Gin Shiro Bekko (metallic Shiro Bekko), Gin Hajiro (metallic Hajiro) and Shochikubai (metallic Koromo) to name a few. In recent years, after the death of the Japanese Emporer who ruled during the Showa Era, a new Emporer now rules in the new and current 'Heisei' Era. A new variety has been produced in Niigata which, hopefully, will be accepted as the three coloured variety to commemorate this Era as did 'Taisho' Sanke and 'Showa' Sanke in the past. This new variety is tentatively named as 'Heisei-Nishiki', it is a doitsu metallic variety which does resemble Doitsu Yamatonishiki, however the sumi pigmentation falls all over the body but does not resemble Doitsu Kin Showa. I have not yet seen, to date, any examples over 9" long and stability of the 'variety' is not yet known, however the examples I have seen are very beautiful indeed. In view of the fact that the 'variety' is not yet stabilised, I have opted not to include it in any Hikarimoyo classification as of now.

'DOITSU' VARIETIES.

As mentioned before these were developed from German scale-less Carp, most of the varieties described in this section have a doitsu equivalent and in very large shows the doitsu equivalent of Kohaku, Sanke and Showa only are entered in a separate classification of 'Doitsu'. All other doitsu varieties compete against the 'wagoi' (regular scaled) equivalents.

Some doitsu varieties are extremely attractive and are highly prized especially with non-Japanese enthusiasts, moreso than their Japanese counterparts. Without boring the reader, correct terminology for doitsu varieties is quite simply made by putting the word 'doitsu' before the wagoi equivalent. For example:– Doitsu Yamabuki, Doitsu Ginshiro, Doitsu Gin Matsuba, Doitsu Shiro Bekko, Doitsu Ochibashigure etc. etc.

Doitsu Kohaku

Doitsu Sanke

Doitsu Showa

'GIN-RIN'/'KIN-RIN' VARIETIES.

As with doitsu, most varieties mentioned in this section have a 'gin-rin' equivalent, this translates as 'pearl silver reflective scales'. Included in this same classification are rarer 'kin-rin' examples with 'pearl gold reflective scales'. In shows, the classification is stated as 'Gin/Kin-Rin' and usually only applies to Kohaku, Sanke and Showa varieties, other Gin/Kin-Rin varieties compete against their non Gin/Kin- Rin counterparts within their classification. If you are selecting Gin Rin varieties look for a good example of the original variety together with a dazzling Gin Rin effect to the good scale formation.

Again, correct terminology for Gin-Rin varieties is simply carried out by putting the word 'Gin-Rin' before the variety in question. For example:- Gin-Rin Kujaku, Gin-Rin Chagoi, Gin-Rin Asagi, Gin-Rin Benigoi, Gin-Rin Kin Showa etc. etc., the same applies to Kin-Rin varieties. Today there are many bloodlines of Nishikigoi which display 'Fukurin' skin where the white pigmentation especially shows a lustre which resembles a subtle reflective quality. These, however, are not Gin Rin Koi as such and are entered in normal classifications.

Gin Rin Kohaku

Gin Rin Sanke

Gin Rin Showa

CLASSIFICATION SUMMARY OF VARIETIES FOR SHOW PURPOSES.

To avoid confusion I think it prudent to incorporate a separate list of classifications that would apply, in general, to most major Japanese Nishikigoi Shows at the time of writing.

CLASSIFICATION	*VARIETIES WITHIN THIS CLASSIFICATION*
1. Kohaku	All Kohaku with the exception of Tancho pattern and Doitsu or Gin/Kin-Rin examples.
2. Sanke	All Sanke with the exception of Tancho pattern and Doitsu or Gin/Kin-Rin examples.
3. Showa	All Showa with the exception of Tancho pattern and Doitsu or Gin/Kin-Rin examples.
4. Bekko	Shiro Bekko, Aka Bekko, Ki Bekko plus Doitsu and Gin/Kin-Rin versions.
5. Tancho	Tancho Kohaku, Tancho Sanke, Tancho Showa plus Doitsu Tancho and Gin/Kin-Rin Tancho versions of these three varieties only. (Note:- most other varieties produce 'Tancho' patterns i.e:- Tancho Kujaku, Tancho Goshiki, Tancho Hariwake etc. etc.- some also in doitsu or gin-rin versions. These do not compete in Tancho class and are entered in normal classifications against regular pattern-styles.)
6. Utsurimono	Shiro Utsuri, Hi Utsuri, Ki Utsuri plus Doitsu and Gin/Kin-Rin versions.
7. Koromo	Aigoromo, Sumigoromo, Budogoromo plus Doitsu and Gin/Kin-Rin versions.
8. Kin/Gin Rin	Gin/Kin-Rin Kohaku, Gin/Kin-Rin Sanke, Gin/Kin-Rin Showa only.
9. Asagi/Shusui	Asagi, Gin/Kin- Rin Asagi, Shusui.
10. Hikarimuji	Yamabuki, Purachina, Orenji and Hi Ogon, Cream Ogon, Nezu Ogon, Kin Matsuba, Gin Matsuba, Orenji Matsuba, Aka Matsuba Ogon plus Doitsu and Gin/Kin-Rin versions.
11. Hikarimoyo	Hariwake, Hariwake Matsuba, Yamatonishiki, Kujaku, Gin Shiro Bekko, Sakura Ogon, Platinum Kohaku, Kikusui, Ginsui, Shochikubai plus Doitsu and Gin/Kin-Rin versions.
12. Hikariutsuri	Kin Showa, Kin Ki Utsuri, Ginshiro, Kin Hi Utsuri plus Doitsu and Gin/Kin-Rin versions.
13. Kawarimono	Benigoi, Kigoi, Soragoi, Chagoi, Ochibashigure, Goshiki, Kage Showa, Kage Hi Utsuri, Kage Shiro Utsuri, Koromo Sanke, Koromo Showa, Midorigoi, Aka Matsuba, Shiro Muji, Hajiro, Hageshiro, Karasu, Kumonryu, Matsukawabake, Kanoko Kohaku, Kanoko Sanke, Kanoko Showa, Goshiki-Sanke plus Doitsu and Gin/Kin-Rin versions.
14. Doitsu	Doitsu Kohaku, Doitsu Sanke, Doitsu Showa only.

NISHIKIGOI APPRECIATION

It is simple to explain varieties, patterns & classification of Koi, but very difficult indeed to try and discuss the 'appreciation' of Koi, mainly because we are all at different stages of the hobby. It is only the actual experience of seeing many examples of high class Koi in many varieties and studying points such as shape, volume, skin quality, texture of pigmentation and overall distribution of pigmentation to give a pleasing overall impression or, in some cases, a striking uniqueness, before we can reach a stage where our abilities in accurate appreciation can begin.

There is much more to the subject of 'appreciation' than a simple throw-away statement used often which is:- *'beauty is in the eye of the beholder'*, this may be very true when choosing a Koi for one's own collection but it certainly does not apply when judging an important show and the final decision must reflect the rightful Champion.

I have mentioned earlier there are some Koi that are very expensive, literally because they are 'one in a million'. There are also several more produced each year that have the potential to become better than anything produced in previous years, but this will take five to seven years or longer to determine if the potential has been realised.

The expert breeder who selects his own tategoi or purchases them elsewhere is sometimes right and sometimes wrong in his choice after the tategoi have been grown to maturity. The odd one may take 'Kokugyo' in a major show and others may take Supreme Champion in a local show. However it has to be remembered that only one Koi each year can take the Supreme Champion award in the most prestigious All Japan Show. To produce this Champion is the dream of over 1,000 professional Nishikigoi breeders and this is why some selected tosai (Koi born this year) can easily fetch well over £2,000.00 at 4" long. This is all for a Koi that will be grown, on and off, in a mud pond for another five to seven years! A common phrase for a person buying this kind of Koi is that 'he is buying a dream'. Another very apt saying in Japanese Nishikigoi circles is:- 'Man who buys small Koi is not wise and man who sells small Koi is also not wise'.

A point also to note on the subject of appreciation is that, in any pond of Koi, no matter how high or low the grade may be said to be, there is a 'best' and there is a 'worst', the rest fall somewhere in-between. Now the best and worst depend upon the eye of the beholder which brings us back to the earlier statement that we are all at different stages of the hobby!

The usual yardstick for Koi appreciation in Japan is by three main points, listed here in order of importance:-

1. *Pattern.*

2. *Shape/Volume.*

3. *Colour.*

I will try to explain these points individually.

1. PATTERN.

This is the most unique point as no two Koi ever have the exact same pattern. Pattern, however, really only relates to non-metallic varieties such as Kohaku, Sanke, Showa, Bekko and Utsurimono. Many non-metallic varieties have no real pattern, varieties such as Asagi, Shusui, Benigoi, Kigoi, Chagoi etc., this also applies to metallic varieties falling into Hikarimuji classification such as Yamabuki, Orenji, Purachina, Matsuba etc. Pattern in metallic varieties relates to Hikari Utsuri varieties such as Kin Showa, Kin-Ki Utsuri, Gin Shiro etc., plus Hikarimoyo classifications such as Hariwake, Kikusui, Kujaku, Yamatonishiki etc. In the main part all metallic varieties are, more often than not, judged on the depth of lustre and un-blemished head areas rather than pattern alone.

There is no doubt that pattern preference is a personal point of view. Many Kohaku, Sanke and Showa varieties have similar pattern styles but the ones taking Supreme Champion Awards rarely fall into classical 'step' patterns as seen in many early books. Instead they usually display a totally unique pattern which impresses the majority of the judges taking part and, if this is combined with superb shape and colour texture, the uniqueness of the pattern is further enhanced, we are never looking for symmetry in pattern styles.

I feel I should point out here and now that there are no barriers or rules governing the subject of pattern, early books on Koi stated that pattern on Kohaku should never fall on the eyes or nose areas and should never fall on any fins of the Koi. The same books stated that sumi pattern on Sanke should never fall on the head or face areas and that Showa varieties should all have black patterns on the head and face areas. This may have been true a long time ago but this is definitely not true today as a truly unique modern pattern rises above all these early barriers.

A unique pattern which appeals to judges, breeders and enthusiasts alike is something extremely difficult to produce. However, no matter how unique the pattern is, the Koi should be judged on its overall beauty taking into account the unique pattern together with the shape, the skin quality and the texture of the colour pigmentation discussed next. However, if the unique pattern is not complemented with these other very important qualities then the unique pattern alone seldom produces a champion Koi. A Supreme Champion *must* combine Pattern, Skin Quality, Volume and Pigmentation if it is to become the best in the world. Still without wishing to labour the point, if there are, say 20 Koi all with superb skin quality, volume and pigmentation entered against each other, then the final decision for Supreme Champions will, most certainly, go to the one displaying the most unique pattern

As 'unique' pattern is so difficult to produce by the breeder and also very important when judging adult Koi, this is the reason why one only sees patterned varieties taking Supreme Champion Awards at major shows. This also explains why these examples cost many times more than equally superb examples of non-patterned varieties.

2. SHAPE/VOLUME.

As shape is a very important point it is, for this reason, that Mature and Adult sizes in the All Japan Show are entered in two separate sections, one for Males and the other for Females. The Supreme Champion is almost always a 'Jumbo' Female although there have been a few isolated exceptions to this in recent years. Generally speaking, female Koi take on a more imposing shape than males of the same size and are generally far more expensive to purchase than males of the same quality.

This is not saying that 'biggest is best' but there is something special in the way that a jumbo Koi presents itself. These Koi give an overall impression of calmness and power that is only apparent when the Koi has been grown to its peak and still retains a superb pattern, skin quality and pigmentation.

(It is true that edges to patterns may be far crisper in smaller Koi between 18″ to 24″ and this is where the aspect of volume comes in and allowances have to be made.)

One point is very true about shape/volume and that is that any deformities are severely penalised when judging, this is one aspect of Koi where symmetry is vital. The skeleton of the head and mouth areas are closely scrutinised as well as the fins and the way in which the Koi swims; any deformities found will result in the Koi being down-pointed in a show.

3. COLOUR.

This is also a difficult point to communicate, early Koi books once stated that the red has to be the brightest possible, the sumi pattern to be as black as jet and the white ground as white as driven snow. Again this once may have been true many years ago but much more has been learned since then as to how pigmentation develops in certain bloodlines. Today there is a more flexible approach taken with the emphasis on quality of pigmentation as opposed to the requirements as defined in the early Koi books.

Today there is no doubt whatsoever that true high grade red pigmentation is derived from 'orange-red' and not 'purple-red' which may look very striking in small sized Koi, but will almost certainly produce 'windows' of white pigment, or fade away totally in later years.

High grade white skin is a delicate creamy white in texture which seems to have a 'depth' to it. This is to say it gives the impression that, if one gently scratched it away with ones fingernail it would still retain its original quality.

As far as sumi (black) pigmentation is concerned, this depends on age of the Koi and the bloodline in question. In adult sizes sumi pattern should be as black as is possible but smaller sizes of good potential display 'brown-black' in Showa varieties and 'grey-blue-black' in Sanke varieties.

The colour, or lustre in the case of metallic varieties also play an important role in selection of champion Koi in varieties other than Kohaku, Sanke, Showa etc.

To try and explain the appreciation aspect further perhaps the following fictional situation may produce some similarities:- If, on entering an art shop, you saw a painting that really impressed you and the assistant informed you that it was by a local artist and only cost £30.00. You decided to buy it and, on leaving the shop with your bargain, you saw another painting which, to your tastes, was terrible. The assistant, seeing your dislike, informed you that it was a very famous painting by an equally famous artist and cost £1,000.00! You still do not like the painting and yet the price still remains the same!

This may, in some way explain the price of Koi and how our tastes may change as we become more involved and more experienced in the overall hobby. As I have been told on many occasions, it would not do if we all liked the same thing. For my part my tastes in Koi have changed dramatically over the years, hopefully for the better, but I find them no less fascinating as a result.

Unfortunately, the subject of Koi appreciation has produced many self professed 'experts' full of their own self importance. On many occasions I have overheard comments from such people directed at a particular

Koi such as:- "Pity there is not enough sumi" or "Pity it is not balanced"(whatever that may mean) or "If it had more pattern near the tail it would be a good Koi"etc. etc. It would be amusing indeed to ask this expert to draw a 'perfect' Koi, I think the result would be interesting to say the least.

In truth we should look at any Koi as a whole. There will never be a 'perfect' Koi in the truest sense of the word, but there will be thousands of superb Koi, admittedly each with a little imperfection here and there, but nonetheless, superb.

On another tack, there are many so-called 'music lovers' who play a record or CD in order to listen out for recording faults and imperfections in the musicianship, rather than to enjoy the overall effect of the music itself.

Every Koi should be looked upon as an individual work of art, irrespective of how it has been classified as far as grade is concerned. Rest assured that the Koi within your pond are all unique and if you love them, then that is the most important factor.

Incidentally, during one visit to Japan to purchase stocks I came upon a most beautiful Koi around 15" long. In truth it was a Showa - but only just! To look at the Koi it was a magnificent Shiro Utsuri with gleaming white skin and a superb black pattern, however the lips only were bright red. (kuchi-beni) For show classification purposes it was Showa but really of no use in view of the tiny red pigmentation, and it could not be entered in Utsurimono class- thought she was magnificent, someone else also thought the same and purchased her from under my nose for £700.00. So much for standards and related prices!

Finally, on the subject of Koi appreciation, it is impossible to assess a single Koi without having others to compare it with or against. In other words, for showing purposes, a Koi is as 'good' or as 'bad' in comparison to other entries within the same classification and size grouping.

IMPORTING NISHIKIGOI

It is only in recent years that there have been non-stop direct flights from Narita Airport, Tokyo to London, Heathrow and Gatwick Airports. Prior to this, due to flying restrictions over Russian air space, the route was via Anchorage, Alaska, on the polar route where re-fuelling had to take place. This journey took around 19 hours, the non-stop flight has now cut this down to around 12 hours. This reduces the time in which our Koi are packed within a carton by some 7 hours which is a very great advantage, but it does not mean the operation is safe — far from it!

To begin with, one cannot simply arrive in Japan with the purpose of buying Nishikigoi unless a shipping agent has been arranged in advance. There are still only a handful of reliable shippers in Japan who are very experienced in packing Koi for export on long-haul flights. These shippers are usually located near Narita Airport and, obviously, make a commission charge for their services.

Many of my Koi are purchased in remote areas of Japan and have to be packed in cartons and forwarded to my shipping agent by road transport. The breeder knows exactly how to pack these stocks at his premises at around 5.00pm. to ensure safe arrival at 8.00am. the next morning at the shippers' premises. This packing method uses a large amount of water in the carton as internal road freight charges are only calculated on volume and not weight. This is not so in the case of air freight where weight determines freight costs.

The shipper is advised by the breeders as to how many cartons of Koi will arrive and at what time the following day. He must then prepare water to receive them and keep them for several days without feeding in order to ensure that the Koi do not pollute

their own water during shipment. A conscientious shipper will also check the stocks for any parasitic problems on arrival at his premises and take remedial action if required.

Once there are sufficient stocks to warrant a shipment then air freight space can be arranged with the chosen air line. A minimum of 100 kilos is needed to obtain the best freight rate for live fish between Japan to the UK at 1520 yen per kilo (£9.80 at time of writing). The internal packing methods for transportation within Japan cannot be used for export methods unless astronomical freight costs are to be met. For example, a breeder would pack one 20" Koi in one carton for internal transportation, the carton would weigh around 30 kilos and only cost 2,500 yen (£16.00) for delivery. If this method was adopted for export, the cost of airfreight would be £294.00 for the same Koi. This would also be disastrous for the Koi as excessive water in the bag would not allow enough oxygen to inflate the bag and losses would most definitely arise as a result. Instead far less water and much more oxygen is used for export packing purposes.

In cool water temperatures a higher packing rate can be made per carton as dissolved oxygen content is higher, in warm water temperatures packing rates have to be reduced accordingly.

I have been asked on countless occasions as to the freight cost of a carton of Koi from Japan to the UK and my answer is always the same, — How much does the carton weigh?" At the time of writing a jumbo female, say 28" or so, could be packed and the overall carton would weigh around 60 kilos actual; this would come to £588.00. If a carton was packed with 50 small Koi it would probably weigh 11 kilos actual which would then be £107.80, there is no fixed price for a carton of Koi as such.

Once air freight space has been arranged, the expert shipper prepares water for shipping the day prior to making the shipment. The water contains cooking salt at 0.5% and Elbagin or Parazan D at the required rate; this water is also heavily aerated for 12 hours or so. Cartons are also prepared the day prior to the shipment and layed out in preparation, each carton has a triple strength vinyl bag inside with the neck folded open to receive water when packing actually commences.

Typical preparations for export packing in Japan.

Packing commences around 6 hours prior to departure of the flight and usually between 20 to 40 cartons make up a standard shipment. Once packing is complete, a freight forwarding company collects the shipment and delivers it to the Japanese

Customs to pay the customs entry charge of £129.00 before delivering it to the air line.

From commencement of packing to arrival at London on a good day it is around 18 hours when the Koi are inside the cartons. Customs clearance in the UK can take between 90 minutes and up to 6 hours on rare occasions.

Contrary to popular opinion, there is no in-flight insurance available for live fish from Japan to the UK, and, as such there is always a high risk involved in any shipment such as this. Every Koi dealer in the UK is very concerned when his shipments are in the air, if a situation arose whereby Heathrow was closed due to fog and the flight had to be diverted to Paris, for example, the whole shipment would be lost!

As soon as the flight touches down, our clearing agents try to get urgent clearance through UK Customs and pay the VAT content which is levied for both air freight charges and invoice value of the Koi before final release can be obtained.

Airline cargo staff carefully loading a Koi shipment into standard Airline container.

Taking delivery of a consignment of Koi at Heathrow.

Immediately the shipment is released to us, the cartons are opened and the Koi carefully transferred into prepared transportation containers. These units hold half a ton (110 gallons) of water and have zip tops to retain the water and the Koi during travel. Pure oxygen is supplied by gentle diffusion from air diffusers during travel from the airport to our premises.

The water in these containers is prepared in advance to the packing temperature of the water as advised by the shipper. The water contains cooking salt at 0.5% and Elbagin, if any delays occur in road travel through congestion or accidents then the Koi are safe from harm. For anyone thinking that importing Nishikigoi is a simple operation, I assure you it is not and experienced people are required at both ends in order to try and reduce the risks.

Koi transferred into transportation containers.

BUYING NISHIKIGOI.

If you are planning to purchase stocks, the best advice I can give is to visit as many outlets as possible before making your purchases. In the UK Koi can be found for sale in pet shops and countless garden and water garden centres; these outlets cater, mainly for the general garden pond keepers who outnumber the serious Koi keepers many, many times over. These outlets generally serve their customer demands by stocking Koi which can be sold cheaply; usually their stocks come from Israel, Singapore, Thailand and the UK. Small Koi from 2" to 6" form the majority of sales in these outlets although larger sizes are often displayed. Many avid Koi keepers in the UK purchased their first Koi from this type of outlet and gained valuable experience in keeping methods with these stocks purchased at very reasonable prices. Whilst there is little comparison between these and the most general grade Japanese Koi produced today as far as shape, quality, true variety and pigment-ation is concerned, the Japanese breeders cannot hope to compete on prices due to the current exchange rates between the Yen and Sterling.

Also in the UK, there are several specialist outlets, many mentioned in the 'Beginnings' section of this book who cater for Koi enthusiasts who collect Japanese Koi; some of these outlets carry stocks of Japanese Koi as well as those from other countries, others stock only Japanese Koi.

When visiting any outlet with a view to purchasing Koi, make a mental note of the conditions given to the Koi as well as to the Koi themselves, look at the well being of the stocks and the prices asked, never make the mistake of mentally pricing Koi by size.

If you are a newcomer to the hobby it would be a good idea to ask a more experienced Koi keeper to accompany you in your viewing trip who can advise if dealers visited have a good reputation for their overall business dealings and can give genuine advice and an after-sales service if required.

Do not expect any dealer to have good quality Japanese stocks at all times, usually the best time for high class selections is between November to February and April to June when supplies of these can be found in Japan.

If you are new to the hobby, try to purchase stocks that are two years old or over and are a minimum of 10" long, these are relatively strong and far easier to keep for a novice than those between 4" to 6" long. Small Koi are fine for the experienced keeper but, like babies of other forms of life such as kittens, puppies and humans, they are weaker and require more attention than do more adult versions.

With regard to actual prices of Nishikigoi imported from Japan, it is almost impossible to define an accurate price for a particular Koi. Some Koi that appear, by price quoted, to be particularly cheap can, in truth, be expensive, whilst others can represent ex-cellent value for money.

For example, if one finds a 12" Kohaku at one outlet which is priced at £100.00 and another 12" kohaku at another outlet which is felt to be twice as good as the first, do not expect the second one to be £200.00. Once a certain quality is reached then a 25% estimated improvement in pattern can make the price five times or more. These prices are governed by the Japanese breeder which reflects the total price landed to the importer after all costs have been met.

It has always been my wish that more enthusiasts could visit Japan to see the prices with regard to the quality in Japan, then add to this the incidental costs and the risk factor before putting a final price to the Koi on arrival to the UK. Most reputable dealers will be only too happy to explain why one Koi costs this whilst the other costs that, it may be bloodline, it may be pattern and so on which always reflects the actual buying price of the dealer who, like any other business has overheads and costs and has to be profitable if he is to stay in business.

There are very few individuals in the UK who can come anywhere near to valuing a Japanese Koi with any accuracy. Reflecting back to my first visit to Japan in 1977, **every** Koi was far better than **anything** I had seen before in the UK, basically because I had never seen examples of these other than in pictures. In truth, I thought I knew a thing or two about Koi, when, in reality, I knew next to nothing at all.

For the first-time Koi visitor to Japan today, this still applies and I maintain the opinion that, for even the most avid enthusiast determined to learn this subject of price structures, six to seven intensive visits are necessary to even begin to understand.

To gain experience in understanding price structures and qualities/potentials of certain bloodlines one must first purchase examples of these and personally monitor development of each example in all stages of growth.

It is totally impossible to evaluate a Koi by looking at its photograph, it is totally impossible to evaluate a Koi by a short cursory glance. Instead one should have the Koi in question placed into an inspection bowl and study it from a distance of between 6″ to 18″, depending on the size of the Koi. If natural light conditions are not present in the outlet in question, ask the assistant to show you the Koi, outdoors in natural daylight and be aware that all Koi look far better in the fading light of the late afternoon.

After many more visits to Japan, I slowly became very aware that there were far fewer Koi which caught my eye and this became more apparent with every visit, at first I believed that the standards of production were falling. In truth standards of production were getting better every year but my demands were getting higher at a far quicker rate, consequently I became far more selective with each visit. In short, my 'eye' was improving with each visit as a result of purchasing thousands of Koi over the years, watching them develop, asking breeder upon breeder vital questions and generally studying hundreds of thousands of Koi over the years.

Today, I personally try to purchase from the breeders whose stocks I have experience with, aspects such as strength, pattern potential, pigmentation potential and growth potential rate highly on my requirements, even if the latter three are not apparent at time of purchase.

"every Koi was far better than anything I had seen before in the UK"

As far as *genuine* Tategoi are concerned, the unfortunate fact is that very few UK specialist Koi dealers will risk purchasing these for re-sale as the average customer would find them insipid, undesirable, incredibly expensive and well beyond their budget. Many would openly class them as 'junk' and that the dealer was profiteering on a royal scale. The average customer cannot be blamed for this as they have no experience of witnessing these rare Koi develop. On the other hand however, these are the Koi that the Japanese collectors would sell their souls for!

As far as actual price of regular grade Japanese Koi are concerned in the UK today, contrary to popular opinion, they are, in fact far cheaper than they were in 1977. In those days the only Koi for sale were Japanese Koi, the pound bought around 1,000 Japanese Yen and English visitors to Japan to buy Koi were rare and deemed to be, by the Japanese, very wealthy indeed. To put all this into perspective, in 1977, in the UK, if you wished to purchase a 14" Koi, you had to ensure you had £100.00 in your pocket. In those days, the average family car cost around £3,000.00, by extending this to the 14" Koi, in reality it cost around £300.00! On top of this the Koi in question could not compare in quality with the worst Japanese Koi imported today.

Furthermore, in Japan in 1977, a cup of coffee cost 300 Yen, in 1995 it still costs 300 Yen, I personally reckon that my purchase price of Koi, quality for quality, has reduced by some 20% over the years.

The problem is, however, today the pound only buys 155 Yen instead of 1,000 Yen, as an example, a Koi costing me 100,000 Yen in 1977 would have meant £100.00; taking UK inflation into account, this would represent £300.00 today. In 1995, taking into account a 20% price reduction it would cost me 80,000 Yen which means £531.00! The Yen also governs all other costs except air fare, (which has reduced significantly in recent years) costs such as internal travel, hotels, food and agent's commission.

Consider the above situation to a Japanese enthusiast and take into account that there has been insignificant inflation in Japan for some 17 years. The Japanese buyer can still buy this Koi for 80,000 Yen; for a Japanese breeder to sell it to a UK dealer for anything less would be financial suicide.

A good dealer will never 'pressure' you into buying a Koi, instead he/she will allow you to leisurely walk round the stocks on display without breathing down your neck. If you need advice and recommendations he/she will give their honest opinions; remember a good Koi dealer always relies on return business and a good reputation.

Buying any Koi should be a pleasurable experience and the decision taken slowly and carefully. The main criteria is that the Koi you purchase are the ones that please you the most and are the ones you want to see every day swimming around your pond.

This book describes why some Koi do become champions, it explains what to look for in a particular variety and why some Koi are very expensive, but no book can dare to try and influence personal taste, this is between the keeper and the Koi!

> *"Remember, a good Koi dealer always relies on return business and a good reputation."*

As far as what to do with your Koi when you get them back home, is a point that can raise more confusion. I personally advise my customers to equalise water temperatures between that in the bag and the temperature in the main pond and release them directly into the pond taking care to cover aeration areas where they may try to jump for several days whilst adjusting to new water conditions. However there are many who advocate that, under no circumstances, should new Koi be mixed with existing stocks until 'quarantine' has been carried out – some advocate for up to 6 months! This usually takes place in indoor containers where water quality is not as good as conditions in the main pond, this, together with cramped conditions and lack of natural light is not nearly as conducive to settling-in a new addition to ones' stocks. I do understand the concern of those who have had bad experiences in this area before but if the Koi are purchased from a reputable outlet and the owner understands the information given in the 'Caring' section of this book then the Koi can be placed into the main pond immediately where they can benefit from the water volume and conditions.

For those still wishing to segregate new stocks prior to adding them to your main pond, do ensure that the separate conditions are adequate for the Koi.

Finally, on the subject of buying Koi, many enthusiasts christen their Koi with pet names, ones that stand out in my mind are:-

A Chagoi known as 'Hofmeister', the brown colour was identical to the lager!

A Kohaku called 'Ray Charles' as it was 'Born to Lose' at every show!

A Gin-Rin Sanke called 'Gary Glitter'.

A Sanke called 'Bubbles'.

A Showa called 'Toni', when I asked why, the wife of the owner told me it was - t'oni one he would ever pay that price for again - if she had anything to do with it!

A particularly gorgeous Sanke called 'Emanuelle'.

A jumbo Doitsu Hariwake named 'Gertie'.

A Showa named 'Bert'.

A Showa named 'Killer'.

A Magoi named 'Chalky'.

A Chagoi of mine called 'The Jumbo Dumpling'

plus a host of 'Flippers', 'Freds' and 'Jaws'.

It is quite amazing that so many Koi enthusiasts look upon their Koi as members of the family, sometimes very important members judging by the amount of care and attention given to them.

On many occasions we are requested to visit and feed a collection when the owner is away on holiday. On one occasion the owner sent her Koi three postcards from where she was staying for a few days!

I can understand the relationship between some keepers and their Koi, there is something very peaceful and relaxing in sitting next to a pond containing a collection of Koi which are special to the owner. It is still a unique experience that hasn't faded at all since I saw my very first Koi.

Since I started selecting Koi in Japan and importing them to the UK for re-sale, I can remember most of the 'special' ones. Details as to the breeders, the sizes when purchased, the customers who purchased them and awards received will always stay with me. Some photographs have been lost over the years, which is not a bad thing, as all could not be included in this book. However, I feel some should be included in this section of the book and given some recognition, for my own part, these Koi will always provide me with many fond memories. Also these are all 'real' Koi that have left Japan as opposed to simply showing the magnificent photographic examples of the finest Koi in the world shown elsewhere in this book, which are financially out of reach of most collectors and will almost always remain in Japan.

This Koi is very famous with many in the UK – it was purchased by Joe Wilmington, on a trip I organised in the early 1980's. The Koi was purchased from Isumiya in Iwamagi, Niigata and was around 21" long at the time. Although the picture does not show the true variety well, she is, in fact, a Kin Hi Utsuri (metallic Hi Utsuri) - in all my visits to Japan, I have only seen less than a handful of this rare variety. She was kept in Joe's pond for several years and eventually won the Supreme Champion Award at BKKS 'Koi '89'. She now resides in a pond in Ratingen, Germany. At the start of 1995, I saw her again and she is better than ever! her skin lustre and condition is breathtaking and she now measures 31".

This Koi surprised me when Nigel Caddock showed me her picture and explained that she was one of 'my' Koi. The picture was taken at a large BKKS Section Show in the South of England where she took Supreme Champion Award in 1992.

During 1987, I took a large party of UK enthusiasts to Japan during November when this Sanke was purchased by one of the party namely Mike Wint who sadly died soon afterwards. It was bought from Mr. Hiroi Seiji near Ojiya, Niigata at 13" long and the sumi pattern very small and faint.

Mike's parents have kept her lovingly and in superb condition since then. The striking sumi pigmentation and pattern arrangement is superb as is the unique head pattern and texture of red pigmentation. The beautiful white ground is dazzling, she now measures some 24" long, a perfect example of an excellent tategoi. Although I am not exactly sure of the bloodline of this Koi, she has all the trademarks of Kichinai Sanke.

I purchased this female Sandan Kohaku from Dainichi in Iwamagi, Niigata during the Spring of 1987 at 12" long when she was just two years old. She was sold to my good friend John Shelton who took 'Best Tategoi' award with her in a BKKS National Show. She was 19" long when this photograph was taken; a classic example of Dainichi Kohaku.

This female Kindai Showa was purchased by Joe Wilmington who was also with my party visiting Japan in November 1987. She was 13" long and purchased from the brother of Isumiya in Iwamagi, Niigata. This Koi has been a favourite of many serious collectors in the UK and has had

a particularly amusing and chequered show career. In 1990 she was awarded 'Best Tategoi' award at BKKS 'Koi 90' when she was 19" long. In the next BKKS National Show, she was disqualified by the judges as being deformed. The next year at BKKS 'Koi 92' she was 23" long and was awarded 'Supreme Champion' prize!

was awarded 'Supreme Champion in Show'. The Koi was sold some six months later to John Pitham of Koi Water Barn and there is now no question at all that she is 100% true Showa!

I purchased this female Showa from Mr. Sakai in Hiroshima during Spring 1989 at 22" long when she was only three years old. One reason I bought this expensive Koi was that the sumi pigmentation, which was in very early stages of development, had a real potential to become very striking in later years. I entered this Koi into a large Dealer's Show held at Stafford during March 1990, but just prior to the judging her entry classification was questioned by two officials. They pointed out to me that the Koi was 'Kage Showa' and, as such, must be entered into Kawarimono classification as opposed to 'Showa' classification; one even pointed out to me that one could see, quite clearly, the 'Asagi lineage'." I pointed out that ALL Koi varieties have Asagi lineage and insisted that the Koi was true Showa and, as such, must be entered in 'Showa' classification. The officials shrugged and said that as far as 'Showa' classification was concerned, she was useless, but as far as 'Kawarimono' classification was concerned, she was superb! I insisted she be entered in 'Showa' classification and, as a result she received 'Third Best Showa in size' award during the initial Judging stage. During the later stages of judging, when all judges participated, she

This rare female Hageshiro with a 'keyhole' head pattern was bred by Mr. Shoichi Hosokai in Wakatochi, Niigata in 1986 at 18" long and three years old. Ian Stewardson purchased this Koi from me on arrival to the UK; I have never seen another example of this 'uniqueness' of pattern since.

There is nothing really special about this 32" female Chagoi, but I had to include her in the book. This is my own 'Jumbo Dumpling'.

I purchased her in November 1993 at six years old and she was bred by Hirasawa in Niigata. She has a very gentle nature, she feeds with no heed to her figure, hence her voluptuous proportions, and yet she fascinates many visitors to our shop. One very young lady called Amy, who lives nearby insists that her parents bring her regularly so she can feed her by hand and stroke her head. If her parents are too busy to bring her, tantrums follow! In 1994, I took her to Koi Shows in the UK and Germany, she is a very well-travelled lady.

This excellent Tategoi was purchased from Mr. Gamo in Isawa, Yamanashi Prefecture during November 1994, she was two years old and a female Sadazo Sanke. She is owned by Christoph Wolters in Dusseldorf, Germany and I wish I could find many other Koi of such quality and potential. This Koi is the type that most Japanese collectors try to find, the Koi is, by no means, 'finished' but I would love to see this develop over the years, a rare and beautiful Koi.

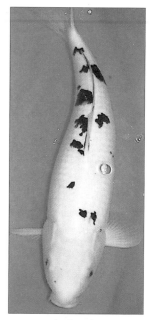

This female Shiro Bekko was purchased in 1986 directly from a mud pond harvest that was taking place in the Niigata mountainsides. We stopped our truck to take photographs and saw the Koi being lifted into a bowl. I purchased the Koi, there and then, from the breeder and took it away for shipping to Tokyo for resting prior to travel to the UK. I did not take the name of the breeder and have never found the mud pond again; however she is still the best Shiro Bekko I have found to date. The white skin almost dazzles, she is owned by John Shelton.

This female Kohaku is covered in greater detail in the 'People' section of the book as it was purchased in 1987 from Mr. Toshio Sakai in Isawa. This Koi took 'Supreme Champion' award at the All-England Nishikigoi Dealer's Show in 1989 when she was around 26" long, the unusual face pattern is very attractive.

A five year old female Sanke that is 25" long and has a skin like a two year old Sanke, the sumi pattern has yet to fully appear and stabilise. This Koi was bred, from Sadazo parent stocks, by Mr. Shoji Tanaka of the Marusyo Company in Yomogihira, Niigata and I purchased her in November 1994. She is owned by Mr. & Mrs. H. P. Mertens of Kaarst in Germany, another Koi I would like to see in two years from now.

Ian Stewardson has owned this female Gin Rin Shiro Uts-uri since 1988, I purchased her during 1987 from Mr. Sakai in Hiroshima at four years old and 23" long. The pattern has always impressed me with this Koi, the volume speaks for itself as the shape is as near perfect as is possible.

circles is an understatement. Many customers still carry the opinion that she is the finest Koi ever to come into the UK and, whilst I do not share their opinion, I can understand why they feel this way. Her overall pattern was complemented by her unique pattern over the left eye, this, together with her white face and the red 'beauty spot' on the right side of her head all contributed to the whole impression. After one year in my ponds, she was purchased by Joe Wilmington, in 1990 she was entered into BKKS 'Koi '90' where she took 'Supreme Champion' award. Today, she is owned by Reiner Behrens in Germany and is now 28" long.

I first saw this Koi at the famous Ojiya No-Gyo-Sai Show in late October 1987, just about everyone who saw the Koi with me raved endlessly about her pattern and intense colours. She was awarded the prize of 'best Showa in size'

and I just had to find out more about her. Her entry card with Polaroid photograph gave the owner and breeder as Mr. Hashino of Tsunan in Niigata and I noted this down. Several days later I made the 90 minute journey to his home expecting to see many other Koi of similar quality, alas there was only one good Koi there - the Showa! He explained that she was three years old and 18" long, she was his best Tategoi to date and her parents were a very old female Showa he had owned for many years and a four year old Matsunosuke Sanke. After three more visits, I finally purchased her and brought her back to the UK. To say she caused a commotion in UK Koi keeping

I included this Showa bred by Mr. Sakai in Isawa for interest value, her parentage comes from female Showa, male Showa and a small amount of male Magoi milt. The reason for using Magoi milt is to try and grow Nishikigoi to the size of Magoi and

still retain the volume of a perfect Nishi-kigoi. As mentioned earlier, no Kohaku, Sanke or Showa has yet reached the magic one metre mark at the time of writing; this is basically because the Nishikigoi of today are far removed from their Magoi origins where one metre sizes are common.

Around 1972, Mr. Sakai decided to introduce 'Magoi blood' once more to some fry in order to try and increase finished sizes. As a result, the fry produced showed more than 80% Magoi and were destroyed, the remaining patterned stocks, however, whilst being of no use for sale, did prove useful for some future male parents.

This female Showa was born in May 1993 and I purchased her in November 1994 at 16" long, the length of her head in relationship to the remainder of her body is greater than the normal ratio, in fact she is nearer Magoi body form than standard Nishikigoi form. This should become more apparent as the Koi grows and we intend to keep her in warm water with good feeding methods to try and make a photographic record of developments over the years.

This female Gin Rin Kohaku is a stunner! She is four years old and was bred in Niigata by Mr. Shoichi Hosokai in Wakatochi, Niigata. She is 21" long and owned by Andy Shepherd. The pigmentation and texture of the Hi is superb as is the Gin Rin effect and the pure white ground. Combine all this with a unique pattern and you have a 'knockout' Koi.

This Koi is not so immediately desirable at first glance however, as far as skin quality and pattern potential is concerned — this is one of the best 20 genuine tategoi I have ever found (see 'Understanding', page 40). Another female Sadazo Sanke bred

by Mr. Gamoh in Isawa, Yamanashi Prefecture, she was purchased in November 1994, two years old and 15" long, the pigmentation now is delicate but dull, whereas the white ground is incredible yet no photograph can do it justice. Colour feeding will produce the pigmentation and texture that is inbred in the bloodline and I make no apology for the pattern. If the pattern remains exactly as it is now and in the same ratio, when the Koi matures to 25" long, I will be more than happy. I would ask the reader to imagine the Koi before you at 25" long, half close your eyes, take it slightly out of focus and imagine what a sight would be before you!

This female Maruten Kuchibeni Kohaku was purchased in 1987 from the annual Spring Tategoi competition held in Ojiya, Niigata. The Koi was two and a half years old and 18" long when purchased, she is of Tomoin bloodline, bred by Mr. Yorijo Hiroi in Takezawa, Niigata. In 1989 she was awarded 'Best Tategoi' at the All-England Nishikigoi Dealer's Show at Stafford and is a particular favourite of mine. Joe Wilmington purchased her from me in 1989.

This beautiful Sanke owned by Ed Clark from Kent, I purchased from Mr. Sakai in Hiroshima during 1986; this photograph was taken during 1988 when she was 28" long. This was another special Koi which captured the hearts of many UK enthusiasts.

The only male Koi shown in this collection — a five year old Gin Rin Showa I purchased in Mushigame, Niigata from Maruju during Spring 1994. Today he is 26" long, he still retains youthful appearance and excellent Gin Rin lustre and the unique head pattern is very striking indeed.

This very striking female Hi Showa is four years old and bred by Mr. Igarashi in Mushigame, Niigata, I purchased her in November 1994 when she was 22" long. My intention is to grow her in an outdoor heated pond for some months before entering her into Koi shows.

NISHIKIGOI SHOWS

The first Nishikigoi Show to be staged outside of Japan, as far as I am aware, was held in my back garden during late Spring 1975. The 'show ponds' were made of blue builders' polythene supported with plastic coated steel mesh formed into a circle. At the time we thought it a giant leap into the future of the hobby, albeit on a very modest scale. Around 100 people attended from most parts of the UK and about 30 collectors showed their Koi.

In later years the standard of UK Nishikigoi Shows improved at quite an alarming rate as more and more interest was shown in the hobby.

A little nostalgia here, I turned this Certificate and Polaroid up just before the final check of the book and decided to include it at the last minute.

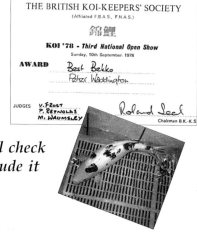

Today there are many Nishikigoi Shows held each year in the UK ranging from local section 'closed' shows which can only be entered by the members through to local section 'open' shows where anyone can exhibit, and then to the major shows, the most prestigious being the British Koi-Keepers' Society 'National' Open Show, usually held during August.

To the avid Koi enthusiast the atmosphere of a good Koi show is something to be experienced, whether one is entering Koi or simply just visiting to take it all in. These are events where enthusiasts can gather to meet old friends from many parts of the country to discuss endless topics ranging from new filtration ideas, new foods, new stocks purchased right through to the decisions

Judging at an early BKKS National Show with Judges (left to right) Pete Reynolds, Val Frost and Malcolm Waumsley, founder members of the BKKS Judging and Standards Committee.

*Judging scene at the first UK Dealers Show, 'Nishikigoi '85',
(left to right) Mr. Masutani from Mihara, Hiroshima,
Chris Ball, Pauline Smith, Janet West,
Greg Jackson and Ron Sharp.*

made by the judges on the Koi entered. In UK major shows there are many dealers attending to take stand space and display Koi and other 'Koi items' for sale over the two day event.

During my early years in the hobby I took part in the organisation and running of many shows for the Society and am fully aware of what it all entails in order to be a success. The BKKS National Show gets better every year directly due to the amount of advance preparation and sheer hard work given free of charge by the elected Show Committee and others. The actual show itself needs teams of experienced enthusiasts to 'bench' or enter the Koi into the show. This necessitates that each one is photographed and accurately sized before placing them in the appropriate display pond in readiness for judging. At all times during the show, teams of officials are on duty to check water readings and aeration requirements as well as making sure any debris is removed from display ponds at regular intervals. These teams also ensure that the Koi are packed in oxygen and returned to their rightful owners after the show has ended.

The judges travel from many parts of the country to give their services, again free from charge. A large show can take almost a year to organise which involves a tremendous work plan to get every aspect right and involves many individuals overall. I believe the hobby needs good shows in order to introduce newcomers to the hobby; the BKKS has played a great part in doing this and should be congratulated. At the 1994 BKKS 'Koi '94' Show there were visitors from all parts of the UK as well as those from the USA, Germany, Holland, Belgium, South Africa and Ireland, all brought together by Koi.

RULES AND PROCEDURES FOR NISHIKIGOI SHOWS IN THE UK.

In the UK, most major shows classify varieties in a similar style as mentioned earlier in the section on varieties and their show classifications as in a Japanese show. As the UK shows do not have a 'Doitsu' classification – there are only 13 classifications. As far as size groupings are concerned the UK generally has six which are as follows:-

Size One, up to 8".

Size Two, over 8" and up to 12"

Size Three, over 12" and up to 16"

Size Four, over 16" and up to 20"

Size Five, over 20" and up to 24"

Size Six, over 24"

The first stage of judging is that each of the 13 varieties are awarded first and second awards within their own size grouping which could give a maximum number of 26 Koi in each size grouping.

The second stage is when these winners (maximum 156) are judged as to first, second and third, irrespective of variety, within their own size grouping, this narrows it down to three Koi per size grouping.

The next stage is when the best three Koi from Size One are compared with the best three Koi from Size Two and 'Best Baby Koi in Show' award is decided.

Next the best three Koi from Sizes Three and Four are judged to find 'Best Adult Koi in Show'.

Then Sizes Five and Six judged together to find 'Best Mature Koi in Show'.

The above three awards also have a second and a third award.

From these three Champions in Baby, Adult and Mature sizes, the 'Supreme Champion' Award is made.

Show rules in the UK BKKS shows are that entrants reserve, in advance, a pond or ponds for their own Koi. Koi from different collections are not allowed to be mixed for fear of any cross infections of disease occurring. One obviously must work within the rules of any Society, but I do sympathise with the UK Judges whose task is far more difficult to complete as a result of the rule. For example, there could be 25 size four Sanke entered in 25 different ponds, the Judges have to 'remember' each one whilst looking at the next, and so on.

RULES AND PROCEDURES FOR JAPANESE NISHIKIGOI SHOWS.

The lavish 'All-Japan Show' has 15 size groupings, Size One being for Koi up to 15cms. and the remaining 14 sizes are in 5cms. size increases to the final one which is for those over 80cms. All Koi are entered by variety and size within the same ponds which makes for easy and accurate judging together with a minimum of legwork.

During 1984 I was invited to assist in the judging of this event which proved to be an 'eye-opener' for me. All judging at this event is carried out on the Friday evening and full results must be displayed in time for the public opening on the Saturday morning. All Koi were displayed in show ponds containing entries in size groups and each entry had a Polaroid photograph attached to the display pond in which it was entered.

A total of 105 judges took part in this particular show; these were appointed by the All-Japan Nishikigoi Dealers' Association and were made up of amateurs, breeders and dealers alike. Before judging commenced, each judge drew a number from a hat which gave the size group he would be judging. As a result, teams of seven judges were drawn giving 15 teams in total.

Each team appointed its leader who was responsible for writing down the decisions made and giving them to the results committee, as well as carrying the final vote should a 'tie' be given by the other six judges.

As there were separate male and female classes from sizes 9 to 14, any team finishing their prime judging early would draw for which male classes to judge.

Judging commenced with each team judging their respective size groups, initially the best Kohaku is selected and 'helpers' move this, together with its' Polaroid photograph to a separate pond prepared near to the size group of entries. The second best Kohaku is then selected and left in the original pond with a '2nd Best in Variety' sticker attached to the Polaroid photograph. This process continued for each variety within the size grouping, at the end of this stage a maximum of 14 'firsts' (one per classification) are displayed in the separate pond for each size group. At the end of the first stage of judging there are 21 ponds each containing a maximum of 14 Koi, each one having been chosen as 'best in variety within its' size grouping'.

The team of judges then selects, by written ballot, the best Koi out of the 14 within their own size grouping and the Koi, together with its' photograph, is moved to a separate pond prepared for all 'Kokugyo' (Champion in size, irrespective of variety). When this second stage of judging is completed the 'Kokugyo' pond will hold 21 Koi, each the best Koi within its' size group.

The next part of the judging can now take place by all 105 judges individually giving their decisions on a secret ballot form to give the following decisions:-

1. The Kokugyo sizes 1 to 3 are judged and the Koi receiving the most votes is awarded 'Grand Champion Baby Koi'.

2. The Kokugyo sizes 4 to 6 are judged and the Koi receiving the most votes is awarded 'Grand Champion Young Koi.

3. The Kokugyo sizes 7 to 9 are judged and the Koi receiving the most votes is awarded 'Grand Champion Adult Koi'.

4. The Kokugyo sizes 10 to 12 are judged and the Koi receiving the most votes is awarded 'Grand Champion Mature Koi'.

5. The Kokugyo sizes 13 to 15 are judged and the Koi receiving the most votes is awarded 'Grand Champion Jumbo Koi'.

These five 'Grand Champions' are moved to a separate pond and from these five Koi each judge then selects, again by secret ballot form, the best one in the pond. The one receiving the most votes is awarded 'Supreme Champion' of the show, the most prestigious award at the most prestigious Koi show in the world!

The All-Japan Show is held in a rented Exhibition Centre near Tokyo and over 750 large trophies and special prizes are awarded for the winning Koi. The cost of staging this event is considerable and this must be re-couped in entry fees for the 5,000 or so Koi entered. As a result costs of entry are:-

Koi in sizes 1 to 3 are charged at 10,000 yen each.
(£64.00 at time of writing)

Koi in sizes 4 to 9 are charged at 12,000 yen each.
(£77.00 at time of writing)

Koi in sizes 10 to 15 are charged at 15,000 yen each.
(£96.00 at time of writing)

As an ending to the section on Koi shows, I was once invited to take part in judging a ZNA Local Chapter show in Hiroshima Prefecture and, after the judging had taken place, we were asked to select the worst Koi exhibited! We did as requested, much to our amusement, and selected a rather doubtful kawarimono-type Koi with only one pectoral fin. The surprised owner of this 'specimen' received a brand new BMX bicycle from a local shopkeeper who specified this award before making his donation!

ZNA Local Chapter Show Hiroshima,

(Above) Judges Mr. Masutani (left), Mr. Sakai (right), and the author.

(Right) Supreme Champion of the same show

*A magnificent example of a Gin Rin Kindai Showa,
she is 75cm. (29.5") long and still retains an excellent
Gin Rin lustre. I also find the head pattern
both unusual as well as pleasing.*

CARING

BOOK 5

'CARING'
Like any other forms of life, Nishikigoi can suffer with parasitic, viral, bacterial & other similar problems. This section is written to give the reader information as to how to identify the problem, how to take the correct remedial action, and how to prevent the problem arising again. It also covers the subjects of handling and feeding techniques.

INTRODUCTION

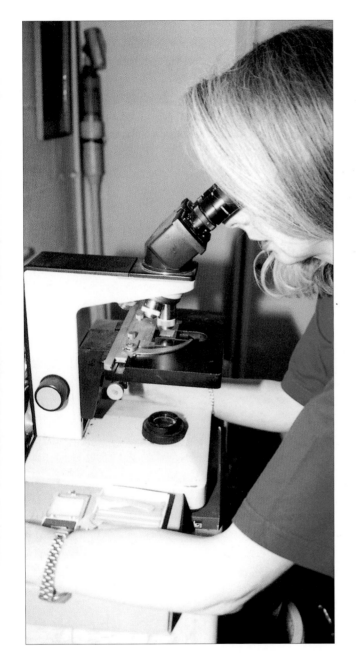

From time to time we all have to attend to our Koi for some reason or other. Sometimes a parasitic problem arises, sometimes a Koi suffers a physical damage due to bad handling, an accident in transportation or a self-inflicted injury occurring inside the pond. Sometimes bacterial problems arise, sometimes care is necessary due to fluctuations in water quality or temperature.

This obviously applies to most forms of life be it human, animal or other fish species. If this were not so we could dispense with hospitals, doctors and veterinarians altogether!

For whatever reason attention is required we should all be able to detect the problem at the earliest possible stage, assess the nature of the problem accurately and know what treatment is required. We must also know the correct procedures in administering the treatment as well as the correct dosage rates and any water temperature requirements which may affect the rates of dosage or use of a chosen remedy.

I do not pretend that this is a simple subject to cover, however, it is a most important subject and vital for inclusion in this book.

Firstly, I must point out that I have no veterinary qualifications whatsoever. My experience in this field has been gathered over the years with much information from the breeders of Japan, other information from the Nishikigoi Research Centre in Niigata, some from practical experience on a day-to-day basis and a proportion learned from 'The School of Hard Knocks'!

Secondly, there are volumes upon volumes of books written by learned and extremely qualified scientists from many parts of the world. These cover, in great detail, parasitic and bacterial problems, detection, medication and remedies for almost every fish species known, from fish farmed for food purposes right through to pet fish, be they tropical, marine or coldwater species.

Thirdly, there are fully qualified Aquatic Veterinarians and Aquatic Consultants who deal on a daily basis with all forms of fish health problems and who are regularly commissioned to attend to Koi problems from time to time.

I have prepared this section of the book purely for the Koi keeper and any remedies offered only apply to Nishikigoi and Carp; this is important as I have no information or experience as to the tolerances of other varieties to these remedies.

The learning curve progresses in any subject and this text is as up-to-the-minute as possible in February 1995. Obviously there are different methods of attending to a single problem and many may prefer their own course of action, others may disagree completely as this is a very complex and sometimes controversial subject. However I can openly state that the remedies recommended here are used, within the specified parameters, on our own stocks and those of our customers should the need arise.

Experience has taught me that a problem, once detected, should be dealt with immediately and correctly. I most certainly do not subscribe to the school of thought that states 'leave it alone and it will go away'. The more vigilant and experienced keeper can detect most problems at a very early stage which makes a cure relatively easy to effect. The longer the delay in time taken to apply a remedy to a particular problem will result in a longer time taken in effecting a cure.

The reader will note that, some remedies specified, are antibiotics; antibiotics and their usages are strictly controlled in any form of animal treatment in the UK, and these can only be obtained from a Veterinary Surgeon by prescription.

Earlier in the book it was mentioned that 'we do not keep Koi, we keep water' and it is well known that many problems arise from bad water conditions in general. These vary from cramped conditions, (usually in so-called 'quarantine' systems), fluctuating water temperatures, inefficient filtration systems producing toxic water readings, plain bad management or a lack of understanding. The amount of 'stress' (sic) caused to Koi having to endure any of these conditions can, and does, reduce natural resistance of the Koi which can then allow a secondary problem to manifest itself. This secondary problem would seldom arise if the prime water conditions were in order.

I used the word 'stress' which I personally loathe and think is the most over-used word on the whole subject of fish problems in general. It is also the biggest 'cop-out' if a problem cannot be accurately diagnosed and then the word 'stress' comes to the rescue like a knight in shining armour! I prefer instead, a more simple, open and factual reason for the start of a problem

It is also the biggest 'cop-out' if a problem cannot be accurately diagnosed the word 'stress' comes to the rescue like a knight in shining armour!

rather than an all-encompassing single word answer that, for many, is the end of the subject. Tell me a Koi is suffering because of high ammonia readings and I understand. Tell me a Koi is suffering from sunburn and I understand. Tell me a Koi is in a bad condition because it has jumped out of a pond, or has a heavy infestation of Dactylogyrus, or the pond has been over-dosed with this or that, and I understand. But please do NOT tell me it is suffering from 'stress' — this I do not understand!

Koi do not have to be wrapped in cotton wool, they are Carp and strong fish in comparison to many other species, even taking into account mans' interference with them. All they really need is a good, stable environment and good food. I accept that, from time to time, correct anti-parasite medications will have to be used in order to eradicate natural water-borne parasites, these are unavoidable in outdoor ponds and the subject is covered in detail in this section of the book but, generally, if other problems occur, they are, in the most part, avoidable.

SECTION 1.

Parasitic Problems.

Before going on to diagnosis, treatments and remedies etc., the following points are important to your Koi, your system, and your own understanding if problems are to be kept to a minimum and treatments, if required, are to be effective and safe.

a. Ensure you know the exact volume of every system you run.

This includes total water in pond and filtration system, the dosage rates for all effective medications used for the eradication of all types of water-borne parasites are measured exactly for the overall volume of water within the system. The most accurate way of arriving at the final figure is to fill the system initially via a flowmeter and log the result accordingly.

Please be aware, the dosage rates specified are accurate, a 15% underdose can be ineffective whilst a 15% overdose can be dangerous, NEVER try and 'guesstimate' your water volumes.

Flowmeter

As far as the anti-parasite medications specified are concerned, these are not 'fish treatments' in any way, they do nothing medically for the fish themselves. Instead they are used to eradicate the parasite that is irritating the Koi, a more accurate term for these would be that of 'pesticides'.

b. Ensure you understand Parasites, what they are, where they come from and what they can do if left un-checked.

Water-borne parasites that infest our Koi can be initially divided into two sections, namely the ones we can see with the naked eye and the ones we cannot see with the naked eye. They ALL feed from parts of our Koi, be it the mucus membrane, the dermal layer of the skin or the bloodstream and flesh. They NEED this sustenance in order to live and reproduce, and, in ideal conditions, they can, and do, reproduce at alarming rates. Each adult lays many eggs, many do not require a partner to reproduce, some stay in the mucus membrane of the fish, others fall to the base of the pond and others are taken into the filtration stages. These eggs will hatch and the cycle will continue with a far greater infestation potential unless something is done to halt the process. They live for a relatively short life span (weeks only) which varies with water temperatures, and need to find a host (Koi, in our case) within about 48 hours after hatching from the egg or else they will die from starvation.

In nature these parasites are kept to acceptable levels because of natural stocking rates where the majority of newly hatched larvae cannot find a host to attach themselves. A Koi pond is usually stocked at least 100 times heavier than a natural pond and, as such, is both a potential fast food paradise as well as a luxury hotel for the parasites as most freshly hatched larvae can find a Koi to feed upon within a very short time and thus the cycle continues.

The parasites usually are introduced to our Koi ponds as follows:-

Even though fish parasites are species specific, frogs, toads and newts can carry some of these parasites and their eggs.

New stocks of Koi, even the most fastidious dealer cannot guarantee that every Koi sold has no parasite eggs attached to it.

A common source of introduction is by way of bird droppings. Many of our wild birds drink in the margins of our ponds, lakes and rivers, the eggs from microscopic parasites are many times smaller than the microscopic parasite itself and the bird has no idea that these have been taken inside. If the bird droppings are deposited in a Koi pond, then there is every possibility that the unharmed eggs will hatch.

Newly purchased water plants can also have unhatched eggs of parasites on them.

If this breeding cycle is left to escalate to very heavy (epizootic) proportions, within a Koi pond it can result in heavy losses. Eventually the infestation will damage the fine mucus membrane on the gill filaments of the Koi which, in turn, reduces oxygen intake to the brain. Secondary bacterial gill decay usually follows and deaths occur. Other secondary problems resulting from that of a prime parasitic infestation can be bacterial infestation visible as ulcerations on the body of the Koi. The prime parasite bores a hole of entry through the protective mucus membrane and into the body of the Koi, this hole of entry is a perfect area for harmful bacteria to colonise and infect.

If we understand and accept the above and also accept that we can never totally eradicate the problem permanently in an outdoor situation, then we are well on the way to controlling the situation safely and effectively by using accurate forms of eradication. In turn, this will keep our Koi free from potential damage at all times.

Please note, the anti-parasite treatments recommended later are all pond dosage methods as used widely by Japanese breeders controlling similar situations. In the UK there are many who recommend that these parasites are eradicated by short-term bath treatments. In view of the fact that, as mentioned earlier, the parasite, the egg and the free-swimming larvae can also be on the pond base and in the filtration system etc., I have never understood the reasoning nor the effectiveness of this approach.

Please also note, the medications and dosage rates given in this section are intended to be used with an adequate filtration system running as normal. If biomass is seriously affected by these dosage rates, then the problem is within the biological stages of the filtration system which are not of enough efficient surface area or water flow is not supplied to all surfaces at a constant, required rate. If this is the case then the biological stage of the filter system should be improved upon accordingly.

c. Detecting signs of parasites.

In the early stages, a few Koi with a mild infestation of parasites will show signs of 'flashing', usually on their sides, on parts of the pond where they can scratch in order to try and dislodge the creature that is irritating them. Some also jump out of the water to try and dislodge the parasite in the same way whilst others may have a visible milky 'cast' appearing on the mucus. At this stage, food is taken as normal. Incidentally, Koi do not 'jump' out of the water naturally as do, say trout, when rising for a fly. Many think that, when a Koi jumps out of the water, it is playing or exercising – more often than not this is a sign of parasitic problems where it is trying to dislodge the parasite causing the irritation.

In the middle stages, if this is left unchecked, the 'flashing' becomes more exaggerated and all Koi will start to show similar symptoms, food is still taken, though not as readily as usual. Pectoral and dorsal fins show signs of 'twitching' at this stage, the milky 'cast', if present, intensifies.

In later stages of infestation, the Koi become visibly weaker with no interest in food, they lie on the pond floor or 'hover' in mid-water, usually showing signs of heavy respiration and are not nearly as alert when one approaches.

All these signs are indicative of parasitic activity but the actual family of parasite or parasites responsible can not usually be detected by the naked eye. Obviously, if effective action is taken in the early stages the problem will not be so stubborn to eradicate as it is in the later stages.

I am of the strong opinion that my Koi prefer not to have parasites. They behave better without these pests annoying them. There are other schools of thought that vary from 'You'll never catch me putting any of these chemicals into MY pond' to 'I only put a medicine in MY pond in Spring' - my honest advice is, if parasites are present, eradicate them before more serious problems arise.

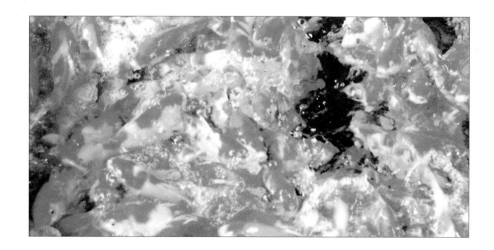

d. How to eradicate the parasites.

If there were one 'magic medicine' that eradicated all parasites then life would be much simpler, unfortunately, this is not the case. Different types of parasites require different chemicals to eradicate them successfully and some of these chemicals vary in dosage rates depending on the water temperatures within the pond at the time of treatment. In view of this, before any eradication treatment is used, the actual parasite to be eradicated must first be determined accurately and it is no use in trying to guess which type of parasite is responsible.

If the wrong medication is used it will have no effect on the actual parasite causing the infestation, and, whilst it will not harm the Koi stocks, it will allow the parasite to continue its cycle.

It must be pointed out here that, whilst the chemicals and dosage rates specified will eradicate the particular parasite and the newly hatched larvae, usually within two to six hours of application, the unhatched eggs, however, will remain protected and unharmed. In view of this, I have recommended a follow-up dosage to destroy these, after hatching, and before they have time to mature and reproduce.

As many of the medications prescribed can produce a toxic chemical reaction with some metals, it is vital that no metals are present in a pond system, other than the safe ones such as brass, phosphor bronze and stainless steel etc.

Do not pump pond water directly through copper, cupra-nickel or similar heat exchangers.

If possible, try and fit an efficient purification system to your mains water supply to remove heavy metals within the water supply prior to usage in your pond.

e. Handling of Chemicals and Medications.

WARNING:- The chemicals and medications specified, are all safe to use in all Koi ponds at the dosages stated, for the eradication of water-borne parasites. However, it must be pointed out that they are potentially hazardous to humans if abused.

Store them in a cool, dry place well away from children and pets. When handling these wear rubber gloves, do not inhale powder or vapour, wear a mask if possible and on no account take internally. Wash hands after use.

After putting any of these medications into a pond system it is advisable to wait for around 15 minutes to allow the medication into the filter stages and then to by-pass any sand filters used by turning the multiport valve to 're-circulate' position and to switch off any ultra-violet tubes being used, this prevents the dosages from being removed too quickly. After 24 hours these can be used once more.

SPECIFIC PARASITES AND METHODS OF CONTROL/ERADICATION.

a. Parasites visible to the naked eye.

ARGULUS OR FISH LOUSE.

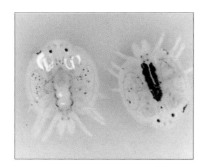

Argulus or Fish Louse.

This parasite and its eggs are commonly introduced to Koi ponds by frogs and toads. It is easy to detect, especially on the fins or white skin of the koi as this gives a perfect background, the size varies between 1mm to 5mm for adults. All are green/brown in colour and they attach themselves to the Koi by suckers and, as well as harming the tissue of the body by constant sucking, they also cause further harm by injecting a poison which causes inflammation and bleeding.

LEECHES.

These are very uncommon in purpose built Koi ponds and more common in heavily planted garden ponds and bog gardens. They are easily visible, resembling a small, flattened worm between 5mm to 20mm and dark brown/red in colour, they attach themselves to the fish by means of a sucker.

Eradication methods for the above:- Both these parasites can be destroyed very quickly at pond water temperatures over 48 degrees Fahrenheit by the use of 'Masoten'. This is an organophosphate-based drug manufactured for the purpose of the eradication of some water-borne parasites, by the Bayer Company of Japan. Although not mentioned on the specification sheet

supplied by the manufacturer, I would not use this product below 45°F.

Method 1:– Masoten Powder at the rate of 1gram per ton of pond water. Measure out quantity required and mix in a plastic bucket with pond water. Ensure all powder is dissolved (it takes on a pale blue colour when mixed) and pour round the perimeter of the pond.

OR Method 2:– Masoten Liquid at the rate of 5ml per ton of pond water, mix and distribute as above.

Second dosage as per above, in water temperatures between 48 to 58 degrees Fahrenheit use again after 10 days. In water temperatures above 58 degrees Fahrenheit use again after 7 days. The use of Masoten on its own as per this method does not colour the pond water in any way.

LERNEA OR ANCHOR WORM
(Japanese word- Ikari-mushi)

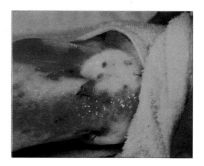

Lernea or Anchor Worm
attached to body of Koi.

This parasite can be very troublesome if left unchecked, the adult can reach 12mm in length and is grey/white in colour. It attaches itself to the fish by use of its hooks or anchors, usually by boring into the skin tissue by first getting under the scale. In this situation the body and tail of the parasite is only visible, which resembles a short cotton thread. This infestation should be attended to quickly in order to avoid secondary bacterial infection at the point of contact.

Eradication method for the above:- There is no chemical available to kill this parasite without also killing the Koi; in view of this the use of DIMILIN POWDER is recommended. This chemical can be used safely at any water temperature, its action is that of sterilising the adult and larval stages of Anchor Worm which ensures that all eggs produced, after Dimilin has been added, will not hatch.

Method:– Dimilin Powder at the rate of 1 gram per ton of pond water, measure out quantity required and mix in a plastic bucket with pond water, ensure all powder is dissolved and add to perimeter of pond, this will give a 'muddy' appearance to the water.

Second dosage as per above, in water temperatures up to 58 degrees Fahrenheit, use again after 10 days, in water temperatures above 58 degrees Fahrenheit, use again after 7 days. This will ensure that any eggs, unhatched at the time of the initial dosage can now be sterilised after hatching. At this moment in time all reproduction cycles have been terminated but both live and dead anchor worm are still attached to the Koi and these should be removed to prevent secondary bacterial problems.

Four to five days after the second dosage, all Koi should be inspected individually under anaesthetic, (see later section on this procedure) once anaesthetised, the entire body including mouth, gills and ventral areas should be carefully inspected, another popular point of contact is directly behind the dorsal fin. All Anchor Worm should then be removed very carefully by tweezers, ensuring that the head and anchors are removed, not just the body and tail. Once removed, the point of contact should be disinfected with a suitable topical dressing. (see later section)

Note:– If difficulty is experienced in removing live Anchor Worm, a strong solution of Potassium Permanganate crystals should be prepared by mixing 1 gram into 25mls hot water. Dip the tweezers into this solution prior to removing the parasite, once the solution touches the body, it results in the Anchor Worm releasing its grip immediately.

Removing Anchor Worm.

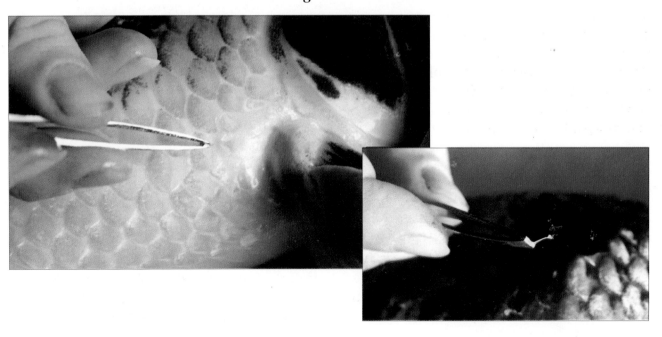

b. Parasites not visible to the naked eye.

To be totally accurate in detecting which parasite is responsible for the infestation, the Koi keeper should have access to a microscope which will cope with a 400 times magnification.

These are simple to use and, once the parasites can be identified by inspecting a small sample of body mucus, the correct method of eradication can be applied to destroy the parasite/s found. It is safe to assume that if one Koi is found to have a parasitic infestation of some kind, then all the Koi within the system will also be infected and usually only one or two Koi need to be examined by taking a mucus sample.

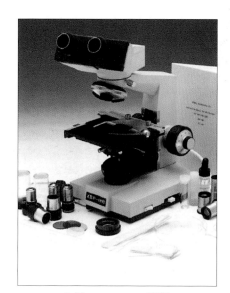

Microscope Kit

Recommended method of taking a mucus sample from a Koi for one who is inexperienced in this operation is as follows:-

■ Prepare a bowl or similar container which is large enough to hold the Koi from which the sample is to be taken.

■ Add 2.75 gallons (12.5 litres) pond water to the container, mix into this 4 to 5 grams of MS222 fish anaesthetic thoroughly by hand.

■ Prepare a damp towel flattened out on the floor next to the container.

■ Carefully net the chosen Koi and transfer it into the bowl via a handling net.

■ Ensure the water covers the gills of the Koi, the bowl can be tilted to give greater water depth.

■ After two to four minutes the Koi will start to become calmer as the anaesthetic begins to take effect and will soon turn on its side motionless.

■ At this point, place the Koi on its side on the towel and cover the eyes with the edge of the towel, (this has a further calming effect)

■ Take a glass slide and gently scrape it along the flank of the Koi in a direction towards the tail, i.e. 'with' the line of the scales, not against them. A sample of mucus will now be on the slide, take a cover slip and scrape the mucus sample to a central position on the slide before placing the cover slip on top to sandwich the sample between the slide and cover slip.

■ Carefully place the Koi back into the pond, within two to three minutes it will begin to swim as normal.

■ Place the mucus sample under the lens of the microscope and bring the sample into focus.

Note:– This is the standard procedure as to anaesthetising a Koi, once the operator has confidence in usage of this, it becomes a very simple operation. Do remember that all forms of anaesthesia work on a time to strength basis; if more anaesthetic is added to the water initially, the time taken for the Koi to be anaesthetised will be quicker and, conversely, if less anaesthetic is added to the water initially then the time taken will be longer for it to take effect. If the Koi has to be anaesthetised for long periods, say 15 minutes or more, then it will have to be more strongly anaesthetised than it would have to be for a simple mucus scrape. Please also remember that a Koi left too long in anaesthetic will not come out of it alive. If you are not confident to anaesthetise your own Koi without supervision, do check with a fellow enthusiast or dealer who will probably go through every aspect with you. As mentioned earlier, it becomes far easier with practice. For an experienced handler, mucus scrapes can be carried out safely and quickly without the need for an anaesthetic.

Now we have the mucus sample under the microscope, we can determine which parasite/s are present by comparing them against the ones shown next. This selection should more than cover the range of microscopic parasites ever likely to infect your Koi.

GYRODACTYLUS (skin fluke)

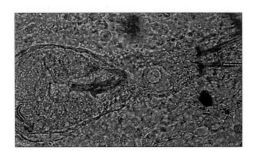

Gyrodactylus.

DACTYLOGYRUS (gill fluke)

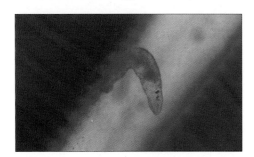

Dactylogyrus

The above parasites are common in our Koi ponds, they both attach themselves to body, fins and gill areas and can do great damage if they are not eradicated.

EPISTYLIS

Epistylis

This parasite is not so common in the UK but can be very serious if not checked when the entire body breaks out in contusions. The unique 'bell' shaped colonies of the parasite are easily detected at around 40 times magnification. Generally, after eradication methods have been completed successfully it is often necessary to use a medicated bath treatment in order to regenerate damaged tissue.

Damage caused by a serious infestation of Epistylis.

CHILODONELLA

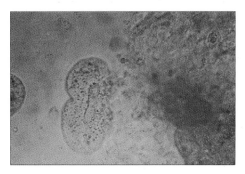

Chilodonella

This parasite produces similar symptoms to Costia and Trichodina mentioned later, it is not so common in UK Koi ponds but I have seen outbreaks on several occasions.

WHITE SPOT
(caused by Ichthyophtirius multifiliis)

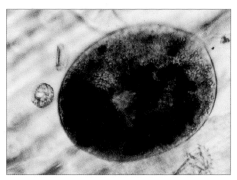

White Spot

This is a protozoan parasite which usually manifests itself in cold water periods. The 'effect' of it can be detected with the naked eye, especially on red and black pattern areas in the form of hundreds of white spots around the size of a pin prick in diameter. The actual parasite, however, can only be detected by microscope. The reproductive cycle of this parasite from tomite to adult stages is rapid and early attention is vital. They attach themselves to the inside of the outer layer of the skin which makes it more difficult to eradicate than other parasites. The parasite generally does not survive in Koi ponds at water temperatures over 68 degrees F.

Generally, all the aforementioned parasites can be destroyed, both in adult and larval stages, providing the water temperature is over 48 degrees Fahrenheit, by adding the following three medications together.

1. **At pond water temperatures between 48 to 55°F and above 73°F.**

   Measure out Zinc-free Malachite Green crystals at 0.25 grams per ton pond water, mix this in a container with warm water to ensure all crystals are fully dissolved.

   Measure out Formalin (Formaldehyde 36% solution) BP grade or 'ANALAR' grade at the rate of 15 mls. per ton of pond water and add to Malachite Green solution.

   Measure out Masoten Powder at the rate of 0.3 grams per ton of pond water, mix this in a container with a little pond water to ensure all powder is dissolved then add to Formalin and Malachite Green solution.

   Empty solution into large plastic bucket and fill to top with pond water, stir again and pour around pond perimeter, water will turn dark blue/green in colour.

   Second dosage as follows:- Temperature between 48 to 55° F, after 10 days. Temperature over 73° F, after 5 days.

2. **At pond water temperatures over 55°F and up to 64°F.**
   As above, but add Formalin at 20 mls. per ton of pond water.

   Second dosage at same temperature, after 8 days

3. **At pond water temperatures over 64 and up to 72°F.**
   As previous, but add Formalin at 25 mls. per ton of pond water.

   Second dosage at same temperature, after 6 days.

Warnings regarding the above – do not use at water temperatures below 48 degrees F and never use Formalin if cooking salt is present in the pond water. If cooking salt is present the above medication is not effective without Formalin and, as such, should not be used. It should also be pointed out that Formalin can prove to be dangerous in water with a pH reading of over 8.0.

Note:- If Dactylogyrus infestation is very high, on some occasions the above medication is not totally effective to eradicate all. If this is the case then the above should not be used, instead use the following, but only at water temperatures above 62 degrees Fahrenheit.

For stubborn Dactylogyrus infestation, at water temperatures above 62°F, use MASO-TEN POWDER at the rate of 1.5 grams per ton of pond water, mix and distribute as per instructions for Argulus/Leeches. Note:- DO NOT USE THIS RATE OF MASOTEN WITH ANY OTHER CHEMICALS AT THE SAME TIME.

Second dosage at same temperature, after 7 days.

The following parasites generally are not usually successfully eradicated by the previous medications in the UK.

TRICHODINA
(Cyclochaeta)

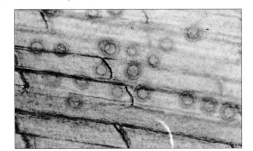

Trichodina

Another protozoan parasite, this one resembles a flying saucer in shape and spins rapidly when viewed under a microscope.

This is usually one which gives problems in warm water periods and causes excessive mucus secretion and vegetation of the skin and gill surfaces, this results in branchial respiration which, in turn, finally weakens the Koi.

COSTIA

A high magnification is needed, between 100 to 200 times to see a Costiosis infestation. The small stages of this parasite can be detected as crescent shaped and spinning rapidly. It usually manifests itself in cold water periods and signs of infestation give the appearance of a white cast on the mucus membrane due to vegetation of the skin. This gives a similar visual appearance to that of infestation by Trichodina and Chilodonella seen in warm water conditions, if left unchecked it can result in respiratory difficulties. Costia cannot survive for more than one hour without a fish it can attach itself to, it also cannot tolerate water temperatures above 86°F.

If these are found under microscopic examination of the mucus, they can easily be eliminated at all water temperatures by using one of the following chemicals:-

1. Potassium Permanganate crystals, BP grade.

   Method:- Measure Potassium Permanganate crystals at the rate of 1.5 grams per ton of pond water. Mix in a large plastic bucket with water on the point of boiling, ensure all crystals are dissolved and leave to stand for 30 minutes. Stir thoroughly once more and pour solution around perimeter of pond. The water in the pond turns dark brown/red in colour.

   Second Dosages:-
   At water temperatures above 68° F, after 7 days.

At water temperatures above 60° F and below 68° F, after 9 days.

At water temperatures below 60° F, after 12 days.

Warning on usage of the above remedy. This chemical seriously reduces dissolved oxygen content especially in warmer temperatures, always increase aeration whilst this medication is being used.

OR

2. Acriflavine Powder Neutral, BP grade.

Method:- Measure Acriflavine Powder at the rate of 1 gram per ton of pond water, dissolve in a plastic bucket with hot water, ensure all crystals are dissolved and pour solution around perimeter of pond. Water in pond turns yellow/green in colour. Incidentally, this also is sometimes effective for the eradication of White Spot, mentioned earlier.

Second Dosages for Acriflavine, see temperature bands for potassium permanganate.

Note:- In my experience, although Trichodina and Costia can be partially eliminated by using Malachite Green and Formalin, Potassium Permanganate is far more effective.

In closing this chapter on parasitic problems, the medications stated for eradicating specific parasites are accurate and effective as stated but I feel I must stress the following in order to prevent any mistakes resulting from any misunderstandings.

NEVER use Masoten at any rate higher than 0.3 g/ton water with any other chemicals.

NEVER use Formalin without also using Malachite Green.

NEVER mix Malachite Green, Potassium Permanganate and/or Acriflavine together.

NEVER use any of the chemicals mentioned if salinity is present in the water exceeding 0.1% (1 kilo per ton) – it is far better to have no salt present at all as this can react with the chemicals used.

ALWAYS double check dosage rates PRIOR to applying them; NEVER become complacent with this aspect of treatment.

SECTION 2.
Viral and Other Problems.

1. PAPILLOMATOSIS.

This problem has only been detected since 1981; it is only found in a cold water situation and can affect any Koi over one year old. It rarely survives at water temperatures over 63°F. Symptoms are circular grey/white protrusions up to 7mm in diameter and are conical, the tip standing some 3 to 4 mm off the body. They are most commonly found on the fins of the Koi but do appear on the body, especially in Doitsu varieties. If the growth is cut off in cold water temperatures it will return and more damage is done by removing it in the first place. Many collectors in the UK refer to this as 'carp pox'- (a notifiable disease) - which it most certainly is not. To date, there is no cure for this virus, however it has no adverse effect on the health of the Koi and, as soon as water temperatures exceed 63°F, the manifestations disappear altogether and no signs of the problem are visible. Usually this will return again as water temperatures fall. It is not suspected to transmit from Koi to Koi as are parasitic problems; those enthusiasts with Koi showing these symptoms have no cause for concern.

2. HIKUI. (HE-COO-EE)

A problem which has escalated in the UK since the late 1980's and is causing concern with several collectors of high grade Koi.

This virus affects only the red pigmentation of Kohaku, Sanke and Showa varieties and is more likely to affect those with high quality red pigmentation.

It never occurs on other pigmentations or on any other varieties of Nishikigoi.

It manifests itself as a kind of skin cancer to the red pigmentation when small areas become orange/yellow and a small lump appears at this point.

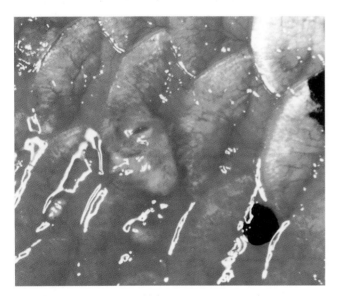

Red pigmentation displaying 'Hikui'

It most certainly affects the appearance and the value of the Koi as this is considered a 'defect' in UK Koi shows. Like papillomatosis this has no adverse effect on the health of the Koi whatsoever but is present in all water temperatures once the virus appears. This also does not readily transmit from Koi to Koi within a system; some are affected whilst others are not. It rarely ever occurs on Koi kept indoors, even in good light conditions, and seldom appears on Koi under 15" long.

I have spoken at length to many breeders in Japan about this problem and all answers point to the filtration systems within the ponds where 'Hikui' is present.

In ponds where filtration units do not allow a build-up of mechanical debris, I have never seen 'Hikui' appear. It is always in ponds which have little or no means of removing debris from under the filter media trays efficiently and regularly that problems with 'Hikui' are experienced. It is important, for many other reasons, that mechanical debris is discharged from the pond system regularly and efficiently to avoid build-up of anaerobic conditions, and my advice to anyone who is experiencing this problem is to take a serious look at all their filtration stages. The filtration systems described in this book will certainly not allow any debris to build up, and, as a result, will not produce the 'Hikui' virus within a system.

Once a filter problem has been rectified, 'Hikui' can be removed gently by cotton bud and the areas disinfected. This may have to be carried out on several occasions before the tumour disappears; there is now a topical dressing made in Japan specifically for this purpose.

3. ULTRA-VIOLET DEGENERATION.

This 'technical' word for simple 'sunburn' was given to me by Professor Roberts of the Department of Aquaculture at Stirling University during early 1982 when I took several examples of some customers' Koi to him to ask his valued opinion. At that time many were of the opinion that this was a rare and mystical disease.

Make no mistake about it, some varieties of Koi can suffer with sunburn. Varieties with non-metallic white pigmentation such as Kohaku, Sanke, Showa, Shiro Bekko and Shiro Utsuri are all susceptible and this also affects their pectoral fins.

In contrast, the black, red and metallic pigmentations of Nishikigoi do not absorb the ultra-violet rays of the sun and these are never subject to the condition at all. High sunlight in crystal clear unshaded ponds produces sunburn problems on the white pigmentation from time to time. If you have Koi suffering with mild signs of sunburn I would recommend that Acriflavine powder is immediately added to the pond at 1 gram per ton of pond water as described earlier and that the pond is partially shaded on a permanent basis, obviously this problem is not contagious. In bad stages of sunburn see bacterial disorders next.

4. ONE OR MORE KOI SUDDENLY BECOME VISIBLY 'BENT' AND SWIM AWKWARDLY.

In my experience there are only three reasons this occurs:-

■ An electrical short within the pond, the nearest Koi to the faulty equipment are the ones to suffer here. The installation of a suitable mains RCD can prevent this occurring. (see section 'Environment')

■ An intense thunderstorm on a very warm day produces a dramatic instant reduction of dissolved oxygen to danger levels and one or more Koi will be affected in this way as a direct result.

■ An overdose of Masoten or similar organophosphate.

The Koi rarely die as a result but will remain deformed forever, the condition is not contagious and Koi affected depend on individual characteristics and levels of resistance and these occurrences are difficult to predict in advance.

5. A KOI DEVELOPS RAISED SCALES ON THE BELLY AND FLANKS IN THE FIRST STAGES.

This usually occurs in cold water periods. This is followed by raised scales developing all over the body which gives a pinecone effect, eyes protrude and the Koi rests, usually motionless on the pond base.

Whilst these symptoms are by no means common, they do occur from time to time and usually fall into two categories namely one we can cure and one we cannot, both problems having similar symptoms. It is a matter of urgency that Koi suffering with these symptoms are given urgent attention to avoid the next stage when the raised scales become infected and lesions break out.

I would recommend that a separate container is filled with pond water and the Koi is placed into this container and aeration is added, cooking salt should be added immediately at the rate of 0.25% salinity (2.5 kilos per ton) and water temperature should be increased very slowly at the rate of 3°F per day to around 60°F. After one day, cooking salt should be increased to 0.5% salinity (5 kilos per ton), when water temperatures exceed 55° F the symptoms of raised scales and bulging eyes should have disappeared. In this case the Koi completely recovers and it is likely that the initial problem was the one of distress caused by long periods of fluctuating cold water temperatures.

In the case when this method of treatment is used and the Koi continues to deteriorate, it will almost definitely be a female Koi that has also developed internal problems whereby her eggs have not been ingested in the usual way. The eggs inside her decay and become foul. On several occasions I have tried to remove all the foul-smelling liquid with no success and, in every case of this I have seen, the Koi deteriorates and death occurs. In truth, only very expert major surgery can possibly assist here. I once witnessed this surgery carried out in Japan by the Niigata Fisheries Institute on a female Kohaku suffering with this condition. The entire belly was opened by scalpel and the area of infection treated, the operation took some 45 minutes to complete. Six months later I saw the Koi, the owner turned her upside down and showed me the belly area, all I could see to prove major surgery had taken place were faint traces where stitches had been made, apart from that, the Koi was perfect.

In both these cases the symptoms are not contagious.

6. BODY OF ONE KOI STARTS TO BECOME THIN EVEN THOUGH FOOD IS TAKEN

All other Koi are unaffected, this condition is rare and I have not seen this now for some seven years. Japanese pathologists find this more common in food fish production and believe it to be a virus close to tuberculosis. I have never seen a single cure for this problem and the Koi will continue to waste away, eventually death occurs, again this is not contagious.

7. KOI IS NOTICED SWIMMING WITH MOUTH PERMANENTLY OPEN.

This is also rare in occurrence and usually only effects small Koi up to 12" long. It is, in fact, a form of 'lockjaw' and, after the Koi has been anaesthetised, the jaw can be manipulated by hand - at first with difficulty but becomes easier after several attempts. On one occasion a complete cure was effected by using an intramuscular injection into the pectoral muscle after manipulation as described above, again this is not contagious.

8. ONE OR BOTH EYES TAKE ON A THICK MUCUS COATING AND SOMETIMES THE EYEBALL BULGES OUTWARDS, IN ALL OTHER RESPECTS THE KOI IS FINE.

The causes are unknown and occurs rarely, in every instance we have come across this a total cure has been effected by the following method:-
A 2% solution is made by mixing 24.5 mls of distilled water with 0.5 gram of Silver Nitrate crystals. The Koi is anaesthetised and this is applied to the eye/s by cotton bud, prior to returning the Koi to the pond it should be placed in a bath containing pond water with a 2% salt solution (1 kilo salt to 49 litres water) for 10 minutes. The procedure should be repeated after 24 hours and, one day later, the eyes will return to normal, again this is not contagious.

9. PECTORAL OR TAIL FIN IS SPLIT SEVERELY.

Usually as a result of harsh netting techniques or bad handling methods, if this is left unattended bacterial problems can occur. The Koi should be anaesthetised and the split fin carefully stitched together and the fin taken back to its original shape by placing the stitches in the soft fin tissue behind both bony rays that are on each side of the actual split. The number of stitches required depends on the size of the actual split but generally the distance between each stitch should be approximately 7 to 8 mm. The area should then be painted first with a 2% solution of Silver Nitrate as described above and then painted with a coating of Friars' Balsam, a sticky antiseptic liquid which is ideal for this application. The Koi can then be returned to the pond, the time taken for total healing depends on water temperatures and can take two to three months in temperatures of 65°F, after which the Koi can be anaesthetised once more and any stitches remaining can be carefully removed.

SECTION 3.

Bacterial Disorders.

As mentioned at the beginning of this section, in my own experience, most bacterial disorders in Nishikigoi are a secondary problem that have developed from another prime problem/incident/ situation that has taken place earlier for whatever reason. These can be listed as follows:-

■ Parasitic problems that have not been attended to quickly and properly and have produced lesions and infection in the skin.

■ Physical damage incurred from a predator or by transportation, this is rare and exceptional.

■ Physical damage self inflicted, the Koi jumped or bumped into the side of the pond nose-first. I ask myself why?- Koi have a very sophisticated radar system, they do not bump into things by choice. More often than not, if something like this occurs there is usually a good reason why and I would generally categorise this as irritation caused by other problems such as parasitic irritation or bad water conditions mentioned on this list.

■ Toxic water conditions breaking down protective mucus membrane.

■ Overdose of medications again breaking down protective mucus membrane.

■ Sunburn in the later stages, see above for early detection and treatment methods.

■ Constant fluctuations in water quality/ temperature.

■ Bad handling, bad netting techniques.

■ Toxic metals in the system.

■ Lack of sufficient natural light conditions resulting in the withdrawal of essential vitamins and minerals thus weakening natural resistance to bacterial infection.

The list goes on, all these can produce problems that vary from minor to extremely serious. They range from frayed fins, rotting fins, nose abrasions, eye infections, raised scales and ulcerations in all areas and all shapes and sizes. One thing is certain, attempts must first be made to try and get the Koi regenerated and well again. Secondly, the reason as to why it happened in the first place must be discovered and steps taken not to allow it to happen again. A 'proper' system, described earlier, once matured fully, rarely produces these problems providing the keeper is vigilant.

General conditions and requirements for healing bacterial problems on your Koi.

A separate body of water, a large aquarium or indoor system, yours or a friends, which has the following facilities:-

a. Good mechanical and biological filtration and an abundance of natural light. Sick Koi must have excellent water quality if they are to recover quickly.

b. A heating system that can be accurately controlled and water temperatures can be maintained up to 80° F., if required at all times of the year.

One of the most significant factors that is required to regenerate fin, scale, skin and body tissue is heat, regeneration of these does not begin until water temperatures exceed 64° F.

c. Excellent aeration to both pond and filtration stages, running at constant high temperatures reduces dissolved oxygen content which has to be replaced by mechanical means.

d. Methods of carrying out heavy water changes if required, mature water of the same temperature is the ideal, a heated and aerated back-up reservoir would be excellent.

e. Accurate water test kits to monitor water qualities — especially pH; ammonia, nitrite and dissolved oxygen plus other necessary items such as a salinometer, accurate gram balance and microscope kit.

Salinometer

This unit is invaluable for giving accurate salinity readings of pond water, it is simple to calibrate and operate.

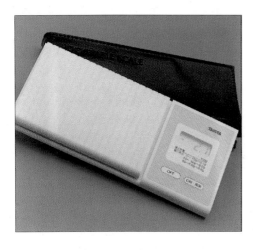

Gram Balance

Small quantities of powder need to be measured from time to time, a small balance such as this will accurately measure from 0.1 gram to 100 grams.

f. A supply of effective medicines to use during the healing process, these are covered later in this section.

Primary treatments required before placing Koi in the treatment pond.

Ensure all parasitic problems have been eradicated and keep a constant check that they do not recur if un-hatched eggs are present.

For serious ulcerations, which have been allowed to get to these stages for whatever reason, an intramuscular injection of a suitable antibiotic is most definitely required prior to placing the Koi into a treatment pond for healing.

As I mentioned at the beginning of this section, ALL antibiotics for use on animals are strictly controlled and can only be obtained from your veterinary surgeon. The overdose, underdose or wrong choice of antibiotic for a particular problem can result in disaster. In view of this I strongly suggest you seek expert veterinary assistance if you have to use an antibiotic injection for your Koi.

I had to think long and hard before including the following information in this book and also had to seek permission to publish the details. I personally feel very strongly that this should be printed as my experience in the usage of the drug, the results it has produced and the Koi it has saved deserves a full coverage. If this saves Koi, then the inclusion of this information is extremely important and it is therefore my moral duty to inform the reader.

The only injection I have used since 1989 was recommended to me by Mr. Toshio Sakai of the Matsunosuke Company in Isawa, he also taught me the method of injection and the dosage rates which, to date, has produced a success rate of over 90% since I began to use the product as specified and with the permission of my veterinary surgeon.

In the years prior to receiving this information, we used, again under veterinary permission, a wide range of injectible antibiotics for Koi with serious ulcerations resulting from a variety of prime causes. Some produced a mild success rate, some a reasonable success rate, others produced 'reactions' due to the density of the antibiotic used, whilst others did little at all. The point of injection varied with these drugs from tail muscle, pectoral muscle, shoulder or gut. It is a pointless exercise for me to mention the ones that I dispensed with many years ago, instead I will give full details of the only injectible antibiotic I can honestly recommend for Koi with serious ulcerations as a result of a variety of prime causes.

The drug in question has the trade name of 'KEFZOL', it is manufactured by Eli Lilley and Company Ltd. and is available in 500mg. and 1 gram quantities. 'KEFZOL' is the trade name for Cephazolin Sodium and is manufactured for human treatment purposes such as Septicaemia, bone and joint infections and skin and soft tissue infections amongst others. The white powder is supplied in rubber-stoppered glass vials, by injecting sterile injection water through the rubber stopper and shaking the bottle well, the injection is ready to use and can only be kept in a refrigerator, after make-up, for 48 hours before becoming ineffective, after which time it should be disposed of.

For Koi injection purposes, 4ml. of injection water should be mixed with 1 gram of 'Kefzol' to produce 4ml. of injectible antibiotic which can be drawn out of the glass vial, at the rate required, by a standard 1.0ml. 'Insulin-type' syringe. These syringes have extremely fine needles which can easily take in the water-like consistency of the solution. By using these syringes for injection purposes, the delicate skin tissue suffers no secondary damages which can result when using larger bore needles needed to inject a denser liquid.

I have used this intramuscular injection on many occasions as a 'one-off' treatment to successfully cure a broad spectrum of bacterial conditions resulting in serious ulcerations and lesions on most parts of the body as well as for healing any secondary fin damages. Specific damages it has healed completely and without being able to detect the original damage has been serious eye wounds, serious ulcerations to the pectoral muscles, serious nose ulcerations and very serious body ulcerations. Only in very rare instances has a second half dosage follow-up injection been necessary. To date, after some five years of using this injection in the dosage rates and methods described below, there has been no secondary reactions manifesting themselves on any Koi treated.

The only qualification I must point out against the latter is that 'Kefzol' should never be used on humans or Koi suffering with liver or kidney problems as permanent damage could result. On only one occasion, during my usage of this injection, did I lose a Koi directly as a result of a later diagnosis of a serious liver infection.

The method of injecting 'Kefzol' is also very important, the total amount used depends on the size of the Koi to be treated, but this amount must be divided in two equal parts and injected on each side of the Koi as illustrated. The point of injection is also very specific and important being in the tail muscle to the rear of the end of the dorsal fin at approximately the position of the third scale above the lateral line. The angle and method of injection is to carefully insert the needle under this scale, in a direction towards the head of the Koi, and gently penetrate the skin tissue beneath the scale. The antibiotic can then be injected into flesh of the muscle just under the skin itself, a deep injection is not necessary at all due to the small amount required and the fine consistency of the liquid to be absorbed readily into the muscle tissue. Obviously, as with any form of injection, care must be taken to ensure no air is present in the syringe prior to use.

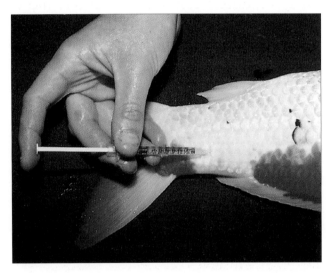

Correct point of injection for an injection of 'Kefzol'.

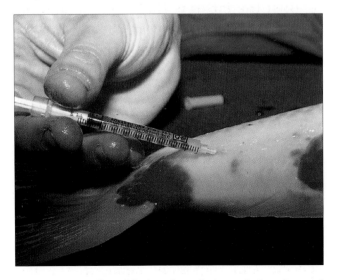

Correct angle of injection for an injection of 'Kefzol'.

The actual dosage rates for injecting Koi with 'Kefzol' are as follows:-

For Koi up to 8" long, do not use an injection, instead see the text following this subject.

For Koi over 8" and up to 9"
— use 0.3ml. per side.
For Koi over 9" and up to 10"
— use 0.35ml. per side.
For Koi over 10" and up to 11"
— use 0.4ml. per side.
For Koi over 11" and up to 12"
— use 0.45 ml. per side.
For Koi over 12" and up to 13"
— use 0.5ml. per side.
For Koi over 13" and up to 15"
— use 0.6ml. per side.
For Koi over 15" and up to 18"
— use 0.75ml. per side.
For Koi over 18" and up to 20"
— use 0.85ml. per side.
For Koi over 20" and up to 24"
— use 1.0ml. per side.
For Koi above 24" use 1.25ml. per side.

For less serious problems detected early, such as minor ulcerations, minor nose damages, frayed and rotten fins and small damages around the eyes and also for Koi which are too small to take an intramuscular injection, I would recommend the following courses of action before the Koi are placed into the treatment pond.

Anaesthetise each Koi individually, any loose scales near the wounds remove carefully with tweezers then, with a soft tissue, gently dry the ulceration and the area around it. It is very important to remove all dead or damaged scales in order to allow the surrounding tissue to be cleaned and allowed to regenerate.

Apply a suitable topical dressing to the area, (there are several available on the market) and leave for 10 seconds, after this, dab the area dry again with a tissue. The Koi is now ready to be placed into the treatment pond.

For Koi with fin infections and physical fin damages, these should be individually anaesthetised and the fins carefully trimmed with surgical scissors or a scalpel to ensure the rot is removed leaving new tissue exposed to grow. The Koi can now be placed into the treatment pond after painting all areas of fin damage with a 2% solution of Silver Nitrate as described earlier. This is far more effective to apply to fin damages than a standard topical dressing which is excellent for body damages.

Once the damaged Koi have been placed in the treatment pond, cooking salt should be introduced to the pond gradually, as follows:-

Day 1. Add cooking salt at 1.5 kilos per ton water.

Day 2. Add cooking salt at a further 1.5 kilos per ton water.

Day 3. Add cooking salt at a further 2.0 kilos per ton water.

This takes salinity to the correct rate of 0.5% (5 kilos per ton water) and this must be maintained for the duration of the treatment. Cooking salt is an excellent disinfectant which has healing properties at this rate and is ideal for use as a base medication in a treatment pond. It is even more effective when used together with other remedies mentioned later.

Unlike other substances mentioned in this section, cooking salt is not removed from a system by filtration etc. it is only removed by water changes and must be topped up accordingly back to recommended salinity of 0.5% when old water is removed and new water added. For example, if a system is running at the recommended salinity of 0.5% and 55 gallons of water (0.25 ton) are removed every day for discharge purposes, then, once the 55 gallons are replaced 1.25 kilo cooking salt should then be added to return to 0.5% salinity. Also when returning healed Koi to original pond, this salinity should be reduced to zero by constant water changes in order to avoid any osmosis problems during the transfer operation. Cooking salt should always be used in preference to table salt which has several additives to ensure it flows freely for table usage.

Finally, time for complete healing and regeneration varies with seriousness of the initial damage, water temperature maintained in treatment pond, your expertise to provide and maintain good water conditions for the duration of the treatment and the basic regenerative and healing capacity of individual Koi. The above guide is based on practical experience, most of the methods were taught to me by the breeders of Japan.

*An ideal time to visually check
your Koi for any problems
is at feeding time*

THE MEDICINE CHEST

To further enhance understanding it is important to include brief details of the chemicals mentioned in the treatment of Koi within this section of the book. Many people in the UK, at least, are still trying to cope with the changeover from our 'ounces and pounds' and 'pints and gallons' to the metric systems, plus temperatures in Celsius and not Fahrenheit which all our children understand perfectly. In view of this some printed conversions may be useful.

a. Weights, Measures and Volumes.

1 ton of water weighs 1,000 kilograms and equals 1 cubic metre = 35.314 cubic feet
= 1,000 litres
= 1,000,000 millilitres
= 220 Imperial gallons.

1 litre of water weighs 1 kilogram
= 1,000 grams
= 2.205 pounds
= 1.7598 pints.

1 pint of water = 0.5769 litres
= 576.9 millilitres.

1 cubic foot of water = 6.23 gallons
= 28.31 litres.

1 Imperial gallon of water = 4.5459 litres.

1 pound weighs 453.6 grams.

1 ounce weighs 28.35 grams.

1 U.S. gallon of water = 3.785 litres.

b. Temperatures.

To convert Fahrenheit to Celsius, deduct 32, multiply by 5 and divide by 9.

To convert Celsius to Fahrenheit, multiply by 9, divide by 5, and add 32.

DESCRIPTION AND USAGE OF OTHER IMPORTANT MEDICATIONS.

'Elbagin' a yellow granular compound, turns water golden yellow.

Used throughout Japan to help with safe transportation of Nishikigoi either in vinyl bag or in oxygenated containers. This is used in conjunction with cooking salt at 0.5% (5 kilos per ton water) and 'Elbagin' at 10 grams per ton of water.

It can be used in a filtered pond together with cooking salt at 0.5% at the same rate of 10 grams per ton of water to effectively reduce fungal infections. Best temperature bands between 68 to 75°F. Water changes are not necessary unless readings begin to fluctuate as the filtration will remove this eventually, its effectiveness used in this way is between 24 to 48 hours.

In an unfiltered 'short term bath' application for urgent attention to fungal infections, it can be used at the rate of 20 grams per ton of water together with cooking salt at 0.5% and good aeration for 24 hours, best temperature range as above.

'Parazan Powder'

This product is mixed with pellets and fed to them to aid speedy recovery after parasitic or bacterial problems. The correct method is as follows:-

Add 20 grams 'Parazan' powder to 200 mls. hot water and stir until powder is completely dissolved. Add the liquid to 1 kilo of good quality Koi pellets and mix by hand in a bowl, ensuring all moisture is absorbed. Spread pellets out on greaseproof paper and allow them to dry overnight in a warm room, feed these over a 10 to 12 day period at normal feeding rates.

'Parazan D'

If bacterial gill decay is a potential problem due to initial parasitic infestation which has been successfully eradicated, this colourless liquid is invaluable and widely used throughout Japan for these and similar problems, notably aeromonas infections.

It can be used in a filtered pond at the rate of 50 mls. per ton of water plus cooking salt at the rate of 0.5%. Best temperature range is between 65°F to 78°F, duration for at least 10 days after which, water changes can be carried out as normal.

It can also be used in an unfiltered 'short term bath' situation together with cooking salt at 0.5% at the rate of 100 mls. per ton of water. Duration for 3 days with good aeration and temperature range as above.

'Terramycin Fish Formula'

A dark green powder made by Pfizer in Japan specifically for use in water to cure a wide spectrum of bacterial disorders.

In a filtered pond use Terramycin Fish Formula at the rate of 50 grams per ton together with cooking salt at 0.5%, best temperature range between 68° F to 79° F. The water colour will change to dark green, duration of this treatment is for 7 days after which normal water changes can be made.

In an unfiltered 'short term bath' situation use Terramycin Fish Formula at the rate of 100 grams per ton water plus cooking salt at 0.5% together with good aeration. Duration of bath for 3 days, repeat if necessary.

A shorter bath dosage is possible for up to 1 hour, exactly same as above but rate of Terramycin Fish Formula increased to 250 grams per ton.

OTHER EFFECTIVE SHORT TERM BATHS

These 'dip' baths are used widely in Japan for quick, eradication of a high level of parasites on the Koi, this is always followed up two days later with pond dosages as already specified.

1. Trichodina. Potassium Permanganate crystals, 20 grams well dissolved in 100 litres water, duration of bath 3 minutes.

2. Dactylogyrus. Formalin, duration of bath 1 hour, with gentle aeration.

    a. At water temperatures up to 50°F, 1 ml. to 4 litres water.

    b. At water temperatures between 50 to 60°F, 1 ml. to 5 litres water.

    c. At water temperatures over 60°F, 1 ml. to 6 litres water.

3. Dactylogyrus and Costia. Potassium Permanganate crystals, 10 grams per ton for up to 1 hour with good aeration.

4. Dactylogyrus, Chilodonella, Epistyilis and Costia. Cooking salt at 20 kilos per ton of water for up to 10 minutes.

Note:- **Only choose ONE of these short term baths within any 48 hour period.**

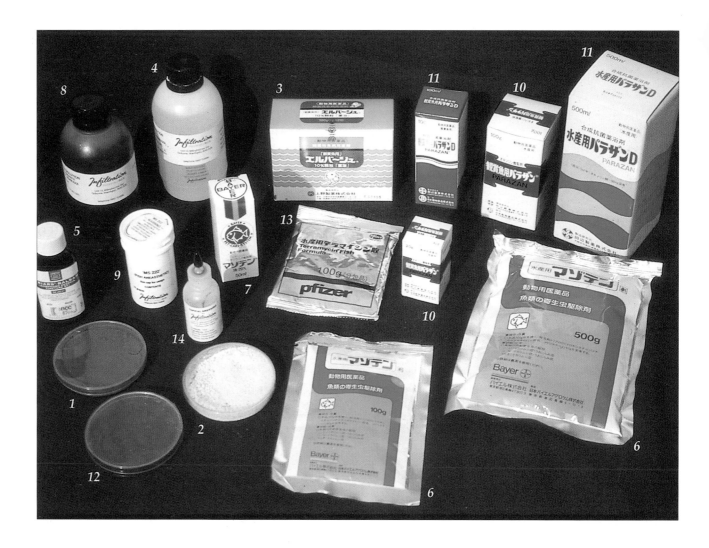

BRIEF DESCRIPTION OF ALL CHEMICALS MENTIONED IN THIS SECTION

ACRIFLAVINE NEUTRAL BP GRADE.
This is a deep orange granular powder consisting of a mixture of 2,8-diamino-10- methylacridinium chloride and of 2,8-diaminoacridine.
(See photograph ref.1)

DIMILIN W.P.
A powdered substance which contains a 25% powder of Diflubenzuron.
(See photograph ref.2)

ELBAGIN.
This is a 10% preparation of Sodium Nifurstyrenate (C13 H8 O5 Nna)
(See photograph ref.3)

FORMALIN.
(Formaldehyde Solution) (HCHO)
This is available commercially in many forms and in many qualities, for Koi pond usage it is recommended to use 'Analar' quality which is the finest quality available in a 36% solution. A 40% solution is also available which contains some methanol for conservation purposes, this is poisonous to fish life and should not be used.
(See photograph ref.4)

FRIAR'S BALSAM.
This balsam is composed of 100 parts benzoin, 35 parts storax, 35 parts Balsam tolu, 16 parts Balsam Peru, 8 parts aloe, 8 parts myrrh, 4 parts angelica and ethanol to make 1000.
(See photograph ref.5)

MASOTEN.
An organophosphate-based drug, available in powder or liquid forms. (The liquid preparation contains 1 gram of active ingredient in 5 mls. liquid.)
(See photograph Masoten Powder, ref.6 Masoten Liquid ref.7)

MALACHITE GREEN, MEDICAL GRADE, ZINC-FREE.
A microscopic dye consisting of green crystals with a metallic lustre, under no circumstances use the grade used for dyeing purposes as this contains zinc chloride which is lethal to Koi. *(See photograph ref.8)* This is a liquid preparation of Malachite Green which is more convenient to use, 50 mls. of this particular solution treats 4 tons (880 gallons) water.

MS 222.
A fine white powder of Ethyl 3 — Aminobenzoate Methane Sulphonic Acid. (Tricaine Methane Sulphonate) $C_9H_{11}NO_2CH_4SO_3$
(See photograph ref.9)

PARAZAN POWDER & PARAZAN D.
Both are derivatives of Oxyolinic acid, and a full breakdown is not available as such.
($C_{13}H_{11}NO_5$)
(See photograph Parazan Powder, ref.10 Parazan D ref.11)

POTASSIUM PERMANGANATE.
($KMnO_4$)
A violet, crystallised substance which should only be introduced for pond dosage when ALL crystals are totally dissolved. As this chemical severely reduces dissolved oxygen content within a system extra aeration should be added as a precaution when using this as an anti-parasite treatment.
(See photograph ref.12)

SALT.
Sodium Chloride ($NaCl$)
Once again, ensure, when using for Koi treatments, that cooking salt is used as opposed to table salt.

SILVER NITRATE.
($AgNO_3$)
A crystallised substance which must be protected from light.

TERRAMYCIN FISH FORMULA.
A 10% strength powder of Hydrochloride Oxytetracycline ($C_{13}H_{11}NO_5$) and made purely for aquatic applications.
(See photograph ref.13)

TOPICAL DRESSINGS.
(See photograph ref.14) A preparation made up from Masoten Liquid, Malachite Green and Terramycin Fish Formula.

HANDLING

From time to time we all have to handle our Koi for one reason or another, perhaps we have to make pond alterations, transport our Koi to a show or inspect them for parasites and so on. Providing this is done with care there will be no damage caused and the Koi will not suffer in any way, the experienced Koi keeper will be aware of this procedure but perhaps the novice will get benefit from this advice.

Correct netting procedures must be learned, a proper Koi net is only shallow and purpose-made for gently guiding a Koi into a container. It is NOT made for lifting a koi out of the water as is a landing net used by anglers. Anyone attempting to do this will most certainly cause scales and mucus to be taken off the body and perhaps cause bruising later. If a certain Koi has to be netted, take great care not to damage other stocks in the process of catching the one you need. Take your time and move the net slowly through the water taking care not to make sudden 'jabs' which will, most certainly, startle the Koi. Never attempt to catch a Koi from behind as it is swimming away from you. This can damage the tail fin as it senses the net touching it and flicks its tail in order to escape and catches it on the metal perimeter of the net support, unlike the actual net this does not 'give'. Always try to catch your Koi by getting your net under its head as it swims towards you. With practice you can guide it to a bowl or a handling net being held by another person, with a minimum of actual contact between the net and the Koi. If you are inexperienced in this procedure it is safer to have a friend to give you a helping hand.

Correct method of guiding Koi towards a handling net.

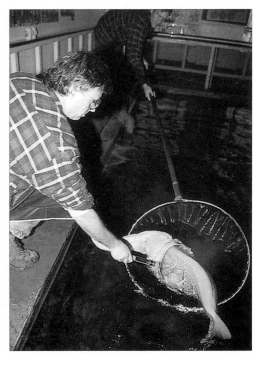

Gently placing handling net over head of Koi, as soon as this is commenced the Koi net is lowered away from the Koi to avoid any damage should the Koi struggle.

The Koi is lifted safely in the handling net, these nets are made from a very fine soft mesh to prevent loss of mucus on the body during lifting.

Correct method of sizing a Koi to ensure any damage is avoided.

The Koi is gently released into a purpose-made container for sizing.

If the Koi has to be guided into a bowl instead, a polythene bag can easily be placed over its head and the Koi and water can be carried in this way to where you need to take it. If it has to be anaesthetised then it is best to carry it from the bowl to the bowl holding anaesthetic mixture with a proper Koi handling net as shown above.

If Koi have to be transported for some distance, possibly to a show, then pure oxygen is vital; many enthusiasts have their own supply of oxygen and a regulating valve.

Adding oxygen to bag for transportation purposes.

You will notice that one bag is placed inside another to give extra strength, a small amount of salt and Elbagin should be added to the transportation water and the oxygen tube inserted. Before oxygen supply is turned on ensure that all air is first squeezed from the bag, add oxygen slowly until the bag is inflated, then seal each bag separately with a rubber band after twisting the neck of each bag several times and folding it over. The bag should then be placed inside a cardboard carton and sealed as Koi travel better in a dark environment. For transportation of Koi to a show, packing rates assuming a standard bag size similar to the above and allowing for a five hour time within the bag, should be as follows:-

Koi above 18" pack one per bag.

Koi above 15" and up to 18" pack two per bag.

Koi above 11" and up to 15" pack three per bag.

Koi above 8" and up to 11" pack five per bag.

Koi below 8" pack 8 per bag.

Try to ensure that larger female Koi have enough depth of water within the bag to give them enough buoyancy so that the vast majority of their own bodyweight does not rest on the base of the box throughout travel.

Transportation/Packing Tips.

When loading these cartons into your vehicle ensure that the heads and tails of the Koi are facing the sides of your vehicle to avoid damage if heavy braking takes place.

Some Koi, when handled for transportation will bleed profusely from the gills and blood is pumped into the transportation water when packing. This is in no way serious and similar to a nose bleed to a human, however, do not transport them in this water, instead re-pack in fresh water.

Some large Koi have a tiny 'hook' on their anal fins which can easily burst a plastic bag. It is always worthwhile to check this whilst the Koi is still in the bowl before packing, if this hook can be felt, it should be carefully clipped off with nail clippers and sterilised, before transportation.

When carrying a large Koi in a plastic bag, always carry the length of the bag in a horizontal position and never the other way as this could damage fins.

FEEDING OUR KOI.

Koi are omniverous and, given the opportunity, our Koi will eat just about anything that is edible. I have heard of Koi taking unusual items such as cornflakes, strawberries, potato crisps, rice pudding and bread and honey as well as many more commonly-used foods such as prawns, peas, bread, maggots, worms and vegetables.

The modern carp angler uses baits that contain just about every flavour imaginable in order to lure his quarry to take the hook. In natural ponds, carp feed on anything that is available, these range from insect life, freshwater shrimps, worms, their own fry and many forms of vegetable matter.

Water temperatures dictate the size of their appetite, in low water temperatures their appetite is low, whilst high water temperatures are accompanied with a voracious appetite. Thus real growth is always attained in warmer water temperatures during Summer months. It is said that growth rates on wild carp start when the water temperature exceeds 58 degrees Fahrenheit and the Japanese Koi breeders say that Nishikigoi only show good rates of growth start when water temperatures exceed 65 degrees Fahrenheit.

Much has been written and discussed as to what to feed, how much to feed, when to feed and to what temperature ranges to feed our Koi and heated arguments can always be produced when these questions are raised. Many advise not to feed below a certain temperature, others say to take care not to overfeed, others recommend special 'Winter' foods for Winter etc. etc. And every Koi food manufacturer will offer reams of 'evidence', scientific data and testimonials from satisfied customers as to why their food is the best that money can buy.

The newcomer to Koi keeping is faced here with a multitude of choices, recommendations, tips and hints that can only serve to confuse and frustrate. Make no mistake about it, the world-wide Koi food market today is a multi-million pound business and has significant potential to increase as more and more take up the hobby.

Make no mistake about it, the world-wide Koi food market today is a multi-million pound business and has significant potential to increase as more and more enthuisiasts take up the hobby

I have mentioned elsewhere in this book that Nishikigoi are not 'coldwater' fish in the truest sense of the word, they most certainly do not 'hibernate'. The ones seen huddled together in Winter, on the base of a pond, some laying on their sides, are NOT doing this out of choice. Instead they are very cold, very miserable and getting weaker by the day and, in my opinion, whether by ignorance or fixed belief of the keeper, this is a cruel way to keep Koi.

As also mentioned, the breeders of Japan whom we all must learn from, never allow their water temperatures to fall below 50 degrees Fahrenheit during the Winter months, many run at 55 degrees and over. No significant growth is made at these temperatures yet very little body weight is lost and the Koi need high Summer water temperatures to give good, healthy growth for the rest of the year.

Some other myths need to be explained here:-

1. ' DO NOT OVERFEED YOUR KOI'

This is printed on the packets of some Koi foods. It is absolutely impossible to 'over-feed' a Koi, as a Koi, and indeed any other ornamental fish, will only eat what and when it wishes to eat. However, it IS very easily possible to overfeed a pond - especially the ones advocated by the 'natural pond brigade', as, in these systems, un-eaten foods can become a major problem when decay occurs. Furthermore the Koi feeding heavily in these systems will produce more ammonias and nitrites which cannot be handled by the filtration stage and more problems occur. In my opinion this warning on the packet should be changed to 'DO NOT OVERFEED YOUR PONDS AND FILTERS'

2. 'DO NOT FEED AT WATER TEMPERATURES BELOW 50° F'

This is usually advice given by many to newcomers to the hobby. The reasons given are that, as metabolic rates slow down in cooler water temperatures, the period that the food takes to pass through the intestines and then to waste takes longer. This could result in the food decaying whilst still inside the Koi, resulting in internal problems. Whilst the basic premise that the metabolic rate does slow down is true, the rest of the state-ment is not. Koi know when they need food and, if they need food, it should be available to them at all water temper-atures, they can then choose whether they wish to take it or not. They also know their own digestive capabilities at all temperatures. If temperatures are so low that this could produce problems inter-nally, then the Koi, at these temperatures, have no desire and no intention what-soever to feed.

It is a simple matter to remove uneaten food

if necessary and many Koi feed quite readily at water temperatures right down to 45 degrees Fahrenheit and below in many cases, depending on the food chosen. In my opinion Koi should be given the opportunity to choose whether they wish to feed or not all year round.

Still on this subject there is no doubt that, when water temperatures are low, the amount of energy produced by the food is significantly reduced. In some instances of very cold water conditions, a Koi swimming from pond base to surface, taking a pellet and returning to the pond base some six feet below would have expended more energy than the pellet could replace. Again, my advice is not to let water temperatures go so low.

In my early visits to Japan I asked many breeders as to the best type of food to feed to Nishikigoi (not fry) and many different answers came back in the replies. However, excluding the following, no other types of feed were recommended.

1. Commercially-made Koi pellets.

2. Koi pellets made to the breeder's own recipe.

3. Lettuce and cabbage leaves (not Spinach).

4. Boiled barley.

5. Crushed toasted barley for small Koi after live foods exhausted.

6. Dried Silkworm Pupae.

7. Water snails crushed underfoot and fed, the Koi take the flesh and spit out the shells.

Several breeders use boiled barley together with Silkworm Pupae on a regular daily basis. The barley is well boiled and left to cool in a large container submerged in the water used during the boiling process. Silkworm pupae is added to the water to around 10% of the volume of barley and mixed well, this is allowed to cool overnight and the water removed the following morning after which the food can be fed. This food sinks to the bottom of the pond.

Dried Silkworm Pupae.

The boiled barley produces good volume together with good skin quality whilst the Silkworm Pupae aids colour enhancement to the red pigmentation. Silkworm Pupae are recommended to be soaked overnight as above or crushed before feeding and, because they are quite hard in texture, should only be used at water temperatures over 65° F. I use these myself as a Summer feed together with a pelletised food.

Lettuce is also an excellent Summer supplement which is very beneficial to the Koi. Koi not used to this food generally take a few days to be accustomed to taking it. It is best to throw a whole lettuce on the pond surface and leave it, initially this may take some days to take but once the Koi have tasted the food it is taken afterwards very readily.

By far the most used foods are floating pellets, many consider these to be 'boring' for the Koi but, in truth, a high class pellet contains everything necessary for every aspect of the diet of the Koi together with a very convenient way of storing and feeding. Should any be left un-eaten it can be removed quickly and easily by net. The actual recipes of a Koi pellet vary considerably in relationship to the desired retail price in respect of ingredients, quality of

ingredients and packaging/shipping costs.

As with most things in this life, one gets what one pays for. As far as high class Koi pellets are concerned the choice of ingredients and quality of them are extremely expensive in relationship to the recipes used in budget-priced versions.

In Japan, there has been years upon years of research into the best ingredients, vitamins and minerals to use for a Koi pellet that will develop a high class Koi to its best possible potential as far as volume, pigmentation and general health are concerned and, as a result, will increase the value of the Koi. Many famous Japanese breeders make their own pellets on a regular basis to their own recipes. Mr. Mano of the Dainichi Company uses a recipe which only contains main ingredients fit for human consumption and he tastes the mix every time before it is machined into pellets. His recipe contains, amongst other items, pure wheatgerm, fresh oysters, pure white fish meal, honey and spirulina for colour enhancement.

What brand of pellet to use, is a question often asked of me and I refuse to be drawn-in here to give a quick one-off single name as to the answer. Instead I will offer a selection of what I consider to be choices which range from good to excellent and prices vary accordingly. This means many will be left out, this is not intended to offend or criticise, by omission, in any way. Many may disagree with the selection here and will choose to stay with their regular brand, however I have experienced good to excellent results with the following brands, mentioned on the following page in alphabetical order:-

1. 'EXCEL'

2. 'HI-GROWTH'
(recommended for feeding in Summer
water temperatures)

3. 'LINA'

4. 'PROKOI'
(recommended for all-year-round
feeding)

5. 'TETRA' FOODS

6. 'SAKURA'
(recommended for all-year-round
feeding)

7. 'WHEATGERM'
(recommended for feeding in lower
water temperatures)

Nos. 1, 2, 3 & 7 are all made in Japan under the Kyorin Trademark and are shipped world-wide by Kamihata Fish Industries Ltd., No. 4 is produced in the UK by Prokoi Enterprises Ltd. and No. 6 is made in Japan and imported to the UK by Infiltration. No. 5, the Tetra' range of Koi foods is wide, varied and readily available at most outlets.

Perhaps the best way to put a food to the test is to give it a serious trial for some six months or so and then try another for a similar period. As mentioned earlier the choice here is endless and very confusing for the newcomer.

As far as how much food to feed is concerned, your Koi will tell you this is how quickly the amount is finished and if they are still looking for more. Try to feed in the morning and evening with an amount that takes about 10 to 15 minutes to be eaten, in high Summer a mid-day feed can be added.

*A famous Kohaku over 80cm. (31.5″) long,
the volume of this Koi is perfect; true 'jumbo'
shape together with excellent finish to the red
pattern make this a deserved Champion Koi.*

CYCLES

BOOK 6

'CYCLES'
The complex 'Art' of breeding and culling Nishikigoi in Japan is covered in this section of the book and as is a guide to breeding Nishikigoi for beginners on an amateur basis.

THE ART OF BREEDING NISHIKIGOI IN JAPAN.

Culling fry, Iwamagi, Spring '94

It must be said, that although there are many Nishikigoi breeders in many parts of Japan, breeding Nishikigoi is not an easy occupation. The modern day breeder has probably grown up with Nishikigoi and may have studied at a Fisheries University for some years after leaving high school. Today there are more items available with which the breeder can use to make the operation less labour intensive than in earlier times as is true with most modern day farming techniques. Nishikigoi breeding is farming in its truest sense. The parents are spawned in Spring and the fry harvested during October after several severe culls.

Still problems can and do occur especially with fry born in the Spring when many can be lost at 3" to 4" with 'sleeping sickness', a virus which only affects small Koi in their first year. This virus can affect whole mud ponds quite suddenly, one day the stocks are feeding as normal the next day all are 'hanging' vertically in the water motionless. There is no known reason as to why this occurs and the only known cure to date has been to add salt at 0.5ppm (5 kilos per ton) - not an easy task to carry out in an outdoor mud pond half way up a mountainside! During Spring 1989 I watched a breeder hiring tankers to transport sea water from the coast to deposit the water into one of his mud ponds containing 21 day old fry all suffering with this virus; fortunately this action saved 75% of the fry and no further problems arose.

Breeding Nishikigoi is, indeed an Art. This is reflected in the breeders from countries other than Japan who try to produce a similar quality to that of Japanese Koi with very little success, as their stocks improve so too do the Japanese stocks and the goal posts are moved once more.

When we refer to 'breeding' in the UK, we usually mean spawning. The meaning in Japan refers to one who grows the stocks, true some may have spawned their own parent stocks yet many others may purchase eggs, fry or larger stocks from other breeders to grow them in their own mud ponds for a Summer period. As mentioned earlier the mud ponds are all man-made, having been carved out of the mountainsides by excavator and the clay compacted by machine to give firm, smooth, snag-free bases to the ponds which allows for easy netting during culling and harvesting.

Sizes and depths of these mud ponds vary depending on the size of Koi to be grown in them, the ones used for growing fry seldom are more than 3 feet deep and many are half this depth. For two year stocks depths range from 3 feet to 4.5 feet deep whilst those for larger sizes can exceed 10 feet deep. Surface areas range from 600 square feet to 5 acres. In every instance stocking rates are extremely low in terms of fish to water volume, newly hatched fry are stocked between 8,000 to 15,000 per 100 tons (22,000 gallons) water, after around four culls between June to October the ones retained will be around 4" long by October. Koi born the previous year having been kept indoors from October to May and are around 5" long are placed into mud ponds usually at the rate of 10 per 100 tons (22,000 gallons) water. No culling will take place for the period these stocks are grown, and by October these Koi will be harvested at around 12" to 14" long.

All these mud ponds are emptied during the October harvest and contain no stocks between late October to late May, outdoor mud ponds are used only for the Summer growing period.

Nishikigoi mud ponds,
Araya, Niigata,
Spring 1992.

Low stocking rates for Koi born 12 months ago, placed in the mud pond in May at around 5" long, mud pond near Yomogihira, Spring 1994.

Larger four to seven year stocks are usually stocked at the rate of one Koi to between 200 tons to 500 tons each (44,000 gallons to 110,000 gallons) One must take into account that high Summer water temperatures can reach 90°F for over five weeks within these mud ponds when dissolved oxygen levels can become a serious problem if stocking rates are too high. During this period aeration is added by air compressors wired into nearby electrical supplies, in other cases portable generators have to be employed where mains electricity is not available.

In just about every instance, the breeder has to protect his ponds from Herons and Shrikes which are numerous in these areas. One can see nylon strings criss-crossed over all the ponds once stocks have been introduced, thankfully theft from human sources has yet not been a problem to date. Margins to each mud pond are meticulously kept free from weeds and vegetation is regularly cropped in order to allow for easy access and to deter snakes such as the deadly Mamushi from resting here.

Mud pond in Aikawa for fry born 1 month previously, note nylon strings and 'scarecrow' to deter predators, electrically powered aeration machine in operation. Photo taken June 1994.

Keeping pond sides free from weeds

Mud ponds are either owned or rented by the breeder and, with the exception of those used to grow this years fry, they are only used to grow tategoi and larger Koi with a real value. The water space in these ponds is never wasted on general grade stocks with no further potential to increase in value, and these stocks are sold in Spring well before parent stocks are spawned.

Before going into detail of the actual breeding techniques used, the Japanese Nishikigoi producer who is constantly striving to better his production is always faced with three major problems that many outside of Japan seldom take into account.

1. The location and purchase of good parent stocks.

Without exception the parent stocks used by any breeder are those of the highest quality and in many cases from the best bloodlines. Often the original purchase prices are fantastic as the vendor also can estimate the potential value of the fry which will be produced. Some, since original purchase, may have been used for many years with good results, others may be recently purchased and quality of fry yet to be discovered. As the breeder only has a certain number of mud ponds in which to grow his fry each year, he must be very selective in his choice of parents as any mistakes will produce stocks that are not worth growing and this cannot be rectified until the following year when a different choice can be made. The wrong choice of parent stocks results in a very expensive wasted year of fry production for one mud pond. Many breeders today are faced with the problem of locating new parents as their own stocks are getting too old. Many parent stocks, whilst mainly looking large, dull, totally unattractive and in many cases deformed with sheer age, still manage to produce the best stocks of fry. Replacing these when necessary is a major problem. Obviously a breeder will never sell any **good** tried and tested parent stocks as these are so difficult to find. To use anything other than very high class parent stocks for a Japanese breeder is a total waste of time and effort as the very few numbers of saleable Koi produced would not even cover the expenses involved to produce them.

2. How to make the correct pairings?

Assuming good potential stocks are located and purchased as new parents, the breeder is now faced with the problem of which male to use with which female to produce the best fry. If this can be determined at the first spawning then making the pairings next year will be far easier (this point is discussed in greater detail later in this section).

3. How to cull?

With existing parent stocks this is no problem to the breeder as he knows exactly how fry from his regular parent stocks develop and can cull accordingly. With new parent stocks, however, this poses a real dilemma. Stocking rates of fry in a mud pond have to be reduced by up to 80% after each monthly cull or the stocking levels will become far too high. Thus the decision as to which Koi to keep and which to throw away, from parent stocks the breeder has no experience of, renders the cull almost guesswork for the first spawning.

The Breeding Operation from Preparation to Completion

MARCH/APRIL.

The Spring thaw occurs, snow water is siphoned from the mud ponds and these are allowed to dry in the sun. After two weeks or so the pond floor is rotavated and lime is added to exterminate any parasites which are still in the mud.

The lime is also useful to increase the pH value of the source mountain stream water which is only between 5.5 to 6.0 at this time of the year and will be used to fill the mud ponds prior to the actual spawning.

Soon afterwards the breeder adds phosphates and minerals to the pond base. Indoor concrete spawning ponds and filtration will be cleaned out thoroughly and then re-filled. Parent stocks (Oya-goi) are selected and separated, males in one pond, females in another.

Mud ponds for fry can now be filled with stream water and very soon the lime content, together with the phosphates and minerals takes the pH value up to between 9.0 and 11.0, and the algae produced turns the water green very quickly. In ten days prior to the planned date for the spawning, chicken manure is added at the rate of 100 to 150 kilos per 1,000 tons (220,000 gallons) of pond water. This produces masses of infusoria within ten days or so, a vital starter food for the fry. Newly hatched fry need conditions where masses of live food are available in abundance from day one, and an environment where food is taken in whenever they open their mouths.

MAY.

During late May the indoor concrete pond is prepared for the spawning pond as follows:-

A purpose made 3 metre x 2 metre x 1 metre deep spawning net is suspended in the spawning pond. This has a dual purpose, it protects the Koi from damaging themselves during the very frenzied spawning activity and also retains all eggs within the net.

A plastic framework is constructed to sit at the bottom of the spawning net. Soft artificial spawning grass (kin-ran) is tied to this at close intervals to give a carpet of grass to the base of the pond in order to induce spawning and to catch the eggs as they are laid and fertilised. The spawning pond is well aerated and contains crystal clear water.

JUNE.

In early June the actual spawning operation is prepared for as follows:-

Note extra spawning grass suspended on pond surface.

Parent Koi are then introduced to the spawning pond. In Japan it is seldom that females under five years old (over 24″) and male parents under four years (over 21″) are used. This is because experience has proven that females under five years old seldom carry enough eggs to make a professional spawning worthwhile whilst males under 4 years old seldom produce enough milt to fertilise all the eggs in a natural spawning.

In a natural spawning method as illustrated here the parent stocks generally are made up from one female to three males. Accurate sexing of parent stocks is covered later in this section of the book, and it should be noted that all parents are bred by variety and bloodline. In this instance these parents are all Sanke from Jinbei bloodline. In a very rare instance I saw a Shusui female used with a Shusui male and a Doitsu Purachina male in order to produce a standard blue coloration as well as a light blue coloration in the offspring. A marked difference was apparent in the fry fathered by the Purachina male when I saw them some six months later as they gave the impression of

Kumonryu as opposed to Shusui. In every case when I have seen Koi being spawned in Japan, a photographic record is always kept of each set of parents used and the date of the spawning marked on the photograph accordingly. In this way there is no confusion the following year if changes need to be made at all.

At water temperatures around 65 degrees Fahrenheit the parents will take one to two days to commence spawning after being placed in the spawning pond. This usually commences around 2.00 am. and takes between 5 and 9 hours to complete.

Note:- In countries outside of Japan, Koi are spawned 'to order' by using a hormone injection of pituitary extract the day prior to spawning. I have asked Japanese breeders many times as to their feelings regarding this method which is widely used in Japan for the production of food fishes. To date all answers have been the same; namely it is fine for food fishes where parent stocks are cheap, disposable and readily available, but for high class Koi it is both risky and not necessary as the breeders can produce as many eggs as they can cope with by natural methods during Spring. The rest of their year is completely taken up in caring for their stocks. They further state that this injection can produce weak strains of fry and also damage parent stocks irreparably.

To continue the subject mentioned earlier in this section- How to make the correct pairings? Several Japanese breeders use an alternative method of spawning especially if they wish to determine which male produces the best quality fry with a given female. This method is carried out exactly in the same way as the natural method illustrated here where three males are placed into a spawning pond with one female. The breeder then waits throughout the night near to the spawning pond until the first eggs are dropped by the female and spawning has commenced. The female is then carefully removed from the pond and anaesthetised, once fully anaesthetised she is gently lifted from the anaesthetic and her belly cradled in an horizontal position by the breeders hands. Immediately her entire body weight is transferred to the belly, all her eggs are naturally released into a stainless steel bowl held under her vent area. These eggs are divided equally by weight to three smaller stainless steel bowls. At this point each male is anaesthetised and milt taken from the vent area by pipette. Each milt sample is mixed with 150mls. of Ringers solution and the solution from each individual male is mixed with one third of the eggs to fertilise them by gentle mixing with a soft brush. Each stainless steel bowl of fertilised eggs carries the photograph of the male responsible for fertilising the eggs. Each bowl of eggs is transferred by large pipette and deposited carefully onto spawning grass in three separate hatching ponds by hand. The photograph of the male responsible for fertilising the eggs within each pond is attached to the hatching pond. When the fry are transferred to separate mud ponds for growing the male used for each pond is noted. During culling it can be seen which male is to be used with the same female next year by checking the pond with the best selection of fry during culling.

Once the spawning is over, parent stocks are removed, before they commence to eat their eggs, and are transferred to outdoor mud ponds for the Summer. The spawning pond containing the eggs is then treated with a mild solution of Malachite Green or Methylene Blue to prevent any fungal infection attacking the eggs, aeration is maintained at all times. A mature female can produce between 120,000 to 200,000 eggs.

Depending on temperature, the eggs will take between three and five days to hatch, prior to hatching eyes can be seen quite clearly.

Koi eggs on spawning grass.

Koi eggs at point of hatching.

Upon hatching the fry can be seen resembling fine slivers of glass hanging vertically to the sides of the net or the fronds of the spawning grass. They remain like this for approximately one day digesting their yolk sac and, at the same time, inflating their swim bladder. Once the swim bladder is inflated the body adopts the normal horizontal position, the fry become free swimming and in desperate need for food. Actual size at this stage is 7mm., colour is yellow.

The fry are now transferred carefully by oxygenated polythene bag to be floated on the mud pond until temperatures are equal when they can be released and 180,000 hungry fry immediately start to feed on millions of infusoria within the pond.

In late June when the stocks are almost three weeks old the mud pond is very carefully harvested and the first cull takes place. Great care has to be taken at this time as fry can easily be damaged with harsh handling. All stocks showing any pattern at all are retained and the rest destroyed, generally around 80% are destroyed at the first cull and 20% returned to the pond. Actual size at this stage is around 12mm.

JULY.

In late July the second cull takes place when a further 50% will be destroyed at this stage. By now all the infusoria and most of the daphnia has been eaten by the fry and supplementary feeding by powdered fry food is commenced. This is suspended in baskets around the perimeter of the pond. Actual size of the fry at this stage is 25mm.

*As there is no natural food whatsoever in these ponds, the breeder feeds his stocks
twice daily, usually at 6.30am. and 3.30pm. Mr. Hiroi ('Choguro') June 1994,
feeding fry born one month previously, with a top-up of Urea
to further stimulate infusoria / daphnia.*

AUGUST.

In late August the third cull is made when a further 40% are destroyed leaving some 10,800 baby Koi around 50mm. long to grow, feeding is now by small pellet twice daily.

SEPTEMBER.

No cull is carried out during September.

OCTOBER.

During mid October the mud pond is harvested, by now the Koi are 10cms. (4") long. 30% are destroyed, and 3,000 are selected for keeping over Winter in an indoor heated pond and the remainder disposed of via a broker or via local auctions at very low prices. By the following May a further 2,300 will be sold and the remaining 700 tategoi will be grown throughout the Summer to reach 14" by October.

To summarise the result from this single spawning, (and many breeders carry out 8 to 10 separate spawnings) from a total of 180,000 eggs produced in this instance, only 7,500 are saleable and 6,800 of these are sold at very low prices, the remaining 700 tategoi are where the breeder must find his profit from. Let us assume that this particular breeder has used 10 sets of parent Koi in Spring, then he will now have some 7,000 tategoi.

Prices are generally calculated on the premise that every egg costs the breeder 1 yen to produce. This covers cost of parent stocks, labour, food, equipment and rental of mud ponds etc. In this case the breeder has produced 1,800,000 eggs, the best Koi produced by the end of the second year will be priced at 1,800,000 yen. The best Koi produced in 100,000 will be priced at 100,000 yen and so on.

The breeder must realise the high prices for the few best Koi produced and, in view of this, **there is not a single chance that any Koi sold at a cheap price will become valuable in future years.**

In the early 1960's this was possible and, on one occasion, an enthusiast purchased a 'job lot' of 50 five inch Kohaku for 500 yen each (then around 50p) In later years one of these became Supreme Champion at the All-Japan Show. Once again, there is not a single possibility of that happening today and a 5" tategoi of high potential is always very expensive. Many of these expensive rarities are often readily purchased by other breeders who are also very aware of the potential. In fact it is said that over 60% of the 'wealth of Nishikigoi' is retained within the breeding community when breeders buy from, and sell to, other breeders. A popular misconception is that tategoi are small Koi only, this is not true and there are good tategoi over 85cms. long and in all other sizes. In small sizes, good tategoi are generally not at all attractive, colours are drab, patterns almost non-existant and prices very high. However, these are usually the Koi chosen by the Japanese enthusiast to bring to maturity and perfection by his/her own keeping techniques.

BREEDING NISHIKIGOI IN THE UK

I first bred my own stocks during 1974 by using similar but far less sophisticated methods as described earlier, many eggs were produced and a large proportion hatched. The parents used were Sanke and Bekko and these varieties were predominant in the fry produced. The fry hatched in early July and I soon realised that my water space was totally inadequate. I bought, begged, borrowed and stole various assorted containers that would hold water and added aeration to all before adding the fry. By then my back garden resembled a very low class water garden centre which was having serious financial problems! From the moment the fry were put into these containers my work started for seven days a week until late September, every day was the same namely:-

6.30am. Take covers off all containers and carefully siphon out all debris plus 25% water. Top up all containers with water from a reservoir tank and trickle water from mains back to reservoir tank to slowly fill up by same evening.

7.15am. Go to local natural ponds with polythene bags and rubber bands and nets. Catch as much daphnia and infusoria as possible. Return home and divide into each container.

8.00am. Go to work.

6.00pm. Leave work and go to local ponds as per 7.15am.

8.00pm. Arrive back home and siphon out containers as per 6.30am., divide daphnia into each container, top up each container, cover each container.

9.30pm. Sandwich and bed.

As I worked six days a week, Sundays could be spent relaxing so I did the above as usual. The rest of the day could be idled away by removing all the 'tobi' (cannibal Koi) who were hell bent on decimating my stocks, checking for any deformed stocks and finding space to put more paddling pools on my now destroyed lawn area.

After one month of this experience of being a Koi breeder, my local ponds totally refused to hand over any further daphnia. My Koi were getting both larger and hungrier by the day and crushed pellets, powdered egg yolk and finely ground beef heart became the menu for the following weeks.

By early September my garden had ceased to exist. The pipework and hoses and containers had taken over, rather like a mini sewage treatment plant. My Koi were fine, all 3,000 of them. My wife and tiny daughter had long since refused to acknowledge my existence and when words were forthcoming the only subject that was mentioned was that of psychiatric aid. It takes much more than these minor setbacks to deter a serious Koi breeder however!

The weather started to become colder and my Koi became noticeably miserable. Not to worry, in my oodles of spare time a pond had been built in the attic of a – wait for it – Fish and Chip Shop some 25 miles away. Access was not a strong point of this pond, this being gained by a wooden ladder. On the good side though it did hold 3,000 gallons of water including the revolutionary new 'undergravel' filtration system. On the bad side however, the lining of the pond leaked on first filling which was only really noticeable when the water, after tracking down two stories of the house decided to exit directly above the main frying range in the Fish and Chip Shop below. The fire that ensued became very famous in the surr-ounding area and a topic of much discussion for many months afterwards. The only other setback, once the liner was repaired, was that of the floor of the attic itself. The timbers started to groan more noticeably as each passing day went by, the plaster on the bedroom ceiling below the pond started to display more and more cracks and tempers were becoming frayed. I offered my opinion that this minor discomfort was a small price to pay for the well-being of 3,000 happy Koi, but the owner of the house refused to share my opinion. As a result, the water level had to be dropped and the volume reduced to 1,800 gallons of water. Immediately the tim-bers ceased to groan and the bedroom ceiling could be repaired and re-plastered with a minimum of fuss. Within seven weeks the owners of the Fish and Chip Shop even spoke to me on one of my visits to change water, feed the Koi and pay the electricity costs for heating and running the system. As I recall the words were – "Here is the Invoice for repairs to the bedroom ceiling."

Still the Koi were very happy and many were over 6" long by now. More to the point many of them were new, rare varieties that had not even been covered in 'Koi of the World', – mainly black in colour with the odd random red or white scale here and there. Some were all white with red and yellow fins, others were all orange with white fins, rarities indeed!

Meanwhile back home, after the containers had been removed as per my wife's request. To be specific it was – "I don't want to see any of this junk ever, ever again!" and, after a new lawn had been laid, garden walls repaired, new trees planted and patios steam-cleaned, our garden was back to normal again. By Christmas that year, after endless new clothes and other gifts, my wife finally started to make food and drinks for me again. My daughter appeared to recog-nise me once more and all was back to wedded bliss, a Koi breeder and his family!

In January and February, the following year, back at the Fish and Chip pond, the odd problem arose. The Koi were growing quite well with pelletised foods when the pump suddenly stopped working. Ammonia levels went off the scale and around 1,600 of my best and rarest tategoi perished, mainly as a result of jumping out of the pond! A new pump was installed, water changes made and the system re-started taking around three weeks to mature and a further 300 Koi lost. I offered the freshly lost ones at a greatly reduced rate to the owner of the Fish and Chip shop, the answer received is diffi-cult and illegal to translate.

By March that year it became clear that my tategoi were no longer welcome anywhere near the vicinity of the Fish and Chip shop. The famous pond had to be dismantled and the Koi had to be re-housed. I prepared, sec-retly, a pond in my garage to house them for a few weeks until they could go outdoors when water temperatures were acceptable. Alas! my secrecy was not quite secret en-ough and, once again, food and drinks were no longer forthcoming.

In July of that year my stocks had fallen to around 750 Koi ranging from 7" to 8" long, **each and every specimen a totally new and incredibly rare variety.** At a forthcoming local Koi show, I decided to take a stand space and unleash them to a Koi-hungry public for sale. My expectations were high, a container was found in which to display them, and final preparations made.

On opening for business, customer reaction was mixed to say the least, questions ranged from "What are they?" through to "I thought it was only Koi that could be sold here" right to "We catch these on maggot in our local pond" (the last one hurt!) Obviously these rude persons hadn't the vaguest idea what rare and unique specimens were displayed there before them. Nor had they the slightest knowledge of the skill, patience, and under-standing that a Koi breeder has to attain before Koi of this class can be produced.

By the end of the day all my tategoi were sold, admittedly only for between £2.50 to £4.00 each, the ones reaching dizzy prices of £4.00 were for a few only that were my finest stocks! I returned home late that night clutching my loot, in total it added up to around £1,900.00, a significant amount of money in 1975. My wife brought me a sandwich, a drink of tea and she smartly relieved me of £200.00 in return.

I then decided to get pen and paper to see how financially viable it was to become a full time professional Koi breeder, bearing in mind that I now had experience under my belt. The figures came out as follows:-

---

YEAR-END ACCOUNTS 1974/5, P. WADDINGTON, NISHIKIGOI BREEDER.

Income:-
Total Sales 1,900.00

Expenditure:-
1. Capital costs. a. Containers/aeration/airstones for garden ponds (now destroyed)
   b. Costs to build Fish and Chip pond and filter (now destroyed)
   c. Costs to build garage pond (now destroyed)
   1. Total 925.00

2. Running costs. a. Electricity costs garden ponds/garage pond.
   b. Electricity/water costs Fish and Chip pond.
   c. Petrol costs to collect daphnia etc.
   d. Feeding costs pellets etc.
   2. Total 955.00

3. Stand/advertising costs, show 35.00

4. Sundries. a. Roof repairs 75.00
   b. Garden renovations 550.00
   c. Clothes/trinkets to wife 400.00
   d. % Show receipts to wife/daughter 200.00
   Total Expenditure 3,140.00

PROFIT/LOSS FOR PERIOD . . . .(£1,240.00)

REPORT re-above:- This is a very encouraging first year for this new venture which only saw a £1,240.00 loss on a £1,900.00 turnover. Mr. Waddington has decided not to claim token labour charges of a modest £1.00/hour but feels it should be recorded should profits for next year take a turn for the better. In all, hours worked to produce the stocks totalled 1,200 plus wear and tear on himself, wear and tear on a vehicle and a pending divorce action.

I hope the reader does not mind my light hearted attempt to add humour to my first and last serious attempt to produce Koi. To qualify this it was very useful as I did learn many valuable lessons in keeping water and seeing how fry develop into Koi. I would not recommend that any inexperienced amateur even considers the task of seriously breeding Koi in the UK if the facilities are as totally makeshift as were mine. My reasons for this conclusion are as follows:-

■ UK water temperatures even in a good Spring and Summer seldom reach 63 degrees Fahrenheit until early July. Assuming a spawning date at the end of the first week of July brings the free swimming stage to around the end of the second week of July when feeding can commence. Fry grown indoors seldom show any pattern or pigmentation as compared with those grown in natural light, it is vital to grow fry outdoors so that regular culling can be carried out before water space runs out.

Kohaku bred by Maruyama, Isawa, Yamanashi.

■ Assuming that water temperatures will drop at the beginning of October, this only gives a maximum of ten weeks feeding time before stocks will have to be housed elsewhere in warmer water conditions. Also if we assume that, during this period, the average water temperature would be around 63 degrees Fahrenheit and compare the situation outlined earlier for Japanese mud ponds where growing time is around sixteen weeks with an average water temperature of 78 degrees Fahrenheit then there is hardly a chance to produce any significant growth rate during this period in the UK.

■ Whilst powdered foods and products such as Liquifry can be used from hatching, these tend to pollute highly stocked ponds very quickly indeed and all fry can be totally lost once even a mild ammonia reading is produced. In view of this, enormous supplies of live foods such as infusoria, daphnia and/or artemia are vital, these quantities are not easy to obtain and maintain.

■ The workload is colossal and just one day of no attention for whatever reason can result in a total loss of stocks. Remember, you could be faced with a minimum hatch of some 20,000 fry.

■ Potential damage to parent stocks during the spawning on an amateur basis must be taken into account.

■ Even by using good grade Japanese parents, the chances of even producing a handful of general grade Koi is remote.

■ Assuming one has reasonable success in producing say 10,000 two inch Koi by early October, where can they be housed for Winter?

There are many other reasons for which I would try to dissuade the reader not to attempt an actual spawning of parent Koi on an amateur basis but for those who wish to learn more about how fry develop into Koi I would recommend that eggs are obtained in a more manageable quantity and these are grown in more manageable conditions. Some UK dealers and breeders have eggs available usually during June/July, many enthusiasts experience 'flock-spawnings' within their ponds from time to time and some eggs can be obtained from these sources.

If you are determined to grow Koi from eggs, I would recommend the following methods:-

1. Find an area in your garden where a cheap temporary pond can be set up for the Summer season, an area of 10 feet by 6 feet is ample.

2. Form a pond perimeter with old timbers or dry laid blockwork to a depth of 15", inside this place half inch deep sheets of polystyrene to the base and walls.

3. Waterproof the area with a double skin of cheap builders polythene and fill to a depth of 12" with tapwater, try to smooth out creases as much as possible.

4. Make an insulated framework with a clear polythene cover to place over the pond every night to protect against temperature fluctuations.

5. Add gentle aeration from an air pump. Approximately 10 days before your eggs are expected to arrive add a beaker full of chicken manure to the pond, find local supplies of good daphnia or culture your own supplies of artemia (brine shrimp).

6. The eggs should arrive on spawning grass, conifer branches or similar material within a polythene bag. Float the bag on your pond and observe temperature equalisation before emptying the entire contents into your pond.

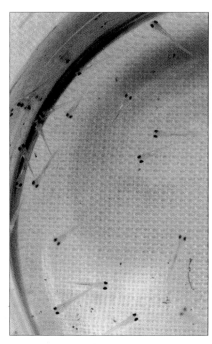

7. It is now a waiting game for the eggs to hatch and this is purely governed by water temperature, look very closely every day for newly hatched fry clinging vertically to the pond walls, a magnifying glass may be necessary as Koi fry are considerably smaller than goldfish fry. Once these have been observed, prepare live food for the next day onwards.

8. The following day the fry should be free-swimming horizontally and feeding on minute infusoria with quick, darting movements. A good initial stocking for this volume of water would be approximately 1,000 fry.

9. Daily maintenance from now on should be tests for pH; nitrite and ammonia plus the careful siphon removal of debris and a daily change of water of between 10% to 15%. It is wiser to use mature water rather than mains water, and, at the same time to ensure that ample food is available.

10. Once the fry begin to grow, look out for the larger fry and remove them as these are almost certainly eating the others, any with deformities should be destroyed. Once the fry reach around 2" long it would be wise to start using dried foods such as good quality crushed Koi pellets with good colour enhancer additives.

After this it is down to your feeding techniques, water management, waste management and temperature control, good luck!

Finally, on this section of the book, if you are determined to spawn your own stocks it is vital that parent stocks are chosen and sexed correctly and that the males are producing milt prior to introducing them to the spawning pond. During mid-June onwards I would suggest you check your potential parents as follows:-

1. Female Parent Koi.

Try to find a single large female to breed with, preferably over 21" in length. A female shape is far more rounded than the male, the pectoral fins on a female Koi are shorter and more rounded in comparison to those of a male. At this time of the year, a female Koi should be full of eggs and plumper than normal. By gently placing her into a bowl and placing your hands underneath the belly and ventral area and along the flanks of the Koi, the flesh should be very soft and spongy to the touch.

2. Male Parent Koi.

The male shape is longer, slimmer and the flesh firmer than the female, the pectoral fins are longer and more pointed at the tips than those of a female. During Spring and early Summer a good test of a male Koi is to place it carefully in a bowl and gently run your fingers along the gill plates. Male Koi produce many small rough, sandpaper-like projections in these areas which are easily detectable by touch. If this is apparent then the Koi is most certainly male. Once this has been determined the next step is to ensure milt is being produced, this can be checked by anaesthetising the Koi and turning the belly upwards. By gentle pressure to both sides of the vent area with thumb and forefinger, a white liquid should appear which confirms that milt is available to fertilise the eggs of the female. Any males not producing this should not be selected for the spawning. Assuming a female Koi like the one mentioned above is being used, I would suggest two to three males at around 18" long are used to fertilise the eggs.

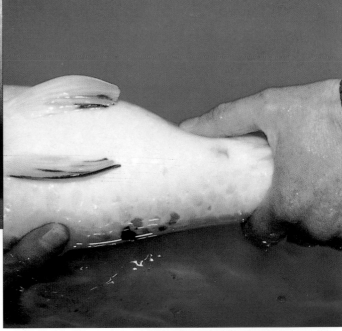

(Above) Male ventral area showing milt.

(Right) Female ventral area, soft, flabby belly containing many eggs.

Other useful tips prior to placing parent stocks into the spawning pond in order to ensure a spawning within one to two days.

■ The parent stocks selected should be kept in separate ponds, males in one and female in another, away from other stocks for at least 10 days prior to putting them together to spawn.

■ Do not feed the parents during this period.

■ Ensure the spawning pond has ample spawning media inside and gentle aeration together with crystal clear water and a water temperature in excess of 65 degrees Fahrenheit.

■ Place the parent stocks into the spawning pond during early afternoon and try to have a temperature differential of 5 degrees Fahrenheit from that of the ponds holding the parents, the sudden temperature change, which does not harm the Koi, acts as a 'trigger' which starts the actual spawning usually the next morning or the morning after.

For those who do not wish their Koi to spawn in their ponds, and I must agree with this, there are several more situations that can 'trigger' a spawning especially in 60° F to 65° F water temperatures during spring.

■ Adding new stocks can 'trigger' a spawning.

■ Air pressure variations especially in thunderstorms can 'trigger' a spawning.

■ Heavy water changes can 'trigger' a spawning.

■ Sudden variations in water qualities can 'trigger' a spawning.

If a flock spawning occurs that is not welcomed, the only real way to end this is to separate the male Koi driving the females until their ardour has calmed!

*I was fortunate to see this Sanke when she won
Supreme Champion award at the 1993 ZNA Show
held in Tokyo, she is 80cm. (31.5") long
and the volume is incredible.*

PEOPLE

BOOK 7

'PEOPLE'

I have tried to include, in this book, a cross section of some of the breeders and a Nishikigoi historian who have continued to amaze me constantly over the years with their knowledge, expertise and total commitment to their endeavours. I feel it's about time that someone gave them the limelight they justly deserve in writing, other than in Japanese. Like the Nishikigoi they produce, no two personalities are the same. There are many others I would have liked to include but time, space and other thieves have not allowed me to do so. One such person is pictured over, Mr. Miya, The Miyatora Company, Araya, Niigata, - famous for Kichinai Sanke.

PROFILES FROM JAPAN

1. Mr. Toshio Sakai, Isawa Nishikigoi Centre, Isawa, Yamanashi Prefecture.

Mr. Toshio Sakai.

I, personally have learned more about Nishikigoi in general from this man than from any other individual. His elder brother owns the Yamamatsu Company in Mushigame, Niigata. My teacher, however, breeds his stocks in Isawa, Yamanashi Prefecture. Both brothers were raised in Mushigame and were taught by their late father who was responsible for developing and stabilising the Matsunosuke bloodline of Sanke and also for producing the first Yamabuki and Aigoromo as well as playing an important part in the development of Shusui.

Today the Matsunosuke Sanke bloodline is world famous, the trademarks being the brilliant 'Hi' texture and pigmentation together with a striking 'jet-black' Sumi pigmentation. The two brothers assist each other with culling and harvesting even though their businesses are over 200 miles apart.

Isawa is a major wine producing area and has several Nishikigoi breeders nearby to Mr. Sakai, notably Mr. Gamo, Mr. Maruyama and Mr. Sakuma. It has a very mild winter climate, a very warm summer period and an endless supply of warm mineral spring water which seldom falls below 62°f. (17°c) at the coldest time of the year.

Mr. Sakai's Koi are rarely cheap and, in some cases, are very expensive but, in my experience, always represent good value for money. He has many breeding ponds in and around Isawa and approximately a further 90 in Shizuoka which are used to grow fry from 30 sets of parents throughout Spring to Autumn. In most instances his best Tategoi are taken to Niigata to be grown in huge mud ponds during the Summer months and, as he points out, to 'tame' the red pigment more to Japanese tastes! The intense pigmentation on his more regular grade stocks find ready volume markets overseas.

Mr. Sakai is a very restless personality, he is never happy with second best and is determined to produce the very first 1 metre Go-Sanke. He has large stocks of 'secret' tategoi which will be offered for sale when they are ready. He never allows his staff to cull his fry and personally culls around 7,500,000 fry each Summer.

His parent stocks produce Sanke, Showa, Gin-Rin Showa, Kohaku, Sumi-goromo, Goshiki and some Kujaku; his brother in Niigata produces Sanke and Kohaku only.

His large retail facility in Isawa is always full of Koi even at times when most other dealers have few stocks for sale, the main reason for this is that Isawa is a very popular tourist area for the Japanese and has many high class hotels. The majority of these hotels have superb Koi ponds as features within their magnificent landscaped gardens; Mr. Sakai designs and installs the filtration systems and 'rents' his Koi stocks on a monthly basis. The hotel guests feed and grow the Koi which come to thousands in total and, if his retail stocks are short at any time he only has to collect a selection of his rented stocks at the nearby hotels.

On a serious note, Matsunosuke is one of the most famous and respected names for high grade Nishikigoi, ranking alongside Dainichi and Hiroshima Sakai. At the All Japan Show held in Tokyo in January 1994, a Matsunosuke Sanke bred in Isawa in 1976 and grown for her first few years next to Mr. Sakai's retail premises took Supreme Champion at the most prestigious event on the world's Koi calendar.

Matsunosuke Sanke, Supreme Champion, All Japan Show 1994.

A glance at the cover of the 'Nishikigoi' book shows that another Matsunosuke Sanke took the Supreme Champion Award again in 1995, perhaps he is trying for the hat trick next year!

On many occasions I have been at the Matsunosuke premises in Mushigame when the brothers have collected their best stocks from the mud ponds during mid October and placed them on display. The modest home served by a narrow road, is almost blocked solid with

Rolls-Royce, Mercedes-Benz and BMW cars complete with chauffeurs bringing the wealthy Japanese collectors to view the harvest.

During many visits to Isawa, Mr. Sakai has spent hours teaching me the finer points of skin quality, texture of pigmentation and Jumbo potential in Koi as well as giving me valuable information on filtration and medication techniques. Between us we only speak in 'Koi Language', on one occasion in 1987, he showed me a Kohaku about 24" (60cms.) and told me I MUST buy it! The price was high and I pointed out that the skin was very yellow, he explained that the Koi had just been harvested from his mud pond nearby and should be kept in a filtered concrete pond in order to 'finish' the pigmentation and the white ground. I purchased the Koi, a little reluctantly, and kept her in an outdoor filtered concrete pond for some six months. The Koi was then entered at the All-England Nishikigoi Dealers Show "Nishikigoi '89" – she was awarded Supreme Champion, and the white skin gleamed!

For me, however, the Matsunosuke Sanke is the most fascinating of his stocks to observe as they develop from year to year. The way the sumi pattern changes and then stabilises is quite unique; in many instances it is difficult to accept that a Koi photographed at three years old is the same Koi at seven years old, so different is the overall pattern.

2. Mr. Minoru Mano,
   The Dainichi Company, Iwamagi, Niigata.

There is an aura of awe and mystique that surrounds the name of 'Dainichi' to Koi enthusiasts the world over. Quite simply, most Japanese breeders, enthusiasts and dealers admit that this man produces the best Kohaku in the world!

Mr. Mano is fairly unique in that he produces his Koi with no previous generations of family experience to fall back on. His father died when Mr. Mano was quite young and he has been born and raised in Iwamagi where his home and business are situated – a shrine which still stands next to his home bore the name Dainichi and thus the name for his business came about.

I asked Mr. Mano how he found the experience to produce so many famous Nishi-kigoi, he explained that, in the early days, he made many errors. He first attempted to produce Yamabuki but his close neighbour Mr. Mano of Isumiya advised him that the grade of his fry was very poor indeed.

He then began to visit other breeders and dealers in the area and asked them the type of Koi he could sell to them – many needed Kohaku with creamy white skin and a constant red texture plus a potential to reach true Jumbo proportions, still retaining the same qualities and youthful appearance. After 20 years of trial and error in using both traditional and modern breeding techniques he began to be well on the way to his goal.

He is, understandably, quite reluctant to disclose details of the original parent stocks that were used to produce the Dainichi Kohaku bloodline, but confirmed that these did have some Tomoin bloodline in them. He further mentioned that his very best female breeder

was found from some of his stocks during a trial breeding. It had been grown and offered for sale but no-one purchased her – he was most relieved that he had not sold her!

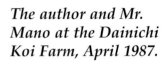

The author and Mr. Mano at the Dainichi Koi Farm, April 1987.

Mr. Mano told me that he breeds around 10 sets of parent Koi each year using Kohaku, Sanke and Showa only, he grows his stocks during the Summer months in 10 very large mud ponds for his large size Koi, around 20 medium sized mud ponds to grow his two and three year stocks and many small ponds to grow his fry for monthly culling.

To highlight the self confidence of 'The Master', Mr. Mano was shown on Japanese network television some years ago 'testing' the water quality in his mud ponds prior to introducing valuable Koi stocks for the Summer growing period. No high-tech water test kits were produced, he simply waded to the centre of the pond clad only in shorts and cupped a water sample in both hands before proceeding to 'test' it in his mouth! A few gargles later he must have determined pH, Nitrate, Ammonia, Nitrite and Dissolved Oxygen contents in this way, - it must have been satisfactory as the Koi were introduced soon afterwards!

At the time of this interview, his largest Koi produced was Kohaku of 90cms., his ambitions for the future was 'to strive for perfection' as well as to breed a Showa which would take Supreme Champion at the All-Japan Show to make the final complement to his Kohaku and Sanke who had already taken this award.

3. Mr. Satoru Hoshino, Ojiya City, Niigata.

I first met Mr. Hoshino during June 1989, I had been looking for an artist who could provide me with paintings of varieties and patterns for this book, he volunteered to do the work after I saw samples of his paintings. When I collected the finished paintings some four months later he said it had taken him almost every single evening in his spare time since June to complete the collection.

Mr. Hoshino is a talented Koi artist and an amateur Koi breeder, but more importantly to me, he is a living encyclopaedia on the history of Nishikigoi! After three long evenings spent with him, a few pads of paper and writers cramp, he accurately bridged many gaps in my research for this book.

Mr. Satoru Hoshino.

Mr. Hoshino breeds Nishikigoi every year purely as a hobby, I asked the varieties of his parent stocks to which he replied – "One set Jinbei Sanke, one set Kichinai Sanke and one set Gosuke Kohaku". I asked how he had Gosuke stock as many breeders had advised me that Gosuke line had long ago been lost. (see Kohaku section on Varieties earlier in the book 'Nishikigoi')

Mr. Hoshino informed me that his great grandfather was the Kunizo Hiroi who originated the Gosuke bloodline from stock purchased in the 1890's, he explained that the line has been kept true in his family since then and now the responsibility falls on himself to ensure the line is continued. He said it has no commercial value at all as the quality is very poor but the historical and sentimental value is great to his family.

I asked him about his views on using petuitary extract injections to induce spawning and he replied by saying he thought they were dangerous to the parent stocks and produced weak fry. I asked him his opinion as to the best Nishikigoi breeder of the time, he gave a quick one word reply- "Dainichi" – a reply I have come to expect!

Mr. Hoshino works as a Government Official in Ojiya City today.

4. Mr. Hiroshi Kawakami, Uragara, Ojiya, Niigata.

Mr. Kawakami is well known to just about everyone concerned with Nishikigoi in Japan. On my first visit to Japan in 1977 I purchased my first 'hand picked' Koi from Mr. Kawakami and since then have dealt with him on many occasions. His family are very gentle and kind, there is always coffee and food ready at every visit, supplemented with a great sense of humour.

He is a traditional Nishikigoi breeder in the truest sense. His grandfather Chuzo Kawakami started the business of breeding Nishikigoi in the same village during 1910 producing Kohaku, his father Torakichi Kawakami started Sanke production during the mid-1920's together with Kohaku. In later years between 1949 to 1953 the bloodline of 'Torazo' Sanke was stabilised. (Torazo was the name of Mr. Kawakami's great great grandfather and translates as Tiger).

The 'Tiger' Sanke bloodline was started by using a female Sanke with a male Kohaku of Yagozen bloodline. Unfortunately, during the very harsh Winter of 1953 the Yagozen male died and, although another Yagozen male was purchased, it did not produce the same high grade stock as that produced by the original male. All Torazo lineage stocks today have all been produced from offspring of the original parents.

Mr. Hiroshi Kawakami (Torazo) showing his fathers' pattern books from the 1920's

Torazo Sanke are very unusual in their development In one year Koi the sumi appears very strong, after two years more the sumi almost disappears and takes on a faint blue colour. True sumi does not start showing until the Koi are four years old and then improves significantly in five and six year specimens.

Mr. Kawakami's son Tsuyoshi is now playing a great part in the running of the business and is very well respected in the Japanese Koi circles despite his youth. Each

year father and son spawn 6 to 10 sets of parent Koi, mainly Sanke and Kohaku but sometimes produce small amounts of Kikusui, Hariwake, Goshiki and Gin-Rin Sanke. The stocks are grown in their own mud ponds in the surrounding mountainsides to grow up to five years and over. Like most other breeders in the area all stocks are housed indoors during Winter with oil-fired heaters providing heat to the ponds.

5. Mr. Sadaichiro Miya, The Miyakoya Company, Ojiya City, Niigata.

The Miyakoya Company is situated a few minutes walk from Ojiya Station and is quite a large complex which consists of a large indoor showroom for the wholesaling and retailing of dry goods ranging from medications, filter media, filtration systems, air pumps, water pumps, books, nets, foods and literally everything to do with Koi. In a separate section of the building there are several concrete ponds displaying Koi for sale in all varieties and sizes. However, Miyakoya is really famous for its Auction House, the first purpose-built Koi auction site to be built in Japan and opened in 1963, dealers from many parts of Japan buy stocks from Miyakoya from time to time.

Mr. Miya is third generation in Koi, his father and grandfather both bred Nishikigoi before him. It is always a daunting experience meeting Mr. Miya, he is always polite and friendly but there is never any doubt as to who is the 'boss man'. I must admit that when I first met him I was a little afraid of him, perhaps the size of the place coupled with his personality and reputation overcame me. He is a very traditional Japanese man and still wears the wooden sandals as opposed to the trainers that most of his contemporaries wear today. In recent years however, he has appeared to be more accessible to me and did not hesitate in allowing me to carry out an interview.

Mr. Miya and his son, the Auction building in the background.

Mr. Miya still breeds Koi but not so many as most other breeders, his Auction takes up a lot of his time and energy, His Auctions are held from the first week in April to the end of November every year, usually two per week. His son has now 'computerised' the auction system which helps the efficiency of the task to get some 30,000 lots through the Miyakoya Auction each year. Lot quantities can vary between 1 Koi to 200 Koi per lot.

He is strong in his opinion that it is still the Niigata breeders who produce the highest grade Nishikigoi in the world and perhaps the Shizuoka breeders who produce the highest volume of general grade stocks. He is always very conscious of the health of the Koi entered into his auction from breeders throughout Japan and controls entries very severely to keep his good reputation.

A few facts he gave me at the interview with him:-

■ The longest Koi to go through his auction measured 90cms.

■ The longest Carp to go through his auction was a 1.2 metre Magoi.

■ The highest price paid for an adult Koi through his auction was 3,000,000 yen (£18,000).

■ The highest price paid for a 1 year Koi (5") through his auction was 200,000 yen (£1,200).

I asked if he rests during the Winter months but he shook his head and replied that he has to work very hard as he and his staff are kept busy trying to keep the heavy snow falls from crushing the rooves of his buildings!

Footnote:- Sadly, three years after this interview took place, Mr. Miya passed away, his son Shinichi now manages the business.

6. Mr. Hasegawa, Ojiya City, Niigata.

I first met Mr, Hasegawa in 1982, he lives with his wife and son in a small detached house in Ojiya City. His full time job is that of a steel construction engineer and breeds Nishikigoi in his spare time as many do likewise in this part of Japan.

One may ask then why I have included him alongside the 'Greats' of the business? – he rents only 10,000 square metres of mud ponds, he does not belong to any Dealers Association. In recent years he has rebuilt his stock ponds in his garage which is a vast improvement on the previous ones but they are nonetheless still small in comparison with other outlets. My reason for including him is that I believe he produces some of the finest Kohaku, Sanke and Showa I have ever seen and does it consistently year after year. His stocking rates, even in his new larger ponds, leave one breathless, and give the impression that there is no actual water in the ponds, just a solid mass of Koi! – and yet every Koi is in perfect condition, a sign of a very great understanding of water quality requirements and the keeping of it.

High stocking rates, excellent water quality, Mr. Hasegawa, Ojiya.

During 1975, Mr.Hasegawa, against his wife's wishes, spent one year's income to purchase Kohaku parent stocks from both Manzo and Tomoin lineages, some years later he located and purchased Sanke parents from Sadazo lineage and Showa parents from original Kobayashi parents.

He breeds only five sets of parents every Spring although he has some fifteen sets to choose from, he also has parent stocks to breed the original 'Cream Ogon' which is something in between Yamabuki and Purachina in colour.

Mr. Hasegawa.

After six weeks of growing his fry he takes his annual two weeks holiday in July to cull down to 50,000 1" Koi from around 1,000,000 hatched. In August he culls again down to 20,000 2" Koi, and by October, he lays aside 2,000 4" tategoi to keep inside for Winter after destroying the other 18,000 during the October cull. The following Spring he will sell 1,500 of these Koi to local breeders and grow the remaining 500 during the Summer.

During October, apart from his 2,000 small Koi, he stocks around 500 two year Koi, 100 three year Koi and 30 Koi four years and over. He is a very modest man who seems genuinely surprised that dealers and breeders from many parts of Japan wish to purchase his Koi. I am not surprised at all, a good example of 'Hasegawa Kohaku' is a wonder to behold, creamy white skin together with the finest texture of orange-red pattern, his Sanke and Showa stocks also reflect a quality few other breeders have yet to achieve.

He has no ambitions to be amongst the 'Names' – he has no plans to expand his business, quite simply, he is happy just to breed his Nishikigoi as a part-time occupation, in short – he is a contented man!

7. Mr. Ichiro Mano,
Isumiya, Iwamagi, Niigata.

Isumiya started trading as a full time Koi breeding outlet during 1947 and are famous throughout Japan for 'Jumbo' Koi. The owner of the company is Mr. Ichiro Mano and at the time of writing in 1994, he is 80 years old, his son Mr. Senichi Mano is 43 years old, his brother also Mr. Senichi Mano who trades next door is 72 years old. The largest Koi ever bred by Isumiya was an Aka Muji which reached 97cms.

Mr. Senichi Mano, Isumiya.

The company farms 1,000,000 square metres of mud ponds in the surrounding area and spawns ten sets of parent Koi each Spring by using natural methods only – convinced that spawning by injection produces weak strains of fry. At the time of my first interview in Spring 1989 their stockholding consisted of 3,500 one year Koi, 500 two year Koi, 150 three year Koi and over 500 older Koi. This stock is made up from 80% of their own bred Koi and 20% purchased from other breeders.

During late June, his first cull of fry (2,500,000) takes around 20 days to complete with a further two to three culls prior to the October harvest. His parent stocks are Kohaku from Tomoin bloodline and Sanke from Jinbei bloodline which he insists is the best Sanke bloodline.

Mr. Mano of Dainichi admits to having Isumiya as a teacher in his early days of Koi breeding, in fact a short five minute walk separates the two famous companies. Today, however Mr. Mano of Isumiya rates Dainichi Koi as the best in the world and also commented on the high quality of stocks produced by Mr. Sakai in Hiroshima Prefecture.

Isumiya is a compulsary stop for breeders, dealers and enthusiasts visiting Niigata during October when all Koi are on display for sale, the pond containing his famous Jumbo stocks is a sight to marvel at!

8. Mr. Hajime Watanabe,
The Jinbei Company, Budokubo, Niigata.

Mr. Watanabe and his son Kazumi breed Nishikigoi in the Budokubo area of Niigata. Hajime's father started breeding Nishikigoi in the 1930's, but it was Hajime who first produced the famous Jinbei bloodline during 1952-1953 after breeding Sanke from the same parent stocks he had purchased some 13 years earlier. These parents consisted of a female Torazo Sanke, a male Tomoin Kohaku and a male Sanke of unknown bloodline purchased from Isumiya.

After 13 years of breeding with these parents he produced a line of Sanke which are very famous today and used by many breeders for their own parent stocks. These Jinbei Sanke are very striking indeed and easily identifiable in adult sizes showing large intense sumi patterns, lots of white ground and extremely bright hi patterns.

Mr. Watanabe & family.

Mr.Watanabe farms 800,000 square metres of mud ponds, he breeds today only one set of Jinbei parents, one set of Showa parents and two sets of Kohaku. He commented that it is easy for other breeders to produce Jinbei Sanke as his stocks are now widely distributed but stressed that culling of the fry is very difficult to do as sumi seldom appears, even after the third culling, and, as a result, most fry look like Kohaku. The development of sumi on Jinbei Sanke comes and goes for up to four or five year five years before the pattern actually begins to stabilise.

After his Spring breeding when 1,800,000 fry are produced, he carries out three severe culls up to October when only 30,000 are kept to sell; of these only 5,000 are retained as tategoi to overwinter and grow. He uses natural spawning methods and in 1993 constructed indoor heated ponds next to his house for Winter storage of his Koi, this method is now widely used by most professional breeders today.

He says that his best Sanke to date is only five years old and 70cms. long, one day he hopes to enter her in the All Japan Show to compete for Supreme Champion. Like many other top breeders Mr.Watanabe rates Dainichi as the top breeder in Japan today.

9. Mr. Yoshio Hiroi, The Yamacho Company, Aikawa.

Mr. Hiroi is a second generation Koi breeder and owns the relatively small business nicknamed as 'Choguro'. He is well known in the Ojiya area as a true 'character' in the industry, is seldom seen without a smile on his face and has a very jovial personality.

By no means is Mr. Hiroi a small-volume breeder, in fact he farms around 400,000 square metres of mud ponds in the nearby fields of the Kawaguchi-Machi area as well as owning several large 'Hot Spring Water' ponds in the Yusawa area. 'Choguro' is unique in the way of breeding and selling his stocks in this area of intense competition, he seldom sells Koi over two years old as most of his stocks are sold at one or two year sizes which accounts for 95% of his sales.

He also produces unusual varieties by experimenting with his parent stocks, over the years I have purchased from him varieties such as:- Goshiki; Goshiki-Sanke; Shusui-Sanke; Doitsu Sanke and Kikusui as well as the variety he is most famous for which is Purachina – a Choguro Purachina has a metallic white lustre that almost blinds!

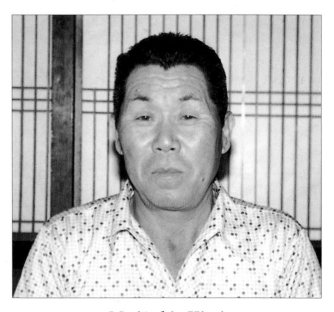

Mr. Yoshio Hiroi.

He uses 8 sets of parents each year and, after culling and tategoi selection, sells around 40,000 one year Koi and between 1,500 to 3,000 two year Koi. On the day I carried out this interview with him he explained that, later that day, he had to drive to Toyama, approximately 90 minutes travelling time, to assist a breeder friend of his to harvest his Koi. He said that his friend was a very nice man and an aquaintance for many years, however he was 78 years old and really should really have retired long ago, but 'Choguro' feared that, if he did not assist him, his friend would attempt to harvest his stocks alone and probably would not be strong enough to complete the work involved. Indeed 'Choguro' is a very good human being.

10. Mr. Takeaki Nishioka.

I first met Mr. Nishioka at Choguro's premises many years ago, he and 'Choguro' are good friends but totally different personalities, Mr. Nishioka is a real, larger-than-life extrovert and is very well known by many in the Nishikigoi business. His Nishikigoi Farm is situated on Shikoku Island in southern Japan and is called Orinaku. During October and November he stays in the Ojiya area to buy and sell stocks before returning, at the end of November to Shikoku.

In recent years he has built a small yet very beautiful facility in Iwamagi which comprises of a small one room house where he stays and sleeps; outside the house are several concrete ponds all tiled in mosaic and very 'different'- though not to my taste. A concrete pad has been built at the front of the facility which has been made for parking his Koi transportation vehicle, this is an enormous brand new truck which appears to be custom-built from stainless steel and carries four, purpose made, two ton transportation ponds and all the necessary oxygen cylinders, valves and equipment. This vehicle is used to ferry large amounts of Koi between Niigata and Shikoku Island – a round trip, in driving time alone, of 24 hours!

Mr. Takeaki Nishioka.

In Shikoku, Mr. Nishioka has been breeding and selling Nishikigoi for over 30 years, his son will continue the business when he retires. He farms approximately 700,000 square metres of mud ponds and spawns 10 sets of parents during Spring. He is famous for high grade and Jumbo Koi and rarely stocks less than 1,000 Koi over 26" long, during the breeding season he employs over 40 staff.

I was responsible for giving Mr. Nishioka a nickname which is sometimes used now by his Japanese colleages, that of 'Rolex San'. He seems to have a different diamond-encrusted Rolex watch for every day of the year as well as many other items of expensive jewellery. Whenever I meet him he is always carrying a leather fashion bag which is reputed to be full of money for any Koi he may wish to purchase. He has a reputation that goes before him and I doubt if anyone would even attempt to touch his leather bag!

I remember once arriving at 'Choguro' to buy two year Purachina to find 'Rolex's' truck and staff there loading over 500 Purachina into the containers. I asked Choguro for some but he said that all had been purchased by Mr. Nishioka and he had no stocks left. I was just about to leave when Rolex San came out of Choguro's house and smiled. I asked if I could purchase some of the stock in his truck as he had purchased everything. He asked one of his staff to take 20 Purachina out of a container and store them in one of Choguro's ponds for me, I asked how much I owed him and he just smiled and walked back into the house! One day I must find time to visit him in Shikoku.

11. Mr. Atsushi Suda, Kowada, Ojiya City.

Mr. Suda has two other brothers producing Nishikigoi, one nearby and the other in Yusawa about 30 minutes drive away. His father was not involved in Nishikigoi and he started as a full-time breeder during 1967.

He is one of the largest 'volume' breeders in Niigata and has recently moved to new premises which are very hi-tech indeed, complete with beautiful house above a modern packing station with indoor display ponds and mud ponds close by. He farms from 600,000 square metres of mud ponds and breeds 10 sets of parents each Spring – varieties include Kohaku, Sanke, Showa, Gin Rin, Hikarimoyo, Hikarimuji, Kawarimono and Gin Rin Kawarimono. His stocks have taken many Kokugyo Awards at the All Japan Show (best in size, irrespective of variety) and once took second best at the very prestigious Ojiya Show.

In any one year he will produce 40,000 one year Koi for sale as well as 2,500 two year Koi, he also has many stocks of older Koi for sale after harvest time. His favourite variety is Showa and he rates Dainichi Kohaku as the finest in the world.

In recent years he has sold many Koi to the USA and has been invited to judge shows there on several occasions – he supplies many Japanese breeders with Nishikigoi from regular to high grade stocks.

As a sideline, he breeds long finned Koi which are very popular in the South East Asian markets.

Mr. Atsushi Suda.

12. Mr. Hiroji Sakai, Hiroshima Prefecture.

Without doubt, Mr. Sakai's Koi farm produces the highest volume of high grade Nishikigoi in Japan. His parent stocks of Kohaku, Sanke, Shiro Utsuri, Showa, Koromo, Doitsu Hikarimoyo and Gin Rin varieties are of the highest quality, mostly from very famous bloodlines.

Mr. Hiroji Sakai.

He breeds his stocks by using natural spawning methods during mid May as Hiroshima area is far warmer than Niigata where breeders have to wait until mid June before spawning can take place. He grows his fry in large outdoor concrete sided ponds with mud floors, the size and numbers of these ponds are a sight to behold and he has many more traditional mud ponds in the surrounding mountainsides.

During mid to late June he makes his first cull which takes him and his staff two to three weeks to complete when over 80% are destroyed and the remainder returned to grow to 2" or so, in the warm water, before the next cull takes place – auto feeders are used to feed small pellets at regular intervals. By the end of August his fry are around 4" long and he then makes one more very severe cull before transferring his tategoi to indoor heated ponds for intensive rearing. These ponds have strong currents and auto feeders to ensure the stocks grow with correct shape, his growth rates are quite staggering with many Koi to 14" long at 13 months old whilst his two year Koi can average 20" in length. The huge volumes of Koi produced by Mr. Sakai enables him to supply stocks all year round.

Shot of concrete sided, mud base ponds, Mr. Sakai, Hiroshima.

During Winter, however, his oil-fired heating costs for his indoor ponds are high and averages out at £500.00 per day! and that is why volume sales are so important for this type of operation.

Many breeders in other areas of Japan are highly critical of this 'broiler' method of growing Nishikigoi and say they are inherently weaker as a result. However there is no doubt that Mr. Sakai is extremely successful both as a businessman and an expert breeder – during October it can take two days to take in the stocks on sale at his farm.

I have bought many Koi from Mr. Sakai and his Shiro Utsuri lines are breathtaking in their skin quality, and with every visit I make to his farm his expansion programme continues. I would not like to hazard a guess as to the investment required to build a facility such as this, it certainly is an eye-opener and well worth a visit.

Koi collected from growing ponds
and placed in sale ponds,
Mr. Sakai, Hiroshima.

*Female Showa, 55cm. (21.5″) long
and still very much Tategoi,
perhaps more will be seen of
this Koi in future years.*

'MYSTIQUE'
There is much of this single word that can be applied to the entire subject of Nishikigoi and there are still many Japanese 'Koi customs' yet to understand. At the time of writing I have visited Niigata on 75 occasions, and know the Koi area covered by a 'guided tour' in this section, like the back of my hand, - still the 'mystique' remains every time I return!

IN CONCLUSION

There must be many other 'Koi-kichi' people reading this book who have never had the opportunity of visiting the Nishikigoi breeding areas of Japan, I sincerely hope you will make a visit there one day. If you do, try to make the trip during October or November and head for the Ojiya area of Niigata Prefecture just after the October Nishikigoi harvest.

This is not the Japan one reads about in tourist brochures, you will never see a traffic jam in this area, trains are not crammed with commuters desperate to get to work on time, people don't rush about like they do in the big cities. Instead this is an area of tall mountains, rock-strewn rivers, countless racing streams, naked rock escarpments and lush valleys with magnificent trees which, in Autumn, display colours ranging from greens; yellows; browns and reds, right through to brilliant crimsons.

In the 50 square mile area of countryside and mountainsides surrounding Ojiya City you will find rice paddies and Nishikigoi mud ponds carved out of the mountainsides in places you would not think possible. You will also find narrow winding roads and villages, some with 'wattle-and-daub' houses that have not changed at all since the turn of the Century, and, at every turn of the road you will find yet another Nishikigoi breeder. This is the area that first produced Nishikigoi and is still, more than ever, the world centre for high grade Nishikigoi production. For myself, and other Nishikigoi addicts I travel with, this area has more of an unique untangible mystique unlike anywhere else I know. This area offers Koi enthusiasts an enchanted and almost magical atmosphere no matter how many times one may return.

As far as the Koi community themselves are concerned, everyone knows each other, they all work very hard, they certainly all seem to help each other, and always appear calm, happy, high in spirits and never lacking in business acumen. They live in 'Olde Worlde' houses in 'Olde Worlde' villages but all have hi-tech trappings as they do in Tokyo, Nagoya and Kyoto. This **is** an area where four-wheel drive vehicles are not just one-upmanship, they are vital, and so every family has at least one. Furthermore they are extremely hospitable people who will never let anyone they know pass by without inviting them into their house for food and drinks. Furthermore, they buy koi from each other, they loan Koi to each other for breeding purposes and yet each and every one has an almost obsessive desire to produce the best Nishikigoi in the world!

I confess I will never be able to comprehend their ways of doing business. No matter how many times one visits them, no matter how many times one buys their Koi, no two visits are anything like the same, much to the total frustration of us Westerners!

To give an example of this, in 1988 I visited a breeder I have religiously purchased stocks from since the early 1980's, basically because they are excellent and always improve once they are sold. This man has a very kind personality and I arrived when he had just returned from his mud pond harvest of larger sized Koi. He was busy and I started to inspect his stocks, after a while I netted a Koi into a bowl and asked him the price, he glanced over his shoulder, thought for a while, and quoted his price to me. I decided to return two days later when he was not so

Feeding stocks, Mushigame, Niigata.

busy and check the price again, on doing just this he quoted me twice the original price. I protested that two days ago he quoted half his current price, but he was adamant and invited me inside for food. The story ended two days later when I visited the Ojiya Show and found that the same Koi had not only taken the award for 'best in variety within the size' – it had also taken the award for 'best in size, irrespective of variety' (kok-ugyo). The breeder came over to me at the show and explained that he had sold the koi to a very famous breeder for eight times the price he originally quoted me. He also expl-ained that he was grateful I did not accept his original price as he would have had to sell it to me for the price quoted. Once I walked away without purchasing the Koi he was then free to quote another price, which he did two days later. He insisted I return to his facility the following day and select

stocks, I did just that, he quoted me prices, I agreed to the prices which were very fair, but when I made payment to him he only took 25% and returned the remainder to me, he smiled and said – "Please Mr. Peter, come back next year and select my best Tategoi once more!" I have learned over the years that there is no fixed price for any Nishi-kigoi, a point that many Westerners can never come to terms with. If I had any record of how many times I have asked a breeder the price of a Koi and have been given the reply – "Oh! I don't want to sell this Koi for three more years, please come back then" – believe me, the man is serious! Incidentally, there is a popular misconception in many overseas countries that the Japanese breeders will not allow their finest Koi to be sold abroad. The truth of the matter is that *anyone* can buy their finest Koi – providing they are prepared to pay the asking price!

Sanke, second prize, Showa, first prize 1987 No-gyo-sai, Ojiya. Both Koi bred by Dainichi Koi Farm.

Often I have heard stories of certain expensive Koi purchased in Japan and shipped for export to other countries, on arrival they are found to be deformed in some way which makes them of no use for show purposes. If a Koi is deformed, generally it will have been deformed since birth. Some of these are not destroyed during culling as their other qualities are exceptional and can be sold as pets at a greatly reduced price where both buyer and seller are happy. In every instance I have heard these complaints the Koi have **not** been purchased from a breeder.

Over the years I have visited Japan to purchase stocks from the breeders in Niigata I have seen several such Koi on display, some have noticeable defects whilst others cannot be detected other than by very close inspection. I can, however, state quite categorically that, on every occasion I have enquired about one of these examples, the breeder has always pointed out the problem with the Koi and why it is only useful as a pet. On other occasions where a Koi is perfect in every way but the breeder is a little concerned about a potential internal problem which may never even arise, this too is always pointed out and the breeder usually

recommends the Koi is checked again on the next visit when he can be sure that everything about the Koi is perfect for sale. The breeders are excellent businessmen, make no mistake about this, but their reputation is very important to them and I have always found them scrupulously honest in their dealings.

As far as the health of their stocks are concerned, it is a very rare thing to see a damaged Koi at any of these breeders, stocking rates are always very high and yet all stocks are in perfect condition, which reflects an expert understanding of water keeping techniques. Many in the UK who have never visited these Niigata breeders find this hard to believe until they witness it with their own eyes. I have yet to see a Sand Filter or an Ultra-Violet clarifier at any of these breeders! Furthermore, if a rare problem arises with a particular Koi, very few breeders attempt to cure the problem themselves. Instead the Koi is taken to the local professional Nishikigoi Veterinary Centre for attention, usually an injection is all that is required but the truth of the matter is that most breeders have no experience in how to do this as the situation rarely arises.

Private breeders auction, Mushigame, November 1992

During research for material for this book, the encouragement given to me by the breeders was very unexpected. On many occasions they arranged evening meetings at my hotel, and, at certain times, if a particular subject could not be covered by common 'Koi Language', they would bring along an interpreter at their own expense in order to ensure I grasped all the facts. These breeders live, breathe, eat and sleep Nishikigoi and never showed any signs of boredom or frustration with my questions, in fact, many suggested other questions I should be asking.

The 'Mystique' of Nishikigoi is absolutely impossible to attempt to explain to non-Koi people and on many occasions it surprises the avid enthusiast. There have been many instances in Niigata when I have been in the company of serious collectors from the UK and other countries, at the beginning of the trip they will state quite adamantly that they are only looking for 'Go-Sanke' varieties (Kohaku, Sanke, Showa and Shiro Utsuri) – the ones for the purist! – they state that 'lesser' varieties have no interest to them. After a few days driving from breeder to breeder, the end-of-day bar conversations always end up on the subject of special Koi seen over the past few days. It is then when an Asagi seen here is mentioned, a Yamabuki seen there, then crops up, I have even heard these people raving about a Kin-Kabuto – a variety said in the early books to have 'no commercial value'! The next night a

When one thinks about it, even the cheapest 4" Koi offered for sale in Japan has been a breeders' tategoi for at least four culls or else it would have been destroyed already along with thousands of others.

Kujaku and an Ochibashigure will be praised and so on. I am just the same in this respect, a superb example of any variety usually has me waxing lyrically for months afterwards; that is part of the mystique.

As mentioned earlier, no two Koi are exactly alike and the grade of Koi produced in Niigata improves with each passing year. I often wonder, where these magnificent mature specimens suddenly spring from? – how many 'secret' tategoi are hidden away in breeders ponds, only to be released when the time is just right? When one thinks about it, even the cheapest 4" Koi offered for sale in Japan has been a breeders' tategoi for at least four culls or else it would have been destroyed already along with thousands of others. How many brothers and sisters are now deemed as tategoi? – very few I would guess. Perhaps it is better to let these mysteries not weigh too heavy, one day the answers may come to light, but by then there will be other mysteries to contend with, fascinating though – isn't it?

I sincerely hope this book has been, and will continue to be useful in some way to the reader, I will leave you with some views and sights around the Ojiya area, perhaps these can tempt you to visit there one day. Who knows – we might meet up and try to learn more about Nishikigoi. To tempt you further I have prepared a map of the area and a key with it to help you find the breeders and, hopefully, the Nishikigoi of your dreams!

KEY TO UNDERSTANDING THE MAP

In recent years, two small hotels have been built in Ojiya with western style-beds, all other hotels use tatami mats for sleeping. I always make my base in Nagaoka City where the hotels have western-style beds and fax machines. The distance from Nagaoka to Ojiya can be covered by train in 20 minutes or by road in 30 minutes. If you are staying in this area for several days for Koi hunting purposes, your days can be taken up without visiting the same breeder twice, there are hundreds of breeders contained within the area of this map. I will try to mention the famous as well as the not-so-famous, but to cover all of them, unfortunately, is not possible.

If mentioning these dealers in this book is termed as advertising, then I am guilty of blatant advertising and not the slightest bit apologetic for so doing. In my opinion it is about time that these people get a little of the credit they rightfully deserve, for without the knowledge, expertise, enthusiasm and determination to succeed that these 'Masters of Nishikigoi' most certainly have, then all of us could never have had the opportunity to see the world famous Nishikigoi that were all 'made' by the descendents of this band of true experts.

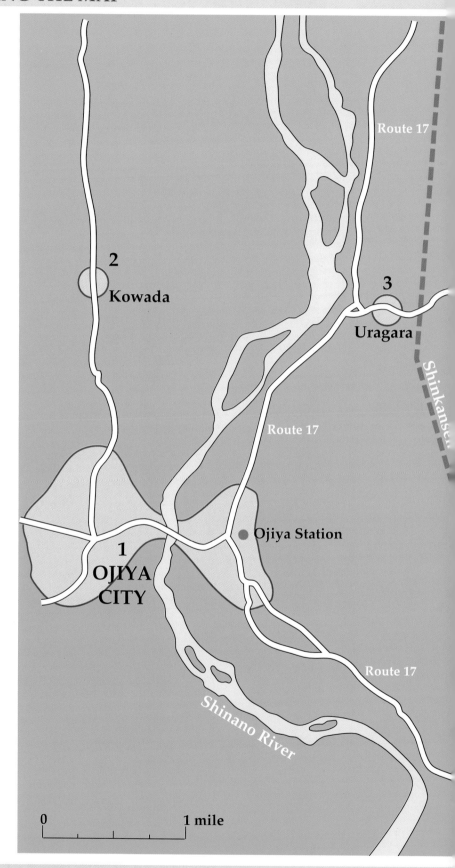

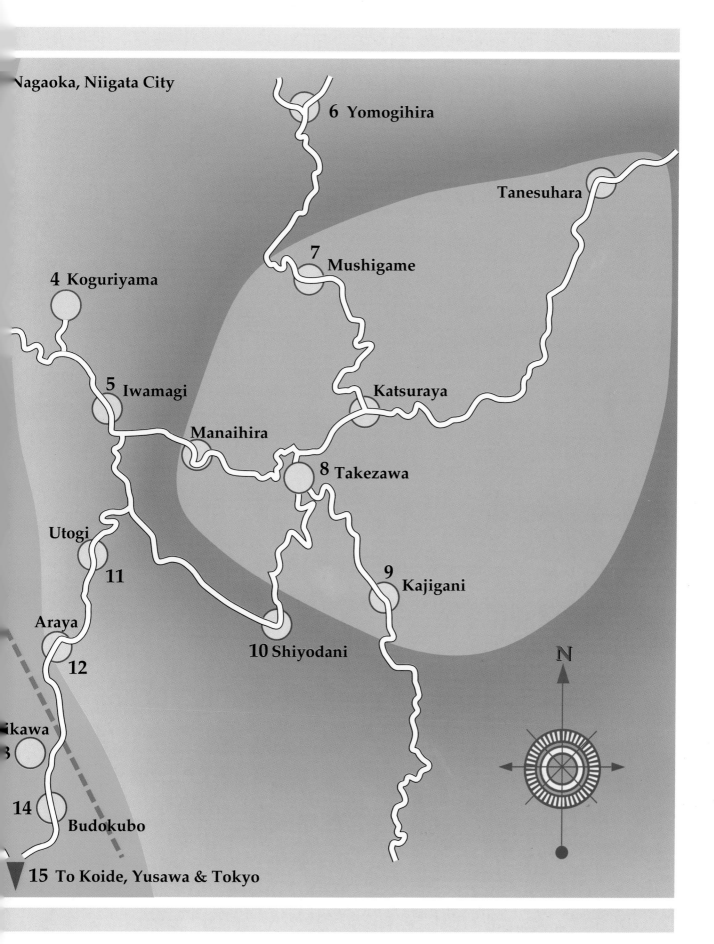

Nagaoka, Niigata City

6 Yomogihira

Tanesuhara

4 Koguriyama

7 Mushigame

5 Iwamagi

Katsuraya

Manaihira

8 Takezawa

Utogi

11

9 Kajigani

Araya

12

10 Shiyodani

kawa

3

N

14

Budokubo

15 To Koide, Yusawa & Tokyo

The Miyakoya Auction

The Shinano River,
the bridge links west and east Ojiya.

Koi harvested from mud ponds,
Hirashin, Kitayama.

1. OJIYA CITY.

A short walk from Ojiya Station will take you to **Miyakoya** where Nishikigoi are available plus a very comprehensive range of accessories such as books, all types of nets, medications, foods, aeration and pumping equipment etc. etc. If you need any of this equipment I suggest you buy here as the breeders only sell Nishikigoi.

Just a few minutes drive from Miyakoya along route 17 towards Uragara, on the right hand side is the facility known as **Kokugyokan** owned by **Mr. Seiji Hiroi,** the owner has no parent stocks of his own, instead he purchases high grade tategoi and grows them in his own mud ponds, always worth a visit.

In Ojiya City, on the west side of the Shinano River, the home of **Mr. Hasegawa** can be found, his Kohaku and Sanke stocks are well worth checking out.

Not shown on the map but a 30 minute drive south-west of west Ojiya will bring you to the adjoining villages of Wakatochi and Kitayama where **Mr. Shoichi Hosokai** and **Mr. Yoshiaki Hurasawa** of the Hirashin Company can be found, both are well known for rarer varieties such as Asagi, Shusui, Kumonryu etc.

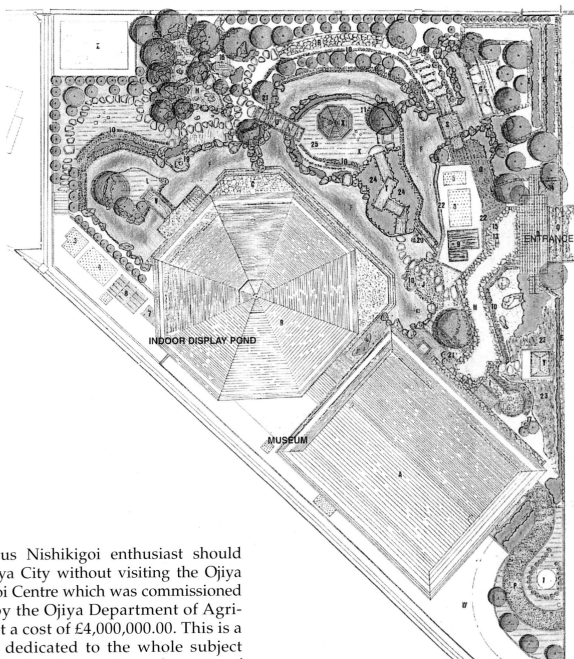

INDOOR DISPLAY POND

MUSEUM

ENTRANCE

No serious Nishikigoi enthusiast should leave Ojiya City without visiting the Ojiya Nishikigoi Centre which was commissioned in 1988 by the Ojiya Department of Agriculture at a cost of £4,000,000.00. This is a complex dedicated to the whole subject of Nishikigoi and comprises of a series of ponds, streams and waterfalls surrounded by magnificent landscaped gardens and walkways. These ponds are crystal clear and full of medium to large Nishikigoi in many varieties. There is also an indoor area which comprises of a large reception area where video films of different aspects of Nishikigoi are shown constantly. The walls of the building display rare items of memorabilia from the early days of Nishikigoi production in this area. The adjoining building houses an enormous formal display pond which holds many large Nishikigoi for all to admire.

This original sketch was made by the Landscape Architect commissioned to design the complex, apologies for the numbers and letters on the sketch, these refer to the key to the design and are all written, naturally, in Japanese on a separate sheet!

Just over the road from the entrance of The Nishikigoi Centre is a store where Nishikigoi souvenirs can be purchased, ranging from T-shirts, sweat shirts, ties, handkerchieves, socks and key rings through to porcelain ornaments and wood carvings.

2. KOWADA.

This area has two good breeders notably **Mr. Atsushi Suda,** famous for many varieties, especially metallic ones and rarer examples, his brother **Mr. Itaru Suda,** nearby in the village of Ikezu, breeds superb Showa and Kin Showa varieties amongst others.

3. URAGARA.

The entrance to this village is highlighted from the main route 17, which links Ojiya and Nagaoka, by this famous statue of a Kohaku, the following breeders in this village, and many others, can all be covered in easy walking distance.

Uragara has many breeders notably the **Maruyo Company** owned by **Mr. Yokio Isa,** who stocks a wide range of varieties in many sizes, nearby **Mr. Katsuyuki Kawakami,** breeds rarer varieties and metallic varieties, many of which are exported overseas. Back on the main street, check out **Kinsuien** owned by **Mr. Tomiei Suzuki,** who breeds Gin-Rin Showa and Goshiki varieties.

Mr. Hiroshi Kawakami produces 'Torazo' Sanke and high grade Kohaku mainly and a visit here is always worthwhile. On leaving the village of Uragara, **Miyaishi** is situated on the left under the Shinkansen line, this is a lavish outlet which supplies many Koi to collectors from overseas, the indoor display ponds are magnificent, just about every variety is available here.

'Torazo' – Uragara.

4. KOGURIYAMA.

On the road from Uragara towards Iwamagi, look out for a left turn just before a narrow tunnel, (a large Koi sign with an arrow is the landmark) – by taking this left turn it brings you immediately to Koguriyama and many breeders all within this tiny village. **Satoshi Hiroi** of the **Yagozen Company** breeds here, and here is the ancient home of this famous bloodline of Kohaku. Nearby, in easy walking distance are breeders such as **Otsuka, Shinosei, Shinoda, Hiroi** and **Hiroki.**

After leaving Koguriyama head back for the entry road towards the main road and turn left into the tunnel towards Iwamagi. After exiting the tunnel in 50 yards on the left is the tiny facility owned by **Mr. Takeaki Nishioka** just before the Nokyo auction site on the right. This is usually worth a look as he stocks some high class Koi here prior to transportation to his main base in Shikoku.

5. IWAMAGI.

This tiny village is the home of **Isumiya,** famous for Jumbo Koi for many years.

Isumiya, Iwamagi.

The facility is situated on the right hand side of the main road, in recent years this breeder has many magnificent jumbo size Yamabuki Ogon for sale, don't miss his brother's smaller facility next door. Continue on this road for a few hundred yards, on the left hand side a large traditional Japanese house will come to view, next to this are the largest indoor Koi houses you will see in Niigata, this is Dainichi.

Dainichi, Iwamagi.

Reputedly the Koi breeders' breeder! the most famous outlet for high grade Nishikigoi in the world at the time of writing. The ponds just seem to go on for ever, hallowed ground indeed for the Koi enthusiast.

On leaving Iwamagi the road splits and several routes can be selected, the already narrow road now becomes narrower and twists and turns upwards into the mountains. The shaded part of the map is an area known as Yamakoshimura which translates as Yamakoshi Village. This is a bit of a misnomer and causes much confusion to foreign visitors as Yamakoshi Village is, in actual fact, an area which comprises of all the villages shown within the shaded area. In view of the fact that any route can be taken from Iwamagi it is less confusing if I now simply name the villages and mention the breeders living there.

6. YOMOGIHIRA.

Nestled high in the mountains, this village has two very famous breeders, notably **Marusyo,** owned by **Mr. Shoji Tanaka,** the selection here is generally Kohaku, Sanke and Showa in many sizes, the quality is very high and this outlet is always well worth a visit. A few yards away you will find the **Sanroku Company** owned by **Mr. Koroku Hoshino,** again mostly Kohaku and Sanke here, and all of very high quality.

About one mile away on the outskirts of the village you will find **Mr. Komei Kaneko** of Kujaku fame, trading from Nigorisawacho.

7. MUSHIGAME.

Again, high up in the mountains and this village probably has the largest number of Nishikigoi breeders per square metre, than any of the villages on this map.

Home of the famous **Matsunosuke Sanke** bloodline, owned by **Mr. Toshiyuki Sakai,** don't miss this outlet whatever you do, stocks usually comprise of 80% Sanke and 20% Kohaku, most over 80cms and several over 90cms! – It's a guaranteed drool! **Mr. Kazuto Igarashi.** Stocks vary at different breeders every year, no two visits are ever the same, grades, selection, varieties, sizes and prices vary considerably on every visit. In October 1994, this outlet got our vote of commendation for the best selection of Nishikigoi in Niigata from **any** breeder we visited on that trip. To describe the quality of the Nishikigoi on display on this visit is very difficult as superlatives rapidly run out, his parent stocks of Sanke are from Sadazo lineage, his Kohaku stocks are from Dainichi mixed with Sensuke and he also produces some magnificent Showa. During this trip we returned over twelve times just to make sure the stocks were as good as we thought, – they were, don't miss it! Other breeders here include **Shintaro, Tokosho, Nagashima, Matsuda, Marusada,** and **Maruju** amongst many others.

Yamamatsu, Mushigame.
(Home of Matsunosuke Sanke).

8. TAKEZAWA.

This village has been associated with Nishikigoi for well over one hundred years and recently the monument (pictured left in 1985 at the old site) which was always displayed on the roadside between Mushigame and Katsuraya, has now been rightfully re-sited at Takezawa and denotes the actual birthplace of Nishikigoi.

Breeders in this village are numerous and all are in easy walking distance of each other, a few are listed as follows:- **Yamakoshimura Nishikigoi Sogo Centre** owned by **Mr. Shogo Sakai,** thousands of cheap Koi in all varieties and sizes here, **Gontaro** owned by **Mr. Kentaro Hoshino, Takatatsu** owned by **Mr. Tatsuji Takano** who produces varieties such as Gin Shiro, Gin Rin Ochibashigure and Shusui, **Hoshiyone** owned by **Mr. Takeo Hoshino**, good Sanke here, and **Mr. Yorijo Hiroi** for high class Nishikigoi.

The first cull, Takezawa village, Spring 1994.

The October Harvest, photograph courtesy of Mr. Satoru Hoshino, date unknown but estimated around 1970, taken in Takezawa after 15 metre deep mud pond harvest, note trolley winched up and down banking for transportation of Koi from pond to containers.

9. KAJIGANE.

A few breeders here notably **Mr. Motoichi Fujii.**

10. SHIODANE.

Another tiny village, don't miss **Hoshikin** owned by **Mr. Katsushige Hoshino** for superb Kohaku, other breeders here include **Oyaji, Kurabe** and **Koi No Kansuke.**

Small mud ponds taken near Shiodane, Spring 1994.

11. UTOGI.

Here look for **Marukin, Marusaka** and the new facility of **Marusei,** owned by **Mr. Seitaro Hirasawa,** as well as high class Sensuke Kohaku and Sadazo Sanke, he has superb Doitsu Hikarimoyo and many Yamabuki and Chagoi approaching the magical one metre mark, always worth a visit.

12. ARAYA.

Home of Kichinai Sanke, bred by **Miyatora,** another place never to miss. Just up the banking is **Miyako** owned by **Mr. Seiichi Miya** who breeds many varieties including Kumonryu, Goshiki and Doitsu varieties.

13. AIKAWA.

Here you will find **Yamacho (Choguro), Mr. Tadashi Ogawa** and **Yamasan.**

14. BUDOKUBO.

Several breeders here including **Jinbei,** home of the Jinbei Sanke.

15. KOIDE.

This area is around 30 minutes drive away from Ojiya, there are many hot spring ponds here where some breeders can keep Koi through Winter although nowadays many prefer to store them in modern indoor systems. **Uonuma Nishikigoi** owned by **Mr. Hirioe Yamaguchi** is a high class outlet only stocking very special Koi, and is another breeder who has no parent stocks but chooses to buy tategoi and grow them to maturity in his own mud ponds. A short drive away will bring you to his father **Mr. Yorijo Yamaguchi,** a famous Nishikigoi personality who breeds some of the finest Showa in Niigata. Other breeders in this area are **Odaira, Kanefuji, Takahashi** and **Nishikigoi No Oyoshi,** many unusual varieties can be found here.

Culling at Miyako.

Many of the breeders mentioned here in 'Mystique' and 'People' are true, real-life heroes on mine and I am very honoured to have had the pleasure of knowing them for many years as well as being an avid student of theirs. In October/November 1995 I will finally realise my lifetime ambition by proudly presenting them with a copy of this book – although they have no idea what it says! I will bow to them, or shake their hands and say, in very poor Japanese – "Do-mo Arigato" (Thank-You) as a token for the pleasure they have given myself and many other Koi enthusiasts from Japan and all over the world and, at the same time, perhaps I will have 'spread the word' in some way and put something back into the hobby.

Without exception, these breeders know every parent Koi they own; they know where they found the Koi; they know how much it cost; they know which bloodline it came from and they know every special Koi they have produced. They have an affinity with these parent stocks that is very apparent to me, they care for them as they would their own family and, if one should be lost (usually due to old age) they are most genuinely distraught.

All Koi have some beautiful aspects but the 'special' Koi that these people produce are true 'magic'. Compare them to the finest wines, the finest cigars, the finest race-horses, the finest motor cars that the world can produce and these 'special' Koi are right up there amongst them.

Give the rest of the world these parent stocks and not a single good Koi would be produced! Give the rest of the world the parent stocks together with Niigata water, mud and air temperatures and still not a single good Koi would be produced! Believe me – you need these 'masters' to complete the complex subject of world-class Nishikigoi production – this is also a large part of the 'Mystique".

IT ACTUALLY HAPPENED!

By being involved in the overall hobby of keeping Koi for some 24 years, I have come across, or heard about, many situations, conversations, events and experiences, some were total disasters, some were failures, some were funny, others were hard to believe and yet all of them, apart from the final light-hearted nonsense – (which I have been bullied into printing), actually took place. Every hobby has these kinds of stories and time, eventually, will reduce the pain felt at the time the disasters or failures took place, and one learns valuable, albeit costly, lessons from these. The funnier cases, however, seem to get funnier with the passing of time. I have listed these down, in no particular order, for inclusion in my book and tried, where possible, to leave actual names out, myself being the exception. There are very serious sections in 'Koi-kichi', perhaps this part will help to give a sense of balance by relating some aspects of the 'lighter side'.

Bernard Channing, owner of Japanese Water Gardens, fervently searching for his last golf ball!

■ I was once assisting a friend to finish off his 'state-of-the-art' Koi pond, he was at the stage where his three large filter chambers could be formed by concrete inside the perfectly-formed shuttering. A concrete company pumped the concrete evenly into the shuttering and my friend started to ensure it was all compacted properly with a large vibrator rod. The concrete company left site and the vibrator rod was still being operated in order to finish the job. I then heard a creaking and a groaning coming from the next garden, I looked over the fence just in time to see a brick-built garage, complete with timber roof and steel door totally collapse before my eyes. The debris destroyed a greenhouse and a flower bed before the damage was complete. My friend commented that 'single brick garages are not very stable' and continued with the vibrating rod. I left before his neighbour returned from work later that day!

■ A customer visited my shop and saw a 'Shishi-Odoshi' operating near a landscaped pond, he asked me what it was and how it worked. This bamboo gadget is translated as 'Deer Scarer' and is sited in a Japanese garden today for ornamental purposes. The purpose it was originally used for was to deter deer from eating valuable plants and vegetables. The operation is very simple, an upright piece of bamboo is placed in the ground and an horizontal one is attached to it to pivot freely. A constant flow of water is fed to the spout of the horizontal bamboo and when the hollow bamboo becomes full of water it pivots down to discharge the weight of water. As a result, the empty pipe returns to horizontal level and is checked by a stone and the process continues. When the pipe hits the stone a noise is made which, according to the Japanese, scares away the deer. My customer was fascinated with this marvel of science and purchased one from me to set up in his own garden. A few days later he telephoned to say that he had placed a piece of rubber on top of the stone, by doing so, the loud 'clanking' noise no longer disturbs his peaceful garden!

■ A dealer whom I supplied many Koi to, sold a very nice Tancho Sanke, about 17" long, to a couple who kept Koi. Two days later they telephoned to say that the Koi jumped out of their pond on the first night and was found dead the next morning. The lady explained that, as there was nothing wrong with the fish, she filleted it, left it in salt water for the day, and cooked it for tea. Her and her husband said it was delicious!

■ A couple I knew who lived on the 10th. story of a block of flats decided to keep Koi, and built a small pond in the common land which surrounded the flats. No permission was asked but no complaints came forth, I asked him, during a telephone conversation, how he hoped to keep it secure from children and vandals. He invited me round and showed me the pond which was protected by a padlocked timber cover on hinges. This padlock had to be opened for feeding and maintenance etc. We went into the flat for a tea and his wife served him his tea to his favourite armchair in front of the television and next to the window. The window overlooked the padlocked pond 10 floors below and next to his chair was a fully loaded, twelve-bore, shotgun!

■ At the time I was setting up my business at Golborne, all my Koi stocks were kept in my ponds at home some 20 miles away. One bitterly cold February evening I returned home from work and was watching television when I had the strangest feeling that my Koi were in real danger. I went to the pond to find them huddled together on the pond base due to the cold water but apart from that they seemed alright and the pond was working normally. I went back indoors but could not settle down at all, some time later I telephoned my two colleagues to ask them if they would assist me to move all my stocks to Golborne immediately. They both suggested we do it the next morning but I insisted on doing it as a matter of great urgency. By the time my colleagues arrived it was midnight and I had already packed some Koi in plastic bags for travel, it was becoming colder by the minute and my net was beginning to stick to the thin ice forming on the water surface. Eventually we had packed all the Koi, transported them to our new ponds at Golborne and finally climbed into beds at 4.00am. The next morning at around 7.00am. I was awakened by the sound of a loud crash coming from my garden. I rushed out to the pond we had

The larger-than-life Ian Stewardson, Koi collector, Bonsai collector and BKKS judge

removed all the Koi from to find that some 4" of ice had formed during the night. The discharge pipe from the bottom drain of the pond, which was only ordinary plumbing tube had frozen solid and shattered, allowing 80% of the pond water to drain away. The heavy sheet of ice had remained in place attached to the pond walls until the weight became heavier, the crashing sound was that of the ice dropping some four feet and shattering the whole base of the pond! Without doubt, had the Koi not been removed, they would all have been crushed by the ice! Since then, I have never underestimated the power of 'premonitions' should they arise in a conversation.

■ One of the most famous and unique Koi ever produced became the Supreme Champion at the All-Japan Show. This was known as 'The Crown Sanke', her photograph is in many books on the subject of Nishikigoi. After the Koi had been awarded the prize, and before the show was opened to the public the following morning, many photographs needed taking for newspapers and magazines. The airstones in the pond which held the Koi were removed for photography purposes, unfortunately the airstones were not replaced into the pond and the building locked for the night. The Koi was on her side the following morning due to lack of dissolved oxygen and, despite many attempts at revival, did not recover and soon died.

■ On one trip to Japan I was selecting Purachina from 'Choguro' in Niigata. After selecting these he invited me into his house for food, at the same time I reached into my jacket for cash to pay him with (cash is the only form of payment a breeder will accept). To my horror my cash was missing, all £36,000 of it in Japanese Yen! 'Choguro's' son took me back to other breeders I had been to earlier that day but no cash was found and panic began to set in. On my return to 'Choguro', I found him with a big beam on his face and he asked me to look at the most expensive item to have ever been netted

from his ponds. It was my bundle of Yen which had fallen from my pocket into a pond, completely soaked! The story did not end there, the next morning I went to my bank in Nagaoka City and asked if it could be exchanged for new notes. The manager said it could but only after it was fully dried out and so I returned to The Nagaoka Grand, my regular hotel. I explained to the manager, Mr. Onozuka, my predicament, immediately he summoned several members of staff to assist. Within five minutes, all my notes were laid neatly on the main counter of the reception desk in the main lobby and guests began to take noticeable interest as to what was happening. Soon an enormous sheet was draped over the notes and three ladies began to iron the sheet, after around 10 minutes the sheet was removed and the notes were perfectly flat and totally dry. Then the cashier piled each one neatly into a bundle and counted them, the amount was exactly correct and there was no need to exchange them for new notes!

■ On one occasion, at my premises, we were installing a new 'diffuser drain' to an existing system. Rather than empty the system, which contained many Koi, we decided to use the services of a local diver. The diver attended and swam down to remove the existing dome cover after which he placed a pipe stop inside the 4" tube exiting from the drain sump. After this we emptied the filter system and the 4" pipe connecting the pond to the drain to allow us to thread an airline down the pipe for connection to the new diffuser top, reasoning that the diver could remove the pipe stop and reach for the airline to connect and site the diffuser top. Simple, we thought, but none of us thought to re-fill the filters and 4" tube prior to sending the diver back down. As a result, the diver released the pipe stop, the pressure of water in the deep pond rushed down the 4" tube taking both pipe stop and divers arm into the tube and holding them there! A pump was set up immediately and the filters completely filled before equal water pressure released the very distraught diver who, thankfully, was otherwise un-harmed. Luckily also the pipe stop was retrieved quite easily!

■ From time to time in Spring, I have spawned several varieties of parent Koi in order to let customers grow the eggs for experience. Only one pond and spawning net is used for this purpose and, when one set of eggs are layed, the spawning grasses have to be removed and given to customers before the next set of parents can be used. In view of this we let our customers know which varieties will be spawned and they can reserve lengths of spawning grass for each variety they need, the only charge raised being that of the spawning grass itself. Before each length of grass is tied to the framework of the pond, a plastic tag is attached to each with the name and telephone number of the customer. Once the spawning is finished, each customer is notified by telephone to collect the eggs. On one such occasion I telephoned a person some 300 miles away and asked him if I should send the grasses by carrier, he told me that the cost of carriage was too high and that he would drive up to collect them instead. He asked me to wait at my premises as he was setting off immediately, we packed the two grasses into an oxygenated bag, my staff left at the close of business that day and I waited. Some four hours later a large car arrived, driven by the customer. (The costs of petrol must have been far higher than the costs of the carriage for the return trip!) By then my evening was over and I was starving, I decided to have a friendly joke with the man. He came to pay me but instead I carefully pointed out two eggs through the clear plastic bag with a pen, – there were hundreds of eggs visible. I said that, if he would allow me to open the bag and let me cut these two eggs away on their little section of spawning grass to avoid damage, I would not charge him for the spawning grasses and refund in full his petrol costs. He eyed me warily and then asked me to point these two eggs out again. I did so and he marked them as best he

could with a marker pen and oh-so-carefully carried the bag, after paying me, to his car. Before he left he said "If those eggs are worth so much to you, they must be worth far much more to me." I have never heard from this man since!

■ Still on the subject of Koi eggs, I had taken some large Koi in part-exchange from a very good customer and decided to use one Shiro Bekko as a female parent in a Sanke spawning. One guy who worked with me at the time and was very experienced in the handling of Koi said that the Shiro Bekko was male and would be of no use. I said that, although the body looked a little slim it was a female and she would hold many eggs as she was a big Koi, but my friend was not at all convinced. In view of this he produced a large bowl, filled it partially with water and asked me to net the Koi so he could lift it into the bowl for closer inspection. I pushed the Koi over to him in the net and he started to lift her, he had only lifted her some 6" out of the water when eggs started to pump out of her body at an alarming rate. Within seconds, his trousers, shoes, hands and face were covered in Koi eggs as were the floor of the building and surrounding areas and the two of us just dissolved into fits of laughter.

■ During the early days of the hobby, one man decided to really promote Koi keeping in the UK and approached the British Koi-Keepers' Society. He explained his plan and pointed out that, in return for his services, he should be rewarded by becoming Chairman of the Society. The forthcoming AGM decided against the offer and the matter appeared to be closed. This, however, was not so and, within a few weeks, articles started to appear in newspapers and Koi publications to the effect that Her Majesty the Queen was soon to be presented with a gift of several specimen Koi from members of Zen Nippon Airinkai in Japan. A leading lady member of the BKKS immediately wrote a letter to the Queen to enquire if she actually had a Koi pond and enclosed press cuttings accordingly. Within days a reply came back from the Royal Household saying that Her Majesty had no knowledge of Koi and no formal offers of Koi as a gift. The press cuttings continued and rumours of the imminent arrival of a full Japanese television crew to take full footage of the 'presentation' began to appear and an actual date, time and location of the 'presentation' announced. The BKKS then began to take a real interest in the matter as the location was on the banks of the River Thames directly in front of the Houses of Parliament. Later the reason for this was discovered to be that the film of the ceremony was to be shown in Japan and the Japanese public would assume that the Thames at this point would be on the Queens' private land and so the Koi, when released, would be her own personal property for her private enjoyment. The date approached, a huge marquee was erected on the Thames embankment, show ponds were erected to receive the Koi, security measures taken and the Japanese TV crew arrived in force. A few days before the event, the gentleman organising all this appeared on a popular lunchtime TV programme complete with Koi and a Japanese exporter of Koi. On the morning of the event caterers delivered cases of champagne, wines and mountains of food. Waiters appeared, a public address system played background music and soon the Koi were delivered and displayed in the show ponds. Soon the guests started to arrive, Japanese dignitaries, politicians, show business personalities and the like all gathered and began to make a start on the refreshments. At the 11th. hour, the leading lady member of the BKKS, mentioned earlier, arrived on the scene, together with representatives of the Ministry of Agriculture, Fisheries and Food and the RSPCA. The representative from the Ministry pointed out that Koi can only be imported to the UK for keeping in enclosed ornamental waters or aquaria and most certainly can not be introduced into our eco-system. The representative of the RSPCA further pointed out that this stretch of the Thames was badly poll-

uted and the stocks would die within a few hours which would constitute cruelty to animals. With these two warnings levelled, the organiser decided to make the film as normal but not to show any Koi being reeased as such and the Koi were removed elsewhere later that day. I do not know if the film ever made Japanese television but the organiser did get enormous publicity for Koi as he promised.

■ Every Koi dealer must have experienced situations like this next one and that is where the husband or wife begs not to let the other know of the actual cost of a Koi being purchased. This never arises when both husband and wife are interested in buying Koi but certainly does when only one is the Koi keeper. On one such occasion, a customer always told me to quote 10% of the actual price of a Koi if his wife accompanied him on a visit. On my main pond I started to display some Koi in a bowl and prices were asked, each time I quoted one tenth of the actual price the lady winced visibly. Four Koi were finally to be chosen from in order to get to two actual purchases and prices were asked again, the two Koi were chosen and the other two released to the pond. At this point another customer approached the lady and asked the price of the two Koi returned and she obliged by telling him. The customer promptly rushed over to me and told me he would purchase these Koi! It took several tricky minutes to disentangle myself from the situation.

■ In the early 1980's, my shipper telephoned to say that a Koi breeder, who was a close friend had inadvertently produced thousands of 'Gin Rin Magoi' by mistake and wondered if there would be a market for them as price was very cheap. I had never seen nor heard of this 'variety' but asked him for two cartons to be shipped with the next shipment. Unfortunately I did not ask as to the size and, on arrival, found them to be 2" long and the two cartons contained a total of 400 Koi! – all jet black with gin rin scales. How to sell them was going to be a problem and so I advertised them in the BKKS magazine as a 'rare' variety, so 'rare' indeed that I could only allow each member of the Society a maximum of 10 at £2.50 each. (At that time the Society had over 4,000 members! - not so 'rare'.) I forgot about these until, one morning, the telephones at my shop went berserk. These were members ringing to reserve their 'quota' of Gin-Rin Magoi by quoting their BKKS membership numbers and offering their credit card numbers for payment. We all began to explain to each customer that it was a joke and that the variety cannot be so rare if we can supply 10 per member, we further pointed out that they could have one or two if needed. Alas the more we tried to explain the situation, the more adamant the customers became and insisted on having their rightful 'share'. In the end I had to import a further 1,000 to supply the orders. As a footnote to this, I have seen many of these Koi fully grown, some over 26" long and superbly shaped Magoi, although the gin rin effect has long since disappeared, and an excellent investment for £2.50!

The reason for inclusion of this picture is, that when we were deciding which photographs to use for each book cover, Nigel Caddock came up with this for Book 6!

■ Quite recently, we returned to the UK from a visit to Germany where we were asked to inspect several collections of Koi over there as well as to give design ideas for future pond systems. We took the ferry from Hull to Rotterdam and drove to Germany in a large truck, after everything had been completed we returned and exited the ferry at Hull Docks one cold grey morning. As we were leaving the docks we were asked to pull over to one side by the Customs Officials on duty and climb down from the cab of the vehicle. Questions were asked as to if we had anything to declare and when we said we had nothing to declare they asked for keys to the vehicle in order to inspect the contents. We were then ushered into a small building to wait until the check was completed in full. After about 15 minutes four more officials entered the building and asked us as to which of us was the diabetic, when the reply came that none of us were, we were asked to return to our truck. When we got to the truck we counted 14 people working through every inch of the vehicle from the cab to the box behind and then the penny dropped! In our medical kit were hypodermic syringes, injection water and gram upon gram of fine white powder in unlabelled containers and sealed glass bottles. This was MS 222 Anaesthetic and an injectable antibiotic purely for Koi medication, we knew what it was exactly and tried to explain but, on reflection, we had returned through Holland and the Customs Officials were rightfully suspicious of our cargo!

■ In Japan there have been many unforgettable experiences, on my first visit I woke up in the middle of the night desperately in need of a glass of water and was wary of drinking tap water (I later found out that Japanese tap water is totally safe) – I went to the refrigerator in my room and found a cup of mineral water which I downed in one gulp before finding out it was Sake instead.

■ On another early occasion, whilst visiting a very expensive Koi outlet in Tokyo with a party of fellow enthusiasts, superb Koi were being shown and prices quoted by an interpreter. I thought the prices were extremely cheap and asked if anyone else needed to buy some as I wished to purchase several for my collection. I think I 'bought' six superb Koi much to the amazement of the dealer before the interpreter came over full of apologies to say that she had made mistakes in translating all the prices to me by only quoting 10% of the actual price! In later years during a visit when I escorted 25 UK collectors to Japan, we stayed for two nights in Mihara, Hiroshima Prefecture. One of the party was unfortunately taken ill late at night and the hotel sent for an emergency doctor. The doctor arrived speedily as promised and turned out to be a blind acupuncturist complete with guide dog. This threw us all initially as we watched needles being placed here and there by touch alone, we had no cause for concern as the next morning the person concerned was almost 100% again!

■ Other UK experiences include a customer whose pond needed urgent repairs and the Koi were housed in his bath during the work. When anyone needed a bath, the Koi were placed in polythene bags, the bath scrubbed out and used. After this the Koi went back into the bath.

A telephone call late one Summer evening from a very dear customer to say that sitting on a patio, watching one's Koi feed on a warm Summer evening is the most relaxing experience of the hobby. He further added that, after one or two liberal measures of the Scottish kind, it's surprising how many Koi one actually has!

On a journey to a major UK Dealers' show we transported our best stocks of 30 jumbo Koi for the show to arrive just in time for benching and entry. The Koi were travelled in four oxygenated transportation containers inside the separate box section of the truck without any staff in this box. On arrival at the Show one Koi had jumped and

broken the zip top of the container and died two days later, and, as usually happens, this was the very best Koi of the 30 transported. Never underestimate the power of a large Koi and always have someone travelling within reach of the Koi.

On one occasion, a state-of-the-art pond was made with no expense spared, concrete, glassfibre laminating and beautiful landscaping. When filled the pond refused to hold water, every aspect was checked and double checked, everything was in order and still the pond would not hold water. The only thing that could not be checked was the 4" pipes connecting the bottom drains to the filters, eventually disc cutters and jack hammers wrecked the pond base and exposed the pipes to find that the person who installed them had no idea they needed solvent to glue them together!

There are many other similar tales such as people falling into ponds and filters, an oxygenated bag of Koi exploding due to a spark from a cigarette – fortunately the Koi were fine, and endless supplies of questions that may be genuinely asked but come out very funny indeed, such as:-

"What's the difference between floating food and sinking food?"

A customer came to me for some 4" pipework and I asked him "How long do you want it?" to which he replied "Oh, I want to keep it!"

These, and many more, are all part of the trials and tribulations of keeping Koi!

The last actual text in this book has been included by demand of my colleagues whom I work with on a daily basis and who promised strike action if it was not included! However, in view of the fact that this book will be read in many countries outside of the UK, the background of the text must first be explained in full to these readers, before they actually read it, if the spirit in which it was written is to be fully, or partially, appreciated. If I do not explain this before the text then only the readers who know our business and its location will even begin to grasp what the text is about, here goes:-

Since 1980, my business has been trading from a tiny village called Golborne, this village is now a part of Warrington, Cheshire which is some six miles South. The location is good for our business as it is very close to many main trunk roads and the main motorway networks, which is vital for us as the vast majority of our customers have to travel some distances. I live some twenty miles away and, prior to actually setting up my business there, I had never even heard of Golborne. The casual motorists can pass through the village in a blink of the eye without even knowing they have ever been there, so small is Golborne. In quite recent years, now sadly gone by, Golborne was a thriving coal mining village as were many similar villages in the area. A few years ago, the mine was closed and many jobs were lost. This not only had an effect on the workforce in question, it had a very real 'knock-on' effect to the small businesses which relied on the income from the miners and their families. Although this did not affect a Koi business, as we have very few local customers, it did significantly affect the whole economy of the area. The locals who live in Golborne, however, are made from stern stuff and, once a period of realisation and adjustment had been allowed, a few of us began to see the lighter side of things.

There is an excellent public house cum restaurant in Golborne which is called The Queen Anne as many of my customers well

Mary Riddoch (left) and Rachel Gosling, two Koi Kichi ladies brought together by a love for Nishikigoi

know. After a day's work, many locals call in for a drink and a chat before going home for the evening. These locals come from every walk of life, some are labourers, some are businessmen and others from professional walks of life. In 1992, when doom and gloom surrounded Golborne, the early evening conversation here always reflected the funnier and more optimistic side of things, the main subject being how to revitalise Golborne itself.

Within a few weeks, we had visions of turning Golborne into an 'Independent Monarchy' with it's very own Royal Family, Palace and very own Euro MP, one local who worked at Manchester Airport insisted that Golborne should have its own International Airport, others suggested a large Ski Centre should be built on the slopes of the disused slag heaps of the mine, a Ministry of Tourism was mooted with an underground direct link to the channel tunnel exiting on Golborne High Street, some insisted that Golborne should have its very own University and, within a few more weeks, many, many more such ludicrous ideas were put forward.

Soon afterwards, I was appointed 'Official Head of Tourism to the Monarchy of Golborne' and was given full artistic license to ensure, by any means possible – fair or foul, that Golborne would become the hub of the UK tourist business.

The following text was published in the BKKS magazine in December 1992, before reading this I would point out that there IS a village called Great Sankey near Warrington, the remainder I will leave to the reader and claim artistic license should any inaccuracies of the text be discovered subsequently. I also apologise in advance if some readers do not understand the local Golborne dialect.

The True Origin of Nishikigoi
(Facts explained, fallacies exploded)

The popular belief that Nishikigoi were first produced in Japan has long been viewed with total incredulity by the local historians and populace around the North West Cheshire and Southern Lancashire area of North West England.

History books make references to the existence of Nishikigoi in this area as early as AD 1269 in the chronicles penned by the Lay Monks of Golborne Abbey who harnessed the local abundance of hot mineral spring water to supply their 'stew ponds' in the grounds of the Abbey.

Soon afterwards, St. Columba, on first witnessing the 'Water Kelpie' (later known as The Loch Ness Monster) remarked that – "It (the monster) was far more terryble, yet not nearly so sweete as the famed cullord Carpe of Golburn".

Very much later, during the dissolution of the monasteries, Henry VIII made only one exception to the destruction he wreaked by advising his soldiers of the following Declaration, (the original, signed version of this bloodthirsty directive is still exhibited for all to see in the History department of Golborne Museum, as a constant reminder to all.)

> 'Burne ye, and burne ye goode, all the wretched abbyes and monasteries thru' my kingdom, leave ye not wun man nor wumman alyve nor wun howse standyng – save wun only and that shall be Golburne Abbye, its inmates, its chattels and its bewtifull cullerfull carpe, these shall be preserved for all tyme.'

It is true that these Lay Monks of Golborne Abbey were the unknowing founders of the Nishikigoi industry as we know it today, initially they bred their 'Carpe' to provide food for themselves and the local peasants. Then the original method of cooking their carp was to dig a shallow, saucer-shaped indentation in the ground and line the bottom with flint which was packed very hard, charcoal was then placed on top and fired until it 'burnyd brytely' after which local 'herbes were caste upon in grayte abundynce'. This simple yet very effective forerunner of the garden barbecue was known as a 'Goy', and many public 'Goys' were constructed in the surrounding areas. In later years a significant improvement was made to the usable life of the Goy by disposing of the hard-packed flint and lining the indentation with a compound similar to modern day concrete. Praise must be given to Stanliegh of Teesdale, the inventor of this compound who lived some two and a half hours horse ride away in Re-inford, (today known as Rainford), he christened his compound as 'Re-in' simply an abbreviation of his village. However, I digress, it was a common request in those days to the monks by local peasants and beggars passing through to give them 'Carpe for ma Goy' (soon afterwards this was abbreviated to 'Ma Goy' and later to 'Magoi' meaning Black Carp.) This term was even adopted into the Japanese language many centuries later.

It must be pointed out here that the famous stew ponds, although fed by underground hot mineral spring water, discharged their excess water into the nearby River Golbe. The golden waters of this majestic waterway gave the name to the village of Golborne (still pronounced by locals today as 'Goalburn' which is an abbreviation of 'Golden Burn' or 'Golden River'.)

In the 1350's it is recorded that the combination of three ingredients namely hot mineral water, excessive carp excrement and the 'golden' water of the Golbe was found to produce 'A helthy elixir of plezant tayste, gud for warding off aylements and carbunkyles'. This was readily available in abundance and has been used for centuries as the prime ingredient for brewing and distilling of the potent yet delicately flavoured Golborne Mist Liqueur. Today we find this drink is famous throughout the world and it is still prepared to the original secret recipe handed down by generation to generation. In recent years, in order to try and comply with the present drink laws, 'Golborne Mist L.A.' and 'Diet Golborne Mist' has been introduced with all the marketing campaigns necessary for world distribution. It has received financial success in some foreign countries, yet neither have sold a drop locally!

Back to Nishikigoi, it is recorded in the Golborne Daily Bugle on the 10th. July, 1704, that freak rainstorms caused severe flooding of many stew ponds resulting in many parent stocks being swept into the Golbe. Needless to say, many 'Goys' were also swept away and sadly, only a few have been replaced to full splendour.

Miraculously, in September 1709, the earlier flooding resulted in great success when three local villagers from Warrington started to fish for sturgeon at the salmon ladders on the falls in the village of Great Sankey nearby. After some hours, each one landed a magnificent three coloured carp, each one displaying a pure white body with intense red and black pigmentation. The local police informed the monks of Golborne Abbey who rushed to the scene on horseback, by the time they arrived at Sankey falls several more had been landed. These carp were, thankfully, returned to the Abbey for breeding purposes but not before the monks had made a solemn, holy vow to the fishermen to name them after the area in which they were first discovered. As a result they were named as 'Great Sankey',

over the years this has been shortened to 'Sanke' – one of the most prized varieties of Nishikigoi, even in Japan today this term is used, taken directly from the Nishikigoi breeders of Golborne!

Soon afterwards, the production of Nishikigoi started to take off in Golborne and, in the period between 1750 to 1825, countless Nishikigoi breeders set up to compete against the monks, siting their farms alongside the lush, verdant banks of the Golbe.

It was not long afterwards that many parent stocks were actually found in the Golbe from which many varieties were stabilised, in later years many of these were stabilised into actual bloodlines. Thankfully all this history has been recorded accurately and in minute detail by the first professional chronicler of Nishikigoi in the world who had the foresight to document everything for future generations. From 1710 to 1745 this avid chronicler began to detail every single Nishikigoi item of interest and laboriously record it by quill pen and ink onto parchment. Apparently he led somewhat of a chequered past prior to devoting his life to Nishikigoi, one story says that he had no name as such until he faced local magistrates for a poaching offence. When the magistrate gave him his fine of sixpence and twenty lashes he growled to the local policeman – "lash the Cad, dock his sixpence", from that day forth he became known simply as 'Caddock' and never strayed outside the law again. He lived in a humble abode in a 'down market' area near to Golborne, then known as 'Low Town', as it was then an area where decent people seldom ventured. Since the great earthquake of 1860, when Low Town was completely levelled, it has been totally rebuilt and renamed as 'Lowton', far more respectable today yet it can never boast the historical values of neighbouring Golborne. Still, without 'Caddock' and his chronicles the world would never have known the following vital facts that form major parts of the Nishikigoi jigsaw puzzle.

Excerpts from the 'Caddock Chronicles'

1756. Hughie Greenhalgh, breeding near the Low Town Falls on the Golb produced a beautiful blue scaleless carp in a flock spawning that year. He sold the carp to a local landowner for five pennies which enabled him to buy a much needed pair of new shoes. He simply named the new variety as 'Shoes for Huey', this has now been changed over the years to 'Shusui'.

1761. A strange variety was discovered by Newton-le-Willows breeder Igor O'Hoemow in his one-year stocks. He named it after himself as 'Igorohoemow' but before he could develop the strain to perfection, the Koi was stolen by a nearby breeder, when Igor complained to him the breeder denied all knowledge of the theft and replied – "If tha's sure ah tekken it, then tha' can sue me Igor O'Hoemow!" These two varieties are known today as Aigoromo and Sumigoromo. Sadly the dispute between the two breeders was never settled, eventually, in 1773, Igor finally lost his High Court action and lost all interest in Nishikigoi, two years later he was admitted into Winwick Asylum, totally insane and mumbling – "The Judges know now't."

1777. A 'pine-cone' effect was produced on a white Koi at the Sewber brother's Koi farm. Mathew, the eldest brother, responsible for the breeding of the Koi named it after himself – Matt Sewber, now 'Matsuba'.

By the late 1700's, many local hostelries were built where local Koi breeders could relax after a hard days culling. Today many of these still remain albeit modernised, yet still retaining their original names. The Koi visitor to Golborne should visit these in order to take in the atmosphere surrounding the true birthplace of Nishikigoi, I can strongly recommend the following:-

"THE SPLIT PECTORAL" – North Promenade, excellent ales and serves mulled Golborne Mist on winter evenings.

THE QUEEN ANNE AND CHAGOI" (Her favourite Variety) – Bridge Street, draught Golborne Mist on tap plus a host of gourmet dishes all from original recipes documented in the Caddock Chronicles, try the Flank of Golborne Greyhound in a spicy Asagi sauce – mm! reservations are recommended here to avoid disappointment.

"THE HARDNESS TEST" – Famous Strip Club, for those with that kind of hard core taste, right next to the Ski slope entrance.

"THE WEEPING ULCER HOTEL AND BISTRO" – a 'must' for all those interested in parasitic and bacterial disorders, regular watering hole for hosts of Nishikigoi consultants in the area. The walls of the dining room are covered in detailed colour photographs (courtesy Nishikigoi International) showing lesions, contusions, Hikui, pox and other interesting disorders.

As far as 'Golborne today' is concerned, it is a bustling Nishikigoi community and the world centre for Nishikigoi. During November and December you will find Koi enthusiasts from all over the world and many Japanese breeders find their parent stocks here. The local Tourist Information Centre have maps of the area which detail all the famous breeders and where to find accommodation.

As far as where to start? well, the choice is endless, how about these for starters:-

PLATT BRIDGE AREA – the most famous Nishikigoi farm in the world, the Welshman famous for producing the best Kohaku money can buy, yes it's 'Dai' Neechy himself, recently he's opened an outlet in Niigata, Japan. (Be prepared for high prices.)

✤ WEST GOLBORNE – Tom's Koi Shop, this outlet is managed today by Dave Owen whose famous grandfather Tom, produced one of the finest Kohaku bloodlines ever. Excellent pigmentation and texture are trademarks of 'Tomowen' Kohaku.

✤ CENTRAL GOLBORNE – Infiltration, known by Koi keepers the world over and dates back to 1641 when Sir Cedric Waddye commenced breeding Nishikigoi in Golborne. He met an untimely death in 1669 when defending his stocks from a band of marauders from Sherwood Forest led by a St. Bernard from Channynge, a giant of a man and notable arm wrestler. Fortunately Sir Cedric left behind four children, Ian, Philip, Tracy and Shawn who each inherited 25% of the company. The origin of the company name was, in fact, as a combination of these names i.e. 'Ian-Phil-Trace-Shawn' – long since condensed to Infiltration, history is indeed fascinating!

✤ NORTH GOLBORNE – Adjoining the Golborne Hilton Hotel next to runway five of Golborne International Airport, don't forget to visit the famous Sanke farm, superbly managed by Charles Snosky, descendent of his famous great, great grand-father Matt Snosky.

Issued by the Golborne Tourist Board; Golborne University – Department of Nishikigoi; Air Golborne plc; Golborne Mist plc; and The Trustees of Golborne Abbey with deep gratitude to Henry VIII.

Champion Showa
at the 1995
All Japan
Show

JAPANESE/ENGLISH KOI DICTIONARY

Japanese Word	Pronunciation	Meaning
AIGOROMO	EYE-GOR-OMO	Indigo Blue
AKA	ACKA	Red from Orange
AKA-ME	ACKA-MAY	Red Eye
BENIGOI	BENNY-GOY	Vermillion-Red Carp
BU	BOO	Section
BUDOGOROMO	BOO-DOE-GOR-OMO	Grape Pattern
CHAGOI	CHAR-GOY	Tea-Coloured Carp
CHOMAN	CHO-MAN	Stomach Problem
DAINICHI	DIE-KNEE-CHEE	Famous Breeder
DIA	DIE-YA	Diamond
DOITSU	DOYTZ	German
GIN	GIN (as in begin)	Silver
GIN-RIN	GIN (as in begin)-RIN	Silver Scale
GINSUI	GIN (as in begin)-SUEY	Silver Water
GOSAI	GO-SIGH	Five Years Old
GOSHIKI	GOSH-KEY	Five Colour
GOSUKE	GO-SKAY	(Kohaku Bloodline)
HAGESHIRO	HAG-AY-SHE-ROE	Bald White Head
HAJIRO	HA-JEER-O	White Edge
HARIWAKE	HARRY-WA-KAY	Like a Patchwork
HI	HE	Red from Crimson
HIKARIMONO	HE-CAR-EE-MON-OWE	Metallic Varieties
HIKARMOYO	HE-CAR-EE-MOY-O	Patterned Metallic
HIKARIMUJI	HE-CAR-EE-MOO-GEE	One Colour Metallic
INAZUMA	IN-A-ZOOM-A	Lightning
ISUMIYA	IZ-OO-ME-YA	(Famous Breeder)
JINBEI	JIN-BAY	(Sanke Bloodline)
KAGE	CAR-GAY	Shadow
KAWARIMONO	CAR-WA-REE-MON-OWE	Uncommon Varieties
KICHINAI	KITCHEN-EYE	(Sanke Bloodline)
KIGOI	KEY-GOY	Yellow Carp

JAPANESE/ENGLISH KOI DICTIONARY

Japanese Word	Pronunciation	Meaning
KIKUSUI	KEEK-SUI	Chrysanthemum Water
KIN	KIN	Gold
KINDAI	KIN-DIE	Modern
KINRAN	KIN-RAN	Egg Catcher
KIN-RIN	KIN-RIN	Gold Scale
KIWA	KEY-WA	Edge
KOBAYASHI	CO-BUY-ASHY	(Early Showa Breeder)
KOHAKU	CO-HAKU	Red and White
KOINOBORI	KOI-NO-BORE-EE	Carp Streamers
KUCHIBENI	COO-CHEE-BENNY	Lipstick
KUJAKU	COO-JA-COO	Peacock
KUMONRYU	COME-ON-REE-YOU	Dragon
KUZUGOI	COO-ZOO-GOY	Junk Koi
MANZO	MAN-ZOH	(Kohaku Bloodline)
MARUTEN	MAR-OO-TEN	Crown
MATSUBA	MATS-BA	Pinecone
MATSUNOSUKE	MATS-NOS-KAY	(Sanke Bloodline)
MENKABURI	MEN-CAB-OO-REE	Hood
MESU	MACE	Female
MIDORIGOI	MID-ORI-GOY	Green Carp
MOTOGURO	MOE-TOE-GOO-ROE	Black Colour on Shoulder join
NEZUGOI	NEZ-OO-GOI	Grey Carp
NIDAN	KNEE-DAN	Two Step
NISSAI	KNEE-SIGH	Born Last Year
NISHIKIGOI	NISH-KEY-GOY	Brocaded Carp
OCHIBASHIGURE	O-CHEE-BA-SHE-GOO-RAY	Rain on Autumn Leaves
OGON	OH-GONE	Gold
OJIME	O-GEE-MAY	Completes the Back
OJIYA	O-GEE-YA	(Famous Koi City)
OSU	OSE	Male
OYAGOI	O-YA-GOY	Adult Breeder Koi

JAPANESE/ENGLISH KOI DICTIONARY

Japanese Word	Pronunciation	Meaning
PONGOI	PON-GOY	Good Grade Koi
PURACHINA	PRA-CHIN-A	Platinum
SADAZO	SAD-AS-OH	(Sanke Bloodline)
SANDAN	SAN-DAN	Three Step
SAKURA	SA-KRA	Cherry Blossom
SANSAI	SAN-SIGH	Three Years Old
SENSUKE	SEN-SKAY	(Kohaku Bloodline)
SHIRO BEKKO	SHE-ROE-BAY-CO	White Tortoise Shell
SHIRO MUJI	SHE-ROE-MOO-GEE	White Without Pattern
SHIRO UTSURI	SHE-ROE-UT-SUE-REE	White Reflection
SHOCHIKUBAI	SHO-CHEEK-OO-BUY	Pine, Bamboo & Plum
SHOWA	SHO-WA	3 Colour Koi, produced in Showa Era
SHUSUI	SHOE-SUEY	Autumn Water
SORAGOI	SORE-A-GOY	Blue-Grey Carp
SUBO-SUMI	SUE-BO-SUE-ME	Black falls on White Skin only
TAISHO SANKE	TIE-SHOW-SAN-KAY	3 Colour Koi, produced in Taisho Era
TAKAI	TAK-EYE	Expensive
TANCHO	TAN-CHO	Red Cap
TATEGOI	TA-TAY-GOI	Koi which will become good
TOBI	TOE-BEE	Jump (In Koi it refers to Koi that jump in size by eating others)
TOMOIN	TOE-MOE-IN	(Kohaku Bloodline)
TORAZO	TOR-AS-O	(Sanke Bloodline)
UEDERA	OO-ED-ERR-A	(Breeder, first to develop Gin-Rin)
YAGOZEN	YA-GO-ZEN	(Kohaku Bloodline)
YAMATONISHIKI	Y'MAT-A-NISH-KEY	Japanese Brocade
YASUI	YA-SUEY	Cheap
YONDAN	YON-DAN	Four Step
YONSAI	YON-SIGH	Four Years Old

*Supreme Champion of the 1994 ZNA Show held in
Hiroshima, over 80cm. (31.5") long and combines
'jumbo' volume with a totally unique pattern,
she is nicknamed 'Scarlet Queen'.*

'The Last Word'

新潟県小千谷市

THE LAST WORD

That's it, it's finished, the final check of many 'final' checks over twelve years has been made and it's all in the hands of the printer to produce the final product, from now on it's all beyond my control. The mind takes over now – did I leave any important items out? – will it 'read' as I intended it to 'read'? – could I have improved on anything written? – are there any spelling and punctuation 'clangers'? – how will it be received? etc etc. – it's all very worrying. Consolation comes to me from the fact that *anything* can be constantly improved upon right up to the point where ones' life runs out eventually, together with the fact that nothing is ever 'perfect' in this world.

I know, very well, that this mere book cannot possibly save any of the hard-earned money already spent and wasted by the majority of readers in buying the wrong items that are totally unsuitable to serve the applications for which they were purchased. Hundreds of thousands of 'Koi Ponds' will be made in the future using pipework, fittings, linings, equipment and 'filters' that can never, in a million years, serve the task in hand. As a direct result many Koi from many breeders in many countries will be lost and many real tears will be shed, not simply for the money paid but for the real grief that follows the loss of a precious pet. I have pulled no punches in my writing of this book sincerely hoping that some readers will follow my advice. I wish I could have written a book telling how corners can be cut and still retain perfection. I wish I could have informed the reader how to build a pond on a shoestring. I wish I could have written that keeping Koi is a relatively cheap hobby, etc. etc. etc. Unfortunately I can do none of these things as experience has taught me that there is only one way to do anything and that is the 'proper' way and I have tried to outline the 'proper' way as far as I know it. The reader will note that I have not gone into the technical details of the building and construction methods of a pond as I suggest experts are consulted for each different application. This is also true of details of electrical wiring, gas-fired heater installations and landscaping where expertise is also necessary.

I have re-read this book more than any reader will ever do, before finally going to print and I stand by all that it contains. As mentioned before, many new and wondrous things will come along to improve our hobby in future years and I look forward to experiencing them as one can never stop learning.

I saw my first Nishikigoi in 1972 and fell in love! – it's now 1995 and I'm still hopelessly in love! – being Koi-kichi *is* an addiction folks, beware!

Finishing a long, enjoyable project brings relief together with an emptiness – what to do next?

Once again, I sincerely hope my book has been, and will continue to be, useful in some ways to you. To those of you who have given me encouragement and constantly urged me to finish this book, I am eternally grateful and I pray you will not be disappointed in my efforts.

'Koi' has also another, better known, meaning in Japan, – Love!

'Waddy' July 1995. ∎

Sayonara!